James Kelman

Manchester University Press

Contemporary British Novelists

Series editor:
Daniel Lea

already published

James Kelman

Simon Kővesi

Manchester University Press
Manchester and New York
distributed exclusively in the USA by Palgrave

Published by Manchester University Press
Oxford Road, Manchester M13 9NR, UK
and Room 400, 175 Fifth Avenue, New York, NY 10010, USA
www.manchesteruniversitypress.co.uk

Distributed exclusively in the USA by
Palgrave, 175 Fifth Avenue, New York,
NY 10010, USA

Distributed exclusively in Canada by
UBC Press, University of British Columbia, 2029 West Mall,
Vancouver, BC, Canada V6T 1Z2

British Library Cataloguing-in-Publication Data
A catalogue record for this book is available from the British Library

Library of Congress Cataloging-in-Publication Data applied for

ISBN   978 0 7190 7096 9 *hardback*
ISBN   978 0 7190 7097 6 *paperback*

First published 2007

16 15 14 13 12 11 10 09 08 07   10 9 8 7 6 5 4 3 2 1

Typeset
by Florence Production Ltd, Stoodleigh, Devon
Printed in Great Britain
by Anthony Rowe Ltd, Chippenham, Wiltshire

Vanessa and Cassius, mindörökké

Contents

Series editor's foreword

Contemporary British Novelists offers readers critical introductions to some of the most exciting and challenging writing of recent years. Through detailed analysis of their work, volumes in the series present lucid interpretations of authors who have sought to capture the sensibilities of the late twentieth and twenty-first centuries. Informed, but not dominated, by critical theory, *Contemporary British Novelists* explores the influence of diverse traditions, histories and cultures on prose fiction, and situates key figures within their relevant social, political, artistic and historical contexts.

The title of the series is deliberately provocative, recognising each of the three defining elements as contentious identifications of a cultural framework that must be continuously remade and renamed. The contemporary British novel defies easy categorisation and rather than offering bland guarantees as to the current trajectories of literary production, volumes in this series contest the very terms that are employed to unify them. How does one conceptualise, isolate and define the mutability of the contemporary? What legitimacy can be claimed for a singular Britishness given the multivocality implicit in the redefinition of national identities? Can the novel form adequately represent reading communities increasingly dependent upon digitalised communication? These polemical considerations are the theoretical backbone of the series, and attest to the difficulties of formulating a coherent analytical approach to the discontinuities and incoherencies of the present.

Contemporary British Novelists does not seek to appropriate its subjects for prescriptive formal or generic categories; rather it aims to explore the ways in which aesthetics are reproduced, refined and repositioned through recent prose writing. If the overarching architecture of the contemporary always eludes description, then the grandest ambition of this series must be to plot at least some of its dimensions.

Daniel Lea

Acknowledgements

I would like to thank the Arts and Humanities Research Council and Oxford Brookes University for funding research leave to complete this project. General editor Daniel Lea provided support and detailed, authoritative responses from start to finish. Iain Sim put me up for free and in comfort in Govan countless times. Librarians were brilliant at the following places: Oxford Brookes Library, Headington; Mitchell Library, Glasgow; Bodleian Library, Oxford; Glasgow University Library; National Library, Edinburgh; British Newspaper Library, London.

While I take full responsibility for the errors of judgement in this book, I like to see it as a social, collective product of innumerable conversations, interactions and readings with all manner of friends and colleagues. The list of people I would like to thank includes Ben Ackland, Colin Bisset, Tim Burke, Sandie Byrne, Gerry Carruthers, Cairns Craig, Richard Cronin, Bob Cummings, Elsa Curran, Maddie Curran, Jean Curran, Maureen Deal, Alison Donnell, John Gardner, Alex Goody, John Goodridge, Huw Griffiths, Jenny Hammond, Ron Hammond, Jon Herring, Matt Hodgman, Caroline Jackson-Houlston, John Jolly, Bridget Keegan, Peter Kitson, Vasiliki Kolocotroni, Istvan Kővesi, Pauline Kővesi, Sonya Kővesi, Greg Leadbetter, Graeme Macdonald, Peter Maclean, Dorothy McMillan, Willy Maley, Steve Matthews, Nigel Messenger, Mitch Mitchell, Adam Piette, Rob Pope, Craig Richardson, Johnny Rodger, Adam Rounce, Lynnette Turner, Ian Willings and Woody.

Most of all, I would like to thank my partners Nessa and Cassius for the love in their noise and voices, for their interventions across this book, for their unflagging and vocal support, for Nessa's reading of draft after draft, and for years of prompting and provoking conversation about Kelman. Any value in this book is theirs.

List of abbreviations

AJS   *"And the Judges Said. . .": Essays*
BH   *The Busconductor Hines*
C   *A Chancer*
D   *A Disaffection*
GFB   *Greyhound For Breakfast*
GT   *The Good Times*
HB   *Hardie and Baird and Other Plays*
HL   *How late it was, how late*
LT   *Lean Tales*
NN   *Not not while the giro*
OP   *Old Pub Near the Angel*
SRA   *Some Recent Attacks*
TA   *Translated Accounts: A Novel*
TB   *The Burn*
YH   *You Have to be Careful in the Land of the Free*

1

Introduction

James Kelman: 'one ought to admire him'

> When it comes to contemporary Scottish writers, Todd rates Alasdair
> Gray very highly, though 'he can get over political'. She also admires
> Ali Smith, Janice Galloway and others. Less so James Kelman. 'The
> trouble is, one ought to admire him,' she says, hinting at the pressures
> of academic orthodoxy.[1]

This quotation says it all. Speaking in 2006 as Professor of English
Literature at Aberdeen University, Janet Todd admits to feeling
pressure to appreciate the work of James Kelman. Wittily and cattily
Austen-like, she hesitates to dismiss him, yet she manages to do
it anyway, and all the more sharply for the teasing hesitation. Her
use of the generic personal pronoun 'one' does a number of things.
It suggests that she is of the class which uses 'one' to distance the
speaking subject from what is being said. Even the *OED* suggests
that such usage is associated especially 'with British upper-class
speech' and is 'now frequently regarded as affected'. Todd is hesitant
to admit to disliking Kelman's work, because, as the interviewer
interprets, to do so would be somehow unorthodox, and that would
mean 'trouble'. One implication might be that most literary academics
who claim to like Kelman's work, actually do not. She seems to be
suggesting that Kelman benefits from a silencing political correctness,
a general fear which muffles the fact that actually nobody really likes
Kelman's work much at all.[2]

But critics of Kelman's work have been far from entirely positive.
There is a widespread perception that the world of urban Glasgow
Kelman presents in much of his work is unjustifiably dour and bleak,
a perception this book will work against. A brief survey of recent

protagonists in this critique suggests that Kelman is chief among a school of 'miserablists'. For example, Alexander McCall Smith and Stuart Cosgrove have launched separate controversial condemnations of a 'miserablist' tendency in Scotland's cultural output. McCall Smith is a crime novelist who is averse to Scottish 'miserabilism':

> I feel that those who portray an aggressive, vulgar, debased attitude towards life are conniving in that life, and I think publishers should reject them. I think Irvine Welsh has been a travesty for Scotland. [He] portrays a notion of Scottish miserablism. But most people in Scotland aren't like that.[3]

Admittedly Welsh and Kelman do very separate things in their fiction, the violence and spectacle of Welsh's amoral excesses are hardly matched by anything in Kelman's quotidian world.[4] Nevertheless Kelman is definitely implicated here in the definition and rejection of 'miserablist' Scottish fiction, just as he is in Louis de Bernières' accusation that Scottish writers indulge in a 'transgressive sordid realism', in Kenneth White's claim that Scottish realist writing is like the 'remains of last night's fish supper, sauced up with sordid naturalism'[5] and in Ronald Frame's concurrent charge that Scottish writers are 'locked in a manic spiral celebrating dark subjects'.[6] Although Cosgrove's public lecture was reported widely in the press as having condemned Kelman, he actually values the novelist as an exception in the otherwise dominant artistic recycling of an outdated stereotype of the West-coast hard-man. Still, Cosgrove condemns cultural indulgence in an exaggerated legacy of industrial decline:

> The Scots prefer failure – whether that's the failure of the national football team, the failure of industries, the failure of the parliament. They almost obsess over it. They also love the culture of poverty. They indulge the culture of poverty.[7]

Instead, argues Cosgrove, Scottish artists should re-focus on the positive aspects of Scottish life, past and present, but particularly on its possible futures. Andrew O'Hagan's argument supports Cosgrove's in claiming that Scottish people have a 'drowsy addiction to imagined injury'. But O'Hagan further argues that far from indulging in 'the culture of poverty', Scotland actually has no idea just how impoverished it is:

> Much of its life is, by and large, a mean-minded carnival of easy resentments; it is a place of bigotry, paralysis, nullity and boredom; a

nation of conservatives who never vote Conservative; a proud country mired up to the fiery eyes in blame and nostalgia. It's not nice to think about, but it's there, this kind of Scotland, and everybody knows it's there. [8]

Such generalisations are only of use in portraying a context of heated debate about the urban misery which, rightly or wrongly, is regarded as being dominant in Scottish cultural and artistic output. Cosgrove and McCall Smith combine to say it is exaggerated, fetishised and should be rejected: 'people in Scotland aren't like that'. By contrast O'Hagan suggests that misery is a widespread national reality and pertains because of a sentimental and resentful reduction of the historical past, combined with an ignorance of intolerant modern realities and flattened by a confining 'smallness of vision'. Kelman is always an important constituent in this sort of argument because when he is attacked, as we shall see in the chapter on *How late it was, how late* especially, it is often for the portrayal of a bleak, alienated, subcultural and even 'uncivilised' post-industrial urban landscape.

At the time of writing in 2006, Kelman has become *the* senior Scottish fiction writer of urban alienation. His work is chief among a generation of writers who follow his stylistic lead and, with their own idiosyncratic inflections, to some extent are often seen to loosely compound his worldview. Janice Galloway, Duncan McLean, Agnes Owens, Jeff Torrington, Alan Warner and Irvine Welsh are just five of the many other novelists who would regard Kelman's work as groundbreaking, influential and liberating. As Allan Massie has pointed out,[9] lumping them all together effects a mistaken simplification of contrasting literary projects and techniques. The resultant dominance of their compound 'version of Scotland' is distasteful to some, including Massie, who is also not averse to a little lumping himself: 'the Scotland that the likes of James Kelman, Irvine Welsh and Duncan McLean portray is a fairly mean, nasty, and brutish place'.[10]

By now, Kelman must be used to being disliked, dismissed and disparaged. He has done a fair bit of public disliking himself too. His literary career has always been embattled, and while much of the battle is of his own making, the greater part of it has been produced by the huge gulf between the polite linguistic affectations of the literary establishment and the quotidian world and vernacular language of Kelman's work. It should always be remembered that

Kelman started publishing short stories in the early 1970s, and that his formative period as a writer was concurrent with the height of the British class war. The conflict of ideologies reached its peak in 1984 and 1985 in the miners' strike, the years that his first two novels were published. Kelman maintains that writers like him are never fully accepted by the establishment, but has evidently revelled in maintaining a position outwith establishments of all kinds, and not just academic ones. When the establishment beckons, offers its material riches and cultural power, Kelman approaches, but then withdraws, criticising polemically on the way in and on the way out: such was the case with his controversial Booker Prize shortlisting in 1989, and his eventual win in 1994; such was the case with his high-profile Professorship of Creative Writing at the University of Glasgow, a triumvirate split three ways with two of his closest writing colleagues, Alasdair Gray and Tom Leonard, and from which he split after a brief tenure of just two years from 2001 to 2003.[11]

When he senses that his work is to be judged and potentially changed, by panels and committees, by institutions, by arts administrators, by authorities of any kind, Kelman withdraws. He withdrew for example from continuing with already well-developed work on a film version of his first novel *The Busconductor Hines* because, in order to secure some funding, his script had to be assessed by the publicly funded body Scottish Screen. A production of one of his plays at the Traverse Theatre, Edinburgh, likewise failed to get off the ground because Kelman refused to have his work assessed by a funding committee.[12] For committed and consistent political reasons, Kelman will not submit to expectations and institutional requirements, even and especially when being paid, even when it would be easier, would be politically correct, personally polite and strategically efficacious for his various projects, to keep quiet. Kelman's is the edgy self-conscious voice of protest, the voice which asks awkward ethical questions, the moralising voice which persistently irritates the literary and mainstream arts orthodoxies and establishments, and which rails constantly against the status quo. He challenges the politics of genuflecting politeness, of the naturalisation of respect for hierarchy, is always alert to possible compromise and doggedly follows his own political line over often rough and lonely terrain. He is, however, a highly sociable, communal figure who is passionate and wide-ranging in his support and promotion of fellow writers and artists[13] and of causes that energise him.[14] Kelman is bluntly resistant to and critical of party politics and the institutions of power: he is, by his own definition, a 'libertarian socialist, anarchist'.[15] He has been guest speaker at rallies in Glasgow and elsewhere, a delegate at an anarchist conference,[16] and co-organiser of an alternative intellectual body 'The Free University', set up in January 1987.[17]

Kelman is a grassroots political activist whose focus is human rights trounced upon by the tyranny of the state, and in this he has close allegiances with the Anglophone world's most famous radical intellectual, Noam Chomsky. Chomsky's critiques of the state as primarily serving big business and powerful elites, his analyses of imperial power and human rights violations from Indochina to Iraq, and his reading of university intellectuals predominantly being legitimators of the state, exactly correspond with Kelman's published views. Kelman is not alone in believing that Scotland has been inferiorised through its oppressive relationship with 'the ruling elite of Great Britain' (SRA 71), and though he advocates Scottish independence from British rule as a way out of enforced inferiorism, he is solidly anarchic and existentialist in his rejection of national identity:

> Entities like 'Scotsman', 'German', 'Indian' or 'American'; 'Scottish cul-
> ture', 'Jamaican culture', 'African culture' or 'Asian culture' are material
> absurdities. They aren't particular things in the world. There are no
> material bodies that correspond to them. We only used those terms in
> the way we use other terms such as 'tree', 'bird', 'vehicle' or 'red'. They
> define abstract concepts; 'things' that don't exist other than for loose
> classification. We use these terms for the general purpose of making
> sense of the world, and for communicating sensibly with other
> individuals. Especially those individuals within our own groups and
> cultures. When we meet with people from different groups and cultures
> we try to tighten up on these loose, unparticularised definitions and
> descriptions. (SRA 72)

Putting distance between arbitrary signs of national identification and the possible damage of the signification process if left unqualified, Kelman suggests that no one is free of the powers and politics of prejudice: we are all grouped and treated according to some assumed and exterior marker of collective identity, be it class, gender, race, nationality, language or accent. It is interesting that 'Scotland' does not appear very often as a concept in the novels, and when it does, it is often rendered remote or irrelevant to the identity and lived reality of the presented world. Sammy for example, in *How late it was, how late*, 'didnay really like Scotland. It was his country, okay, but that didnay mean ye had to like it' (*HL* 256). Kelman's individuals show little allegiance to the national cause, because as an entity the stateless nation of Scotland means nothing to them. In part the novel *Translated Accounts* portrays the dehumanising devastation uncritical group identification can cause through what seems to be fully militarised national conflict. While he has been actively committed to various 'campaigning formations' as political pressure groups are called in *Translated Accounts* (e.g. *TA* 169), Kelman resists the coercive temptations of large group identification necessary to official party or nationalist politics. If Kelman's political vision is particularising, multiplying and always context-specific, at the same time he sees a similarity of status between his own culture and language in relation to English hegemony and the oppression of indigenous cultures and languages in nations and peoples ravaged by foreign oppression through colonisation, militarisation, and national, tribal and cultural conflicts.

Kelman's various commitments have been plural and fully engaged. For example, on the invitation of Amnesty International, he spoke at the 'Freedom for Freedom of Expression' Rally in Istanbul in 1992 to highlight the government's intolerance of free expression, imprisonment of writers and the treatment of Kurds in Turkey (*AJS* 385–406). He returned to Turkey in 1997 to try and get arrested for contributing to a booklet which highlighted human rights abuses and was itself 'an act of terrorism under Turkish law'.[18] He attended a conference of the African National Congress in Johannesburg in 1993, before the end of apartheid (*AJS* 7–10). In London he chaired the People's tribunal on Racial Violence and was fully active in the Stephen Lawrence campaign long before it gained massive media and judicial attention.[19] Closer to home he protested against the 1994 Criminal Justice Bill in Glasgow's George Square,[20] and at the time of the Queen's jubilee in 2002 he spoke on Glasgow Green against the status of the monarchy and promoted republicanism alongside Scottish Socialist Party politician Tommy Sheridan.[21] These are just a few of his publicised campaigning activities (for Kelman's own accounts of many more, see *SRA* and *AJS*). With his array of international campaigning contacts, Kelman is now a well-known polemicist in Scotland, standing deliberately outside of the party political system, because he adduces it to be incapable of real or legitimate social progress: for Kelman 'there is no possibility of socialist change' within the established political system.[22]

For all this activism, he claims that his politics have little to do with his creative writing: 'I mean you might have quite a clear political view personally, but it's not going to really get into the way of the fiction.'[23] This separation of his life from his fiction goes someway to explain why the protagonists of his novels, while being consistently critical of the status quo, are never involved in any collective or political action, nor hold out any hope for or take any action towards social change (with the awkward exception of *Translated Accounts*, the only novel not to be focalised through an individual male). In stark contrast to his fictional creations, in life Kelman consistently acts on a seemingly inexhaustible campaigning energy, which must be fired by a hope that change through collective action is possible, even if social transformations can only be localised and by degrees.

'language is the culture'

If his political work reveals his diversity of interests, his creative work has likewise ranged freely through short stories, plays and novels. Kelman's fictional texts are not voiced in standard English, or in standard Scots: occasionally pockmarked by quasi-phonetic rendition, and linguistic markers of locality – always of Glasgow where recognisable – the voices are broadly variable, polyvalent, inconsistent, and rendered in fluid, changing Kelmanese, a style all of his own making. There is nothing 'pure' about his language other than its consistent idiosyncrasy. He has been frequently berated, dismissed, rejected but also fetishised for his choice of 'choice' language. Initially a fan, successful Scottish crime novelist Ian Rankin changed his mind about the efficacy of Kelmanese because his father could not access it:

> Rankin's first book owed a debt to Kelman in that the Edinburgh student publishing house, Polygon, brought out Kelman's first book of stories, which did well enough to fund Rankin's 1986 debut *The Flood* ... Rankin has said how impressed he was by Kelman's use of Scottish vernacular and how he enthusiastically showed Kelman's stories to his father. 'But he said he couldn't read it because it wasn't in English. Now my dad is from the same working-class linguistic community as Kelman writes about. If he couldn't read it, but half of Hampstead was lapping it up, that to me was a huge failure and I decided then not to write phonetically.'[24]

Materially, Rankin's first publication was enabled by Kelman; conversely, and divergently, his avoidance of Kelman's 'huge failure' of formal choice led to Rankin's sales success. Although from similar backgrounds, they follow very different literary trajectories: Rankin cruising snugly in a tight-boxed pop genre, Kelman ploughing the furrowed brow of his tarmac and concrete realism. Seeing Kelman rejected by Rankin senior, Rankin junior decides on a path safely approved by his father and the wider 'working-class linguistic community'. Far from being a model of rebellion, Rankin's representation of his early artistic choice is one of anxious conformity, seeking both paternal- and peer-approval. His Scottish dad will only read 'English'; Kelman's 'Scottish vernacular' is a foreign language 'phonetically' rendered and read only by English middle-class metropolitans. With this logic, Rankin asserts his triumph as the proud artist of the masses, while Kelman is the exoticised fetish of a southern middle class. If Rankin rejects any father figure at all, it is Kelman.

'I was born in Glasgow and live there: this is what I work' is the bald passport of verification, identification and substantiation on the front cover of an early pamphlet of short stories by Kelman.[25] In interview in 1985, he said:

> language is the culture – if you lose your language you've lost your culture, so if you've lost the way your family talk, the way your friends talk, then you've lost your culture, and you're divorced from it. That's what happens with all these stupid fucking books by bad average writers because they've lost their culture, they've given it away. Not only that, what they're saying is it's inferior, because they make anybody who comes from that culture speak in a hybrid language, whereas they speak standard English. And their language is the superior one. So what they're doing, in effect, is castrating their parents, and their whole culture, and saying 'Right, that's fucking rubbish, because it's not the language of books. I speak the language of books, so does everyone I meet at uni, so do the lecturers and so does my new girlfriend, whose father is a fucking book millionaire or something, and they all speak the real way.'[26]

If Rankin's model for his choice of form is paternal approval, strangely enough so too is Kelman's, though the direction of intention differs. If Rankin wants to write *to* his father, and so have his work accepted by him, Kelman's model of origins writes *out* of his family, to make its culture and language accepted as legitimate by both itself and others. The image of 'castration' is highly charged and clearly masculine. Language 'is the culture', is the source of progeny, is the security of future identity, is the fertility of the male line. To wipe out paternal language with the alien 'language of books' is to deracinate, to betray, to make redundant, to de-bollock. Culture here is something quite fixed, something you should remain 'married' to, something that stays behind if the individual develops and speaks away from it; it is therefore social, community-based, familial. It is not portable or individually malleable. In this extract, there are two languages: the language of 'us', Kelman's culture; and the language of 'them' – the 'everyone at uni', extended into the stereotype of the daughter of a 'book millionaire'. There are two languages, and so there are two cultures: us and them. This model of language relations is that of a hostile class war; the hostility is all Kelman's, and what is being resisted is the endemic authority of 'standard English', the supposed 'superiority' of 'the language of books'. The 'language of books' only serves to de-legitimise, belittle and 'other' any other language. Here we might think back to the Professor of English Literature who opened this introduction, deploying as she does an elevated – and what the *OED* suggests is an 'affected' – language usage to dismiss Kelman. Crude proof, perhaps, that Kelman's position is still relevant to the politics of language use in established literary education.

Rankin's choice of standard English coupled with the crime plot has earned him a great deal of money, and he is now undoubtedly a 'book millionaire'.[27] I don't mean to suggest Rankin's financial success necessarily compromises his integrity: after all, as Patrick Doyle says in Kelman's 1989 novel *A Disaffection*, 'Picasso was a multimillionaire communist. So what.' (*D* 169) But early on in his career, Kelman detected a relationship between plot and economic security:

> You don't need any beginning, middle and end at all. All you have to do is show this one day in maybe this person's life and it'll be horror. And it's a case of artistic selection in the sense that – O.K. you've got to know when to begin and when to stop. When to allow the camera to begin and when to cut the camera off. That will assume the artistic mind or perception behind it. But that's all. There's no need to be saying or thinking 'When's the murder or bank robbery going to happen?'. No such abnormal event will occur – the kind of event that seems to motivate almost all mainstream fiction whether in book or screen form. In reality these events are abnormal. The whole idea of the big dramatic event, of what constitutes 'plot', only assumes that economic security exists.[28]

Kelman's artifice is politically intended to wrest the fictional working-class individual from the opium of myth: there are no plots with pots of gold, no mysterious Magwitches bequeathing fortunes, just the occasional accumulator that comes in. Stories with neat endings, with overt denouements or cathartic crises, or even with 'surprise' generated by playing within a form: all of these are products of a fictional world of material comfort. Kelman is the prophet of unsettling discomfiture because he claims as his subject matter ordinary working-class life. 'Ordinary' for Kelman is a social and socialist positive, not a tool of class-based condemnation. Like Raymond Williams, Kelman celebrates the differences in the ordinary: that multiplicity of differences is culture and culture is always ordinary.[29] To ignore the ordinary, or to take its homogeneity for granted, is to ignore the complex truth of lived culture. His conceptualisation of the ordinary, of the everyday, and of the existential, have clear associations with the phenomenological philosophy of Martin Heidegger and Jean-Paul Sartre. Both philosophers emphasise the importance of the consideration of things as they appear now, focusing on existential temporality, on everydayness, on 'being-in-the-world' and on 'facticity'.[30] Both are suspicious and sceptical about transcendental subjectivism, and doubt whether there is 'a neutral transcendental "I" that underlies all acts of consciousness', as Husserl proposed.[31] Kelman, one-time student of philosophy and English at Strathclyde University,[32] is interested in the representation of ordinary factuality in the present moment. This goes some way to explaining why his first four novels are situated in the contemporary moment, in Glasgow, and are chronologically linear. But the impulse to represent the ordinary is fully political too. Ordinary is the primary subject for Kelman's literary project:

> In our society we aren't used to thinking of literature as a form of art that might concern the day to day existence of ordinary women and men, whether these ordinary women and men are the subjects of the poetry and stories, or the actual writers themselves.[33]

Ordinary is defined in terms of literature by its neglect, through its rejection and dismissal by Kelman's contentious version of literary tradition. When he started out in the early 1970s, Kelman regarded classic British literature as being prejudiced against the ordinary, repressive of working-class identities, and demeaning of non-standard varieties of English. This founding view has shown little signs of changing in Kelman's polemics against what he calls the literary 'élite', though, by 2006, university and school curriculums have undertaken massive revisions of the range and variety of literature studied and, implicitly, legitimised, including writers of working-class life like Kelman.[34]

In the 1970s and 1980s, the terms of the class war were pervasive,[35] deployed by all sides of the social divisions. Literary culture at times exhibited a distance from and superiority to working-class life, as one of the most popular novelists of the 1960s and 1970s, John Fowles, exemplifies:

> Once you've done one good novel about the working class, it becomes a very difficult field to go on with because culturally [. . .] it is limited [. . .] the thing with the middle class is that there are far more complex situations, middle-class people are far more complex than working-class people, and therefore, in a sense, it's just giving yourself more room.[36]

Few novelists are so explicit about such assumptions underpinning their work. For Kelman, these prejudices are buried in the assumed and accepted social position of the third-person narrator. While not exactly a canonical text, George Blake's *The Shipbuilders* (1935) is a typical example of what Kelman regards as being characteristic of the third-person narrative voice, which asserts its 'value system'[37] even while its sympathies are nominally with the Glaswegian working class. Leslie Pagan is the son of a Glasgow ship-yard owner. The narrator follows and justifies Pagan's thoughts as he enters a pub which is full of his employees, who are unaware they are about to be made redundant:

> The house was busy, burly men in working clothes and dirty cloth caps two deep along the counter. The ugly tongue of Clydeside assailed his ears, every sixth word a fierce and futile obscenity; they spat much as they seemed to breathe. He saw the scene as one of degradation, and yet, understanding, he neither recoiled nor condemned. They were the men he knew – passionate, strong and true to the core.[38]

Determined to resist such romanticising, animalising, patronising stereotypes of a proletariat described and judged from *without* (a limitation George Blake himself was aware of), Kelman claims to write from *within* that 'ugly tongue of Clydeside'. This is the foundation of Kelman's artistic project. What he decided to do to resist a largely unchallenged literary power structure was groundbreaking and is now well known. He described the politics of his chosen form clearly in 1997:

The establishment demands art from its own perspective but these forms of committed art have always been as suffocating to me as the impositions laid down by the British State, although I should point out of course that I am a socialist myself. I wanted none of any of it. In prose fiction I saw the distinction between dialogue and narrative as a summation of the political system; it was simply another method of exclusion, or marginalising and disenfranchising different peoples, cultures and communities. I was uncomfortable with 'working-class' authors who allowed 'the voice' of higher authority to control narrative, the place where the psychological drama occurred. How could I write from within my own place and time if I was forced to adopt the 'received' language of the ruling class? Not to challenge the rules of narrative was to be coerced into assimilation, I would be forced to write in the voice of an imagined member of the ruling class. I saw the struggle as towards a self-contained world. This meant I had to work my way through language, find a way of making it my own. (*AJS* 40)

This passage points to the aspect of his work about which Kelman is most consistent, and perhaps the stylistic feature which has granted him a uniquely influential position in literature: his decision to make his novels linguistically unified. In the 1970s and early 1980s in numerous short stories, Kelman experimented with a variety of narrative styles, language types and punctuation options: from first-person to third-person; from thoroughly standard English, through to quasi-phonetic transcription; from standard quotation and elision marks to their complete absence.

As many commentators have noted, for the novels, varied though they are, Kelman has developed a flattening of the usual hierarchies that are inherent in narratives where the omniscient or central speaker narrates through a standard variety of English. Characters' spoken words, by contrast, are usually placed inside inverted commas and further separated from the language of omniscience, of narratorial knowledge, by being evidently meant to be working-class, inflected or accentual in some other way. Such a disjunction is evident even in the stalwart texts of twentieth-century working-class fiction, both north and south of the border, though of course there are exceptions which Kelman missed in his generalising assessment of literary history. The conflict between standard and 'vernacular' languages stretches all the way back to Dante, Chaucer and Cervantes, wherein national languages usurped Latin, the established language of law, governance, academia, faith and so, literary respectability. Linguistic diversity due to class and region within major tongues appears in poetry in the eighteenth century, and in fiction in the nineteenth century. But rarely are marginalised varieties of English, especially working-class forms, allowed a dominant position in fiction. Literary language and standard language have often been regarded as the same thing even by working-class novelists; to write in a 'non-standard' variety was to write a 'non-literary' English.

The most cited marker of this conflation is the first edition of the *Oxford English Dictionary* (started 1860; published 1933) which gathered quotations from literature. Tony Crowley and others[39] contend that it was the dictionary makers who established and codified the concept of a 'standard literary language'. The dictionary makers included words according to their literary and textual precedence, not their oral currency; in requiring quotations from printed sources as evidence for each etymological change, they had no choice. But the result was that 'standard' and 'literary' were conflated within the rationale and mechanics of this massively influential standard bearer. It is a testament to the progressive, developing nature of the *OED* project, and to the influence of critics of early lexicography like Crowley, that Kelman is now a cited (literary) source in the ongoing third edition for twenty-one words, including standard lexical items such as 'age', 'brilliant', 'giro', 'moonlight', 'mind', 'minute', 'monosyllable', 'minestrone', 'moaning', 'mocker' and 'lumber', together with non-standard forms such as 'manky', 'mawkit', 'midden', 'midgie', 'Tim', 'maw', 'blooter'.[40] Maybe the inclusion of these words confirms how much more linguistic diversity appears in literature now than in the early twentieth century. Or perhaps the inclusion of Kelman's terms in the central bearer of supposed standard English language suggests that the opposition of standard to dialect, of centre to region, is no longer a convincing or sufficiently subtle map of the relationships between language varieties.

When Kelman assessed British literary history, he felt that the separation between language varieties was illustrative and reproductive of a divided society, of structures of power, of class stratification, and he discussed no Scottish exceptions. He ignores, for example, Lewis Grassic Gibbon who opened up narrative use of a 'folk voice'. As Cairns Craig points out, Grassic Gibbon 'invented a radical narrative strategy which displaces the third-person, omniscient – and anglocentric – author in favour of a narration organised through the voices and the gossip of the folk themselves'.[41] As early as the 1930s Grassic Gibbon was breaking what Kelman asserts were the usual 'rules of narrative'.[42] If Kelman missed these two pioneers, he was very aware of James Joyce's resistance to inverted 'perverted commas', which separate spoken from narratorial discourse; Joyce opted to replace their function with dashes.[43] But still, even a cursory survey of twentieth-century fiction would suggest that Kelman was largely correct about the separation between the language of a narrator and the language of a working-class or otherwise-accented character; Grassic Gibbon and Joyce were exceptions. In 'realist' fictional worlds designed to be entirely sympathetic with working-class culture, in those novels polemically intent on social change, and even where the novelist was of an identifiably working-class background, narrator and character have entirely different linguistic platforms, separated by speech marks, separated by quasi-phonetics or regionalism. In the following quotation, Rab Hines parodies the tradition of representing the poor, in Kelman's first novel:

> you put forward the mouth with head lowered while the slight stoop or curtsey and forefinger to eyebrow the sign of the dross, we do beg ye kindly sir we do beg ye kindly, for a remaindered crust of the bread we baked thank 'ee kindly y'r 'onour an' only 'ope as we might bake 'em more sweetly for 'ee t' nex' time 'appen y'r 'onour as'll do us t' privilege o' robbin' again sir please sir kick us one up the arse sir thanks very much ya bunch of imbecilic fucking bastarn imbeciles. (*BH* 91–2)

This passage of Hines' monologue concludes an invective against social hierarchies, itself initiated by a speculative effusion upon the future of Rab Hines' son Paul, which for a brief spell seems like an urban version of Samuel Taylor Coleridge's 'Frost at Midnight'. Hines wants Paul to eat well and to be a 'big man', to be prepared in body and in mind 'to do it son, control, take control, of the situation' (*BH* 90). As Hines gives voice to the genuflecting humility of the poor before their masters, the writing turns into an attempted realisation, a phonetic rendering of working-class accent – the equivalent of Dick Van Dyke's cockney accent in the film of *Mary Poppins* (1964). The rendering of the cloying and unrealistic accent is evident in the numerous apostrophes indicating an un-aspirated 'h' [h]ere, an elided consonant sound 'th' [th]ere, a missin' final 'g' too, which entirely contrast with the presentation of Hines' own language, thought or spoken. Parodic though it may be of nineteenth-century attempts to manage both working-class voice and material circumstance in fiction, this version of working-class speech is still readily available to us throughout the twentieth century. It is the technique that novelists still often use when wishing to present a non-standard accent in written form: the long list of such novels would include Robert Tressell's *The Ragged Trousered Philanthropists*, Edward Gaitens' *Dance of the Apprentices*, Alan Sillitoe's *Saturday Night and Sunday Morning* and William McIlvanney's *Docherty*.[44] It is not a form which is isolated in the fossils of big-boned British nineteenth-century dinosaurs like Charles Dickens or Elizabeth Gaskell, though it owes much to these groundbreakers. In their novels, narrators talk in standard English. Kelman has written a prefatory homage to Dickens' *Bleak House*,[45] but his own presentation of language differs greatly from his predecessor's rendition of working-class dialogue. The following example of Dickens' version of working-class direct speech is from *Bleak House*:

> 'Yes, I see you once afore at the Inkwhich,' whimpers Jo. 'What of that? Can't you never let such an unfortnet as me alone? An't I unfortnet enough for you yet? How unfortnet do you want me fur to be? I've been a chivvied and a chivvied, fust by one on you and nixt by another on you, till I'm worritted to skins and bones.'[46]

Here the archetypal innocent victim of social neglect talks. The sympathy of the omniscient narrator who is pulling the strings is fully aligned with the 'plight' of the working-class character. Ostensibly, the authorial intention as far as it can be determined does not suggest that such speeches are presented to be ridiculed, sent up, gawked or laughed at. Put simply, the reader is supposed to feel sorry for Jo, to feel enraged at the horror and insecurities of his life, and to feel the itch of political anger about the social injustice that has led to his sorry plight. Novelists like Dickens, Gaskell, Zola and Tressell have an ostensible moral agenda which is all about throwing stark, emotive, fictive light on the realities of poverty and economic insecurity and deprivation in real, identifiable worlds. But the stylistic fact that their narrators write their controlling, knowing, all-seeing narratives in a language whose very omniscience in no small part derives from its recognisably standard spelling, standard punctuation, standard grammar and – in contrast to Jo's speech above – un-phoneticised written (rather than spoken) language, means that there is a huge linguistic gulf between narrator and character, and so between character and reader. The character's voice is trapped in a cage of apostrophes and phoneticisation, which is all the more stark in its contrast to the standard English of the narrator. Narrator and reader collude in feeling standard-English sympathy for, and so discourse distance from, the working-class voice and material circumstance of the character. Narrator and reader become *cognoscenti*, while the working-class character remains a holy fool, and is patronised, made primitive, animalised.

To turn to the more recent past in Scottish literary history, William McIlvanney's *Docherty* makes clear what is only implied in *Bleak House*: the narrator has words and concepts at his disposal far beyond the realm and ken of his working-class characters. The central patriarch, miner Tam Docherty, has a code of honour based on family:

> The one oasis was his family. The rest was work that never blossomed into fulfilment, thought that was never irrigated with meaning. The absence of certitude made a moor of the future, and inarticulacy lay over everything like a blight. He felt grotesqueness in his efforts to impose himself on the forces he was up against, the pettiness of fights with pit managers, the ludicrousness of a family that had two religions. He had perceptions that enabled him to feel the pain, but not the words to make it work for him. He could only endure.[47]

McIlvanney's presentation of Scottish West-Coast working-class speech is quasi-phonetic, dialectal, localised, and separate from the standard English of the narrator's language of this quotation. This is clearly not just a matter of presentation, but of 'articulacy': Tam does not have 'the words' to take control of his world, so his lot is one of unchanging suffering. With this logic, working-class Scots is therefore not the language of control, of agency, nor indeed of emotional expression. The 'blight' of inarticulacy is akin to urban decline, a landscape despoiled, infertile, disease-ridden, dying. A pervasive impoverishment of language, McIlvanney's narrator seems to be suggesting, is both indicative and productive of an absence of 'meaning' in these insecure lives. The problem has to be that the language in which this tragedy is explained is English, even in a novel which makes powerful emotive play with the suppression of Scots in the classroom, when Tam's youngest son Conn realises his own Scots is not to be allowed.[48] McIlvanney himself is similar to Conn in regarding this as a tragedy:

> I spoke Scots until I was five, and I went to primary school, and I was taught English – what I resent is that I was taught English to the suppression of Scots. I think it was necessary that I be taught standard

English in conjunction, as a harmonious marriage, with my own daily speech – it would have been good! [. . .] all I can do, it seems to me, is inhabit the paradoxes as healthily as possible and try to embrace the dichotomies. And I think there *can* be a fruitful union between the two; it seems to me false to seek a reversion, I think you have to inhabit the contemporary situation as healthily as you can.[49]

In that emphasised '*can*', and in the repetition of 'healthily', McIlvanney is positive that Scots and English can and should be combined, that one does not have to exclude, or be superior to, the other. But the fact is that in his most celebrated novel McIlvanney does position English as the language of explanation, of rationality, of articulacy and complex, expressive thought, while working-class, vernacular, Scots is installed in the position of a denuded, spoken language, a language which cannot express the raw suffering of the most populous section of society. If English is the language through which the omniscient narrator explores, explains and accounts for the otherwise inarticulate working class, then a power relationship is ideologically, inescapably embedded in the way we access this textual world. The reader is hand-in-hand with the 'well-to-do' couple who stroll down Tam's street, in disbelief at what they see, class tourists, 'blinkered with apprehension'. Tam challenges them: '"Why don't ye bring ye fuckin' cookies wi' ye? An' then ye could throw them tae us!"'.[50] For these middle-class passers-by, Tam is an animal in a zoo, and because our view of his inner life is simultaneously enabled and stymied by the bars of standard English, no matter how emotionally successful this novel might be in raising awareness of 'those who had committed poverty',[51] no matter the passionate political anger of the narrator, we are always at a remove, always in the place of the articulate tourist, understanding for the most part through the pristine, omniscient legitimacy of standard English.[52]

For all his socialist hope, the cornerstone of McIlvanney's worldview is loneliness. As the family receive news of his elder brother's severe injuries sustained in the First World War, young Conn is numbed by a realisation.

Disturbed by the atmosphere of lost security which his home had held all evening, he sensed a reason that was outside of comprehension – the utter isolation of one man's life. His heart took on a knowledge which his mind would never have, the realisation that in each of our lives everybody else is just a tourist.[53]

If social classes are divided by a 'touristic' lack of proper understanding, by surface encounters jarred with the friction of mutual
suspicion, individuals within classes are likewise separated. This
novel charts a period of transition away from the socialistic, honourable working-class code of neighbours helping neighbours, of
families sticking together, towards a more atomised, materialistic,
capital-driven individualised relationship to work and a commensurate diminution of the status of community. In Conn's atomising
realisation of 'utter isolation', and McIlvanney's separation of the
understanding of the 'heart', from the understanding of the 'mind',
arises a de-intellectualising of working-class mentality which is rein-
forced by a hierarchy of language varieties which in turn embed
within the deep narrative structure a set of binary oppositions, divided
from each other by a hard linguistic boundary: narrator from narrated,
English from Scots, tourist from animal, observer from victim, mind
from heart.

'The human reality'

Kelman works against exactly these sorts of structural separations in
his novels and short stories. His narrators and protagonists use the
same language in terms of spelling, punctuation, vocabulary and
syntax, usually merged in free indirect discourse. After experimental
early short stories, he does not use speech marks or even Joycean
dashes for either direct speech or direct thoughts. This means that
narrator's voice and character's voice are so intertwined that it is
often impossible to separate the two; direct speech and indirect speech,
speech and thoughts, have fuzzy borders in Kelman, as do subject–
object relations. The merging and anti-first-person effects are
repeatedly deployed and have aesthetic and political implications.
Aesthetically the result is a fluidity of position for a merging voice
which conjoins protagonist with narrator to the point where the first
person is almost implicated, without the concurrent limitations of
that first person. Conversations between characters are therefore
demanding to follow, without the usual or standard separation
demarcated by speech marks, especially if there are more than two
characters. For Kelman, neither voice of narrator nor protagonist
should be dominant because that would imply that someone's voice
is lessened, is secondary. A dominant or omniscient voice would
necessarily subject and subjugate other characters to its all-seeing

eye/I. Kelman regards omniscience as a romantic fiction, a superstition, and so it has no place in the realist's toolkit. His narrative strategy is also confirmation of his foundational atheistic existentialism: he does not want for a moment to suggest either omniscience or essentialist notions of the generic narratorial voice. Voices are never omniscient because there is no god in Kelman's universe: the individual experience, or, to use Jean-Paul Sartre's terminology, 'the human reality', is the primary and the consistent focus.[54] The hierarchical power of an omniscient narrator is also absent because of Kelman's anarchic anti-authority politics. In Kelman's polemics, authorities are neither the locus nor the determinants of truth, so fiction should resist the ideological implications of recasting trusted governance in the shape of an omniscient narrator. 'Authorial intrusion is out', Kelman has said. 'I don't thrust my own thoughts down the throats of my characters.'[55] Although the worlds he constructs are full of alienating authorities and hierarchies, it is true that Kelman's narrative forms have no 'powers that be', no all-seeing eyes, no holders of a 'truth', no judges. By and large if a narrator can be discerned she or he will not summarise, contextualise, qualify or analyse the characters' outward actions or inner workings, and this is especially the case in his second novel *A Chancer* (1985). All of these important verbal administrative tasks will be carried out by the thoughts, spoken and unspoken, of the main character himself (and problematically it is always a 'him'); or, they will not be carried out explicitly, but will be left for a reader's own detective work and imaginative play. The neutralisation of the narrator dramatically opens up the role of the reader, as in the following quotation from *A Chancer*, which contains the wedding speech of the protagonist Tammas in its entirety:

> Well everybody . . . Tammas cleared his throat.
> Another man called: A bit of order now for the best man.
> Tammas waited until the talking stopped. Well . . . He cleared his throat again. I'd like to toast the bride. She's the best looking bride I've ever seen. He turned to her and said, Honest Rena, I really mean that. All the best to the two of yous.
> He raised the tumbler of sherry he had been given aloft. There was silence, the faces in the room all gazing at him. It was crowded. The door open widely and people standing visible out in the lobby. Here's to Rena! he cried, and he swallowed the sherry in a gulp.
> Somebody called: To Rena! (*C* 217)

And that is it: Tammas says no more. The narrator does indicate action and dialogue ('he cried', 'he swallowed') but only in an abbreviated fashion. We are given a sense of Tammas' audience by the narrator as a little context, but the directions are perfunctory. No position is taken by the narrator on Tammas' performance, no judgement offered, and no guidance granted at all as to how we should react to Tammas' speech. As John Corbett points out, the narrator is neutral[56] and withdrawn as much as possible. The withdrawn narrator does not put us inside the mind of either Tammas or his audience. The implied position for the reader is that of a guest at the wedding, knowing no more about Tammas' speech before he makes it than the audience does, because access to Tammas' thoughts is almost nought; the narrator is external, and so is the reader. But we also don't know for sure what the audience, 'gazing at him', think either as a group, or as individuals. We can guess that they are disappointed by the brevity of the speech, but the decision to interpret, indeed, construct their reaction in this way, and to judge Tammas for his performance, to be disappointed alongside Rena, is entirely our responsibility, our work and our choice.

This brief example of social awkwardness confirms the root source of Kelman's difficulty: the reader is never explicitly coaxed into a certain understanding of the processes of the narrative by a close relationship with a narrator. It is through the absence of the narrator, through the gap that is left, that the sheer emotive force and necessary interpretative complexity of Kelman's work emerge: the reader has to make sense, has to be active, has to inflect and re-inscribe the actions, words, emotions, that occur in the white spaces on the page. Intimacy with the narrator is just not available, though it often is with the lead characters. Instead, a fully active engagement with the information on offer, normally focalised through the life of a male protagonist, is a necessity for any interpretation. The distinct lack of narratorial guidance and the interpretative free space that opens up, is the place where the awkward 'horror' of Kelman's world is fully realised. This neutralised strategy gestures towards a world where there is no plot, no grand narrative, no neat endings other than departures, no frameworks other than localised, fragile relationships upon which to pin hopes and sureties. Nationality and nationalism are never asserted as an overarching structure of succour or confirmation. As pointed out above, Kelman's characters have little to do with accepted narratives of Scotland or Scottishness; after all, as critic Laurence Nicoll asserts, 'Kelman is not a nationalist'.[57]

To express it more positively, Kelman's world is liberated from the shackles of determinism and plotted conventions; the individual, though often faced with insurmountable odds and institutions which constrict and police, is individually and psychologically free, and their characterisation does not rely upon explanation or rationalisation from a more powerful, more knowing other. The generalisation, essentialism and evaluative panoramic vistas of omniscience are replaced with specificities, localities, orthographic and phonetic variety and robust psychological individualism. Kelman does not present us with a generalised working-class world or society: he presents us with working-class *individuals* to interpret. Society consists of intricate networks of individuals in this fiction, not of reassuring communities or groups fighting for, or showing the necessity of, social change. Kelman's fiction does not present political or social problems which are digested, processed and solved by the agenda of the narrator, or by the devices, resolutions or social conscience of the narrative. Instead the short stories and novels present individuals to watch and to listen to, the spaces around them to be filled in by the coaxed, teased, frustrated, participation of the reader.

Here is a section of dialogue from Kelman's third novel, *A Disaffection*:

I apologise Alison.
What for? She frowned: You dont have to apologise to me.
He nodded.
. . .
. . .
. . .
. . .
. . .
He shook his head. (*D* 159–60)

The standard ellipsis markers are deployed here to portray graphically the extended suspension of conversation after a moment of communicative friction. The five ellipses are bracketed by two simple but contradictory actions by the male, Patrick Doyle. In between these contradictions, there are only dots, for the reader to join up and form some sort of meaning.

Margarined honesty: the language of Kelman's realism

Inevitably there are problems and tensions. If Kelman represents 'ordinary' life he is surely attempting as realistic a portrayal as he can muster, and if he likewise wants to use the language he hears about him, to convey his culture, as unaltered as possible, he will have recourse to 'real' language as opposed (and which he opposes) to the 'language of books'. But what if a 'real' term in common use is not acceptable to Kelman's politicisation of class relationships, and his intention to represent the material details of working-class life? Does committed writing about working-class life always have to be 'realist'?

A small but symptomatic example of this crux of issues occurs in *A Chancer*. Unsurprisingly perhaps, characters in this novel eat bread, sandwiches and toast fairly regularly. At the end of the novel, Tammas is getting himself ready at five in the morning. Before he leaves his sister's flat he has something to eat, outlined as follows:

> There was enough milk for a bowl of cornflakes. But he did not make coffee or tea. He margarined a slice of bread then put some jam on it. He found a plastic wrapper to stick it into. Back in the bedroom he unzipped the side pocket once more and stuffed it in. He stepped to the window and stared out for a time. (*C* 308–9)

One of the manuscripts to *A Chancer* includes a different version of the third sentence in this quotation, which reads instead: 'He buttered a slice of bread then put some jam on it.'[58] In pencil Kelman has crossed out 'buttered' and inserted the word 'margarined'; 'margarined' ended up in the published version. This is the only occurrence of the word 'margarined' as a verb in this novel. In the published version, 'butter' does not appear at all. Bread and toast appear with the adjective 'margarined', for example: 'On top of the table were the salt, the vinegar, and the tomato sauce, a teaplate of margarined bread' (*C* 227). As an adjective 'margarined' is relatively common; but functional conversion of it into a past participle is surely rare.

The use of 'margarined' as a verb can sum up Kelman's language use: its three syllables are somehow awkward as a verb, it makes the reader double-take, and it is full of the politics of representing the economically marginalized and literarily neglected. The question is whether 'margarined' is a natural, expected or common usage. Is it instead an artful and artificial lexical substitution which makes a blunt point: margarine is more common on working-class bread, or at least on *this* working-class bread, than butter. It is a tiny change and it is a word voiced not by Tammas, but by the narrator I have described above as 'withdrawn' and 'neutral'. 'Margarined' as a verb is a derivation from the noun, but is an uncommon one; we might even say it is a *coined* derivation. It might be that the use of margarine as a verb is *not* commonly spoken by working-class Glaswegians. If so, why does Kelman use it? He repeatedly asserts that his written language is the language of 'his' culture, of 'his' class. So why the coined verb 'margarined' which might possibly come only from Kelman?

A little history would help here. Margarine was originally intended as a butter substitute for the poor. Its invention was stimulated by Napoleon III, who supposedly worried about his poor populace not getting enough energy through fat to survive both the severe working conditions of industrialising France and the looming war against Prussia. In 1866 his government launched a competition to invent a cheap fat substitute. When margarine was first produced in 1871, it was half the price of butter. Initially margarine could not compete with butter at all and it was not popular for a long time. In Émile Zola's *Germinal* of 1885, the novel about a French mining community, anxiety over a lack of butter is expressed frequently, especially by women gazing at empty cupboards, but no one mentions margarine.[59] Margarine was unpopular until the beginning of the twentieth century, at which time the source of the fat in production of margarine shifted from animal fat to vegetable oil. The quality and quantity of margarine consumed in Europe and North America developed and expanded rapidly, until today it outsells butter almost everywhere.[60]

Today butter is considerably more expensive than margarine though government statistics on comparisons of consumption of these competing sources of fat suggest that there is no evidence for a class-based division between their use. If we can trust statistics, it seems it is no longer the case that affluent people consume butter and poorer people consume margarine.[61] But Kelman clearly, deliberately and – as the manuscript correction suggests – against his own instinctive initial use of 'buttered', forces a 'margarined' distinction. In *A Chancer*, margarine remains a butter substitute for the poor.

Even if there is a vexed complex of political reasons behind this odd lexical substitution, is the use of the verb 'margarined' 'realistic'? One of the problems of representing working-class life in textual form can be explored through the use of 'buttered' as a generic verb to refer to the spreading of margarine or butter or any such fat spread; I would argue that 'buttered' is used in many working-class varieties (not just in Glasgow) when what is meant is the applying of margarine. However I should admit that this is anecdotal: I'm drawing here on my own experience and discussions with people who grew up, pretty much exclusively, on margarine. If the dominant mode of expressing the way we spread fat on bread is 'buttered', and that includes Kelman himself as the manuscript draft reveals, then the usage clearly includes but ignores the larger proportion of the spreading of margarine that goes on. Kelman forces an explicit, awkward and pointed assertion: butter is not a common feature of urban working-class life as he understands it, or as he wants to represent it. The problem is that the verb-form 'buttered' is much more common than 'margarined', so 'margarined' draws disproportionate attention to itself. Of course a standard Scots or English dictionary is exactly the place Kelman would *not* want us to go for 'verification'. Sure enough, lexicographers only recognise margarine as a noun. So does its use as a verb come from 'real' life or from Kelman's personal politics? Where do we go for 'verification' of his language use? How do we test the verisimilitude, or veracity, of Kelman's fiction? Indeed, should we even be 'testing' his language use against 'real' life?

The analysis above is determined to some extent by an expectation that there will be a rationale for Kelman's change of 'buttered' to 'margarined' which is somehow coherent and consistent. But to require consistency in Kelman's language use, as some have done,[62] is to ignore his intentions and systematic resistance to standard language practice. The following are 'proofing notes for Dent paperback', which was to be a reprint of *The Busconductor Hines* (1984). The notes summarise Kelman's defence of his text and adjustments to be made to the original Polygon setting:

> can the pages be centred? or at least positioned better than by Polygon?
>
> general notes on text: all negations such as didnt, cant, wouldnt etc. not to have any apostrophes
>
> capital letters seem to be missing from certain proper names, and capital letters seem to be tacked onto ordinary names – on occasion (i.e. do not look for consistency in it) certain
>
> very occasionally the word 'realize' is realize and other times the verb realise is spelled realise; please leave as is, and do not seek consistency

occasionally the punctuation seems missing from end of sentences; just leave it like that i.e. missing[63]

Kelman anticipates that Dent will try and regularise his language, and we can assume that this anticipation is born of his previous experience with other publishers.[64] In summary, the fronts on which he is defending his text are layout, punctuation, capitalisation and orthography: the fundamentals of print presentation. We might interpret the anticipated conflict as that between two varieties of English use: between the variety Kelman uses in this novel and the unitary or standard variety to which his publishers might be more accustomed. The repeated order to the editors to 'not seek consistency' reveals just how distant regularised standard print language is from the varying oral variety Kelman is defending.

The best guide to the nexus of issues we are encountering here is Kelman's close writing colleague, Tom Leonard. His prose poem 'Honest' (1976) starts with the speaker worrying over what to write about. An arbitrary decision to write about a fisherman is dismissed as a waste of both his and his readers' time; the resultant book might end up as a book based on other books, serving only the purpose of informing other books still to be written. It would be a book derived from other books and only valuable for the creation of yet other books: its generation, its valuation, would be textual, not concrete; immaterial, not material. The title of the piece suggests that what the speaker is looking for is a sincere (authentic? realistic? true?) subject matter and manner for his writing, and the fisherman is clearly not that subject for our non-fishing speaker. Writing about himself also seems impossible as the resultant persona on the page is not recognised by the author as having anything to do with him: it 'wiz jis a lohta flamin words'. In other words, author and text are separated, not the same, distant. On the page, author is not author, but just text. In yet other words, there is no reality, nor any 'honesty', in the text. The language used to discuss the difficulty of creative beginnings in this Beckett parody is Leonard's own remarkable quasi-phonetic rendition of vernacular Glaswegian, as in the following extract:

Yi write doon a wurd, nyi sayti yirsell, that's no thi way a say it. Nif yi tryti write it doon thi way yi say it, yi end up wi thi page covered in letters stuck thigithir, nwee dots above hof thi letters, in fact, yi end up wi wanna they thingz yid needti huv took a course in phonetics ti be able ti read. But that's no thi way a think, as if ad took a course in

phonetics. A doant mean that emdy that's done phonetics canny
think right – it's no a questiona right or wrong. But ifyi write down
"doon" wan minute, nwrite doon "down" thi nixt, people say yir beein
inconsistent. But ifyi sayti sumdy, "Whaira yi afti?" nthey say, "Whut?"
nyou say, "Where are you off to?" they don't say, "That's no whutyi
said thi furst time." They'll probably say sumhm like, "Doon thi road!"
anif you say, "What?" they usually say, "Down the road!" the second
time – though no always. Course, they never really say, "Doon thi road!"
or "Down the road!" at all. Least, they never say it the way it's spelt.
Coz it izny spelt, when they say it, is it?[65]

What Leonard is 'honest' about here is that it is impossible to convey
exactly how anyone speaks in written form. The closest you can
come to 'honest' rendition is through 'a course in phonetics', but the
writer does not want to paint his work into such a tight, frighteningly
unread, possibly elitist, corner (though as he is at pains to point out
that 'it's no a quiestiona right or wrong', the elitist interpretation is
probably all mine). What he wants to get on paper is both 'thi way
a think' and 'thi way a say': thoughts and speech into printed text.
The distance between what we expect, and what we allow, of spoken
language, compared to what we expect and allow of written language,
is then exemplified in the varying versions of the dialogue, in which
both of the voices change their accent, their pronunciation, when not
immediately understood, 'though no always'. That 'though no always'
is exactly Kelman's point: language outside of standard print, Leonard,
and by implication Kelman, seem to be arguing, is inconsistent. For
these writers, speakers and narrators flip between pronunciations,
registers, lexis and code-switch depending on all manner of shifts in
contexts, intentions, moods and audience. Evoking such a multiplicity
of localised shifts and changes in print – from the strategic changes
to aid understanding as in Leonard's poem, to the rhythmical,
arbitrary, whimsical, or humorous in so much of Kelman – is one
of the key problems on Kelman's stylistic agenda. That print culture
has not presented these linguistic variations is for Kelman testament
to the neglect and dismissal of the material realities of people who
speak non-standard English varieties, and the distance between oral
and textual forms of the language. If 'language is the culture' and
certain varieties of English are ignored, even rejected, by the culture
industry, then for Kelman this proves that whole swathes of the
population are not being considered at all by political discourse.
Kelman's defence of linguistic inconsistency is evidently meant to

be anarchically liberating while also keeping faith with his under-standing of oral speech and 'real' thought patterns. His albeit limited inconsistency within English is meant to gesture towards a libera-tion of author, narrator, subject and reader from the shackles of a language system which carries with it both the burden of formula and the possibility that when it is printed, standard language is at an inherent distance from reality as experienced by those who do not live their lives through this accepted language of power. When standard English surrounds and voices an omniscient narrative position, the contrasting non-standard varieties render their non-standard speakers 'other'; they are made to seem unlike 'us' – that 'us' being the collusive narrator and reader. For some, such as Gilles Deleuze and Felix Guattari, the non-standard speaker is rendered so strange, so other, as to effectively become insane:

> Forming grammatically correct sentences is for the normal individual the prerequisite for any submission to social laws. No one is supposed to be ignorant of grammaticality; those who are belong in special institutions.[66]

Leonard, discussing radical anti-psychiatrist R. D. Laing,[67] delineates exactly the same process of othering of the non-standard speaker.

> The dialect speaker tends to appear in a narrative like Laing's patient in a hospital: there is complicity between author and reader that that speaker is 'other', that the user of such language cannot be the person who has written or who is reading the work. It comes down to language, often the nature of the present tense. Laing demonstrated how language is used to invalidate the access of others to an agreed universal present supposedly shared exclusively by people in related positions of power. In other words, to deny people their full existence.[68]

The 'agreed universal present' is something which both Leonard and Kelman problematise through their deployment of non-standard English at all levels of their narratives, Leonard in verse, Kelman in prose. 'Agreed universals' might be what the homogenous and consistent grammar and orthography of codified standard language enable, enact and support, in seemingly innocuous words like 'buttered'. Leonard makes the point here that there are actually no 'universals' which are agreed – there is always already someone, some language system, some class, which is excluded (and which excludes itself) from the agreement process. 'Universal agreement' would require everyone to have a say, a vote, about language, which is a complex product of culture, not of a formal political process. With this model adopted from Laing, Leonard can claim that standard language cannot possibly speak for, or rather, voice, everybody, and if it does so, can do so only partially and is inherently compromised by the prejudices and the processes of positioning between a subject and an adopted language. If standard language claims to be all about repetition of similarity, regularity, dependability and sanity, then by contrast non-standard language is dissimilar, irregular, unreliable and insane. This is not a binary opposition of equals, because standard language always has the upper hand, the political potency, the power of authority, the major position; it authorises, signs off, the instability of non-standard, inconsistent, forms and it 'others' them, forces them into a minor position. With this logic, if Kelman used standard language in his fiction, he would be othering his culture just as, he asserts, so many other writers did and do:

> Whenever I did find somebody from my own sort of background in English literature, there they were confined to the margins, kept in their place, stuck in the dialogue. You only ever saw them or heard them. You never got into their mind. You did find them in the narrative but from the outside, never from the inside, always they were 'the other'. They never rang true, they were never like anybody you ever met in real life. (*AJS* 63)

In fiction, the marginalised are defined and controlled by the standard practices of omniscient narration. Kelman and Leonard have a moral agenda which works against the hegemony and hierarchies of standard language. Kelman writes a language which is a part and product of a tradition of resistance to the pervasive, invasive dominance of standard language (the sort of language in which this book is written). He resists standard language use for many reasons, but at the core is a belief that its adoption in creative work would necessitate a subservience to a way of understanding the world which is not indigenous to his own culture. He writes in recognisable English, but it is an English deliberately embedded with inconsistency, variation and awkwardness.

French theorists Deleuze and Guattari provide a useful terminology for understanding positively the sort of position Kelman adopts. Because it is a terminology which they raise through their work on Kafka – an author Kelman is clearly influenced by – there is an appropriateness in applying the resultant theory to Kelman.[69] For Deleuze and Guattari, language is forced into a fixed system by linguistic theory, not by actual language use. Language use is always at variance with the standard form; the standard form asserts its unity and regulations for its own political ends. The standard form signals the fixity of the majoritarian position. Usages of language which undercut and play with hybridised versions of the standard are called 'minoritarian', not necessarily because they are used by a numerical minority, but because such usage is outwith the codes established by the language of power – by those who claim the majority position, the major share of political and cultural power. Deleuze and Guattari write:

> The unity of language is fundamentally political. There is no mother tongue, only a power takeover by a dominant language that at times advances along a broad front, and at times swoops down on diverse centers simultaneously . . . universals in linguistics have no more existence in themselves than they do in economics and are always concluded from a universalisation or a rendering-uniform involving variables. *Constant is not opposed to variable*; it is a treatment of the variable opposed to other kinds of treatment, or continuous variation . . .[70]

For Deleuze and Guattari, minoritarian language is dynamic, polyvalent, fluid, inconsistent and variable. 'Expression [in a minor use of a major language] must break forms, encourage ruptures and new sproutings'.[71] Its 'continuous variation' within the major tongue – in Kelman's case this would be English – undermines the power structures which that tongue is always establishing through its language of fixity, of determinacy, of law and control. As Ronald Bogue writes, the 'problem for the minor writer is that the present configuration of the social order is unacceptable, and an alternative collectivity does not yet exist'.[72] Citing Joyce and Beckett as revolutionary writers, who, like Kafka, were part of a 'minority . . . within a major language',[73] they ask questions of language ownership which might usefully be levelled at Kelman too:

> How many people today live in a language that is not their own? Or no longer, or not yet, even know their own and know poorly the major language that they are forced to serve? This is the problem of immigrants, and especially of their children, the problem of minorities, the problem of a minor literature, but also a problem for all of us: how to tear a minor literature away from its own language, allowing it to challenge the language and making it follow a sober revolutionary path? How to become a nomad and an immigrant and a gypsy in relation to one's own language?[74]

Throughout this study, I consider Kelman as a minoritarian writer, as someone who questions the power of majoritarian discourse by foregrounding and questioning his foreignness within English, and the troubled politics of language in Scotland. This book focuses upon the six novels in turn, tracing developments in Kelman's style and subject choices as key political and social contexts shift over time. As Kelman is often at pains to point out, he is not just a novelist:[75] while the novels are its structural focus, this study will refer to Kelman's short story collections, plays and political and critical essays (though in truth each of his genres warrants its own book-length critical study). It attempts to recover Kelman's work as artful literature, conveyed in a highly crafted and actively resourced language, and therefore works against the prevalent, buried notion that Kelman's world is the product of a primitivist, passive mimesis assumed by many commentators to be the only tool of the working-class realist. This book will worry at the manners and modes of the burgeoning Kelman critical industry, questioning its methods, uncovering its raw anxieties, while always valuing its contributions. This book conceives the key interrelated themes of Kelman's work to be class, politics, language and masculinity, and these will be the four main aspects of its foundation. But what has often been neglected in the rush to praise or condemn Kelman's presentation of 'real' worlds, is just how literary, how bookish, his work can be. This study will address some of that neglect through close attention to the texture of his work, to unravel some of his complex literary techniques and devices. He is cautious about the relationship between the culture of the worlds he represents in his fiction, and the often unquestioned preconceptions embedded within the critical discourse of people who write about his work. In response, this study will be self-critical, will question the validity and values of its own methods, hoping that such self-reflective turns do not entirely disable its wider intentions.

Notes

1 Sam Phipps, 'The age of the page', *Herald*, 11 March 2006, 4.
2 For a full account of Todd's work and background, see John Sutherland, 'Janet Todd: A novel mission', *Guardian*, 'Education', 21 March 2006, 11.
3 [Anon.], 'The scribbler', *Sunday Business Post*, 18 January 2004, http://archives.tcm.ie/businesspost/2004/01/18/story460699552.asp (accessed 10/11/2005).

4 The most useful comparative essay is by Drew Milne, 'The Fiction of James Kelman and Irvine Welsh: Accents, Speech and Writing', in Richard J. Lane, Rod Mengham and Philip Tew (eds), *Contemporary British Fiction* (Cambridge: Polity Press, 2003), 158–73.

5 De Bernières and White quoted in Gina Davidson, 'De Bernières scorns "sordid" Scots writers', *Scotland on Sunday*, 26 August 2001, 3.

6 Allan Massie, 'The way to literature's urban kailyard', *Scotsman*, 23 August 2001, 12.

7 Stuart Cosgrove, 'The Edinburgh Lecture: innovation and risk – how Scotland survived the tsunami', 16 February 2005, http://download. edinburgh.gov.uk/lectures/StuartCosgrove.pdf (accessed 10/11/2005). See also Lorna Martin, 'Dreary, deprived, awful – a Scot on the Scots', *Observer*, 13 February 2005, 1.

8 Andrew O'Hagan, 'Beast of a Nation' [review of Neal Ascherson, *Stone Voices: The Search for Scotland* (London: Granta, 2002)], *London Review of Books*, 24:21, 31 October 2002, 11.

9 Massie, 'Literature's urban kailyard', 12.

10 Allan Massie, 'Rude awakening for complacent Scots', *Sunday Times*, 23 November 1997, 19.

11 Although so far Kelman is publicly silent about his leaving Glasgow University, Gray suggests the problems of teaching creative writing at Glasgow increased as time wore on: 'There was a lot of incoming mail and phone calls and thingumajigs. The teaching was comparatively easy. But there were many administrative problems to be tackled. We [himself, and James Kelman and Tom Leonard] felt that after the first year we'd tackled them and that there would be no more, but a new set of problems came up and we realised that every year there would be.' He added that while the writers thought that, as professors, they would be consulted on changes to the running of the course, many were made which they had not sanctioned. Liam McDougall, 'Author and artist Alasdair Gray reveals double blow to health', *Sunday Herald*, 5 October 2003, 3 (McDougall's insertions in editorial brackets).

12 William Clark, 'A conversation with James Kelman', *Variant*, 2:12 (Spring 2001), 3–7.

13 For various accounts of Kelman's enriching sociability in arts and literary worlds of Scotland, see: Agnes Owens, 'A Hopeless Case', in Paul Henderson Scott (ed.), *Spirits of the Age: Scottish Self Portraits* (Edinburgh: The Saltire Society, 2005), 75–80; Sarah Lowndes, *Social Sculpture: Art, Performance and Music in Glasgow. A Social History of Independent Practice, Exhibitions and Events since 1971* (Glasgow: Stopstop, 2003); Ross Birrell and Alec Finlay (eds), *Justified Sinners: An Archaeology of Scottish Counter-Culture (1960–2000)* (Edinburgh: Pocketbooks, 2002).

14 For an account of his influence see Moira Burgess, *Imagine a City: Glasgow in Fiction* (Glendaruel: Argyll Publishing, 1998), 297–314.

15 Kirsty McNeill, 'Interview with James Kelman', *Chapman*, 57 (Summer, 1989), 1.

16 Kelman's attendance at the Anarchist Summer School in Govanhill, Glasgow, 29–31 May 1993 is discussed by Ross Birrell, 'Letter 1', [January 2002] in Ross Birrell and Alec Finlay (eds), *Justified Sinners* [no pagination]. See also Ian Heavens and Jack Campin, 'Review of Anarchist Summer School, May 1993, Glasgow, Scotland', *Spunk Library* http://spunk.org/texts/events/sp000054.html (accessed 27/04/2006).

17 Lowndes, *Social Sculpture*, 90.

18 Stephen Naysmith, 'Author seeks arrest over torture claims', *The List*, 21 March–3 April 1997, 4.

19 See H. Gustav Klaus, *James Kelman* (Tavistock: Northcote House and British Council, 2004), viii. Klaus usefully lists the full range of Kelman's political activities in the 1990s, 55.

20 Ken Smith, 'Kelman fans flames at demonstrations against Bill', *Herald*, 3 November 1994, 3.

21 Kay Jardine, 'Sheridan and his citizens hold an alternative party', *Herald*, 4 June 2002, 2.

22 McNeill, 'Interview', 1.

23 Michael Gardiner, 'James Kelman interviewed', *Scottish Studies Review*, 5:1 (2004), 102.

24 Nicholas Wroe, 'Bobby Dazzler', *Guardian*, 'Review', 28 May 2005, 22–3.

25 *Jim Kelman*, Writers in Brief 11 (Glasgow: National Book League, 1980) [no pagination].

26 Duncan McLean, 'James Kelman interviewed', *Edinburgh Review*, 71 (1985), 72.

27 'Rankin's book sales exceed 5 million copies in the UK alone' says the profile of the author on BBC2's *Newsnight Review* website: http://news.bbc.co.uk/1/hi/programmes/newsnight/review/2016770.stm (accessed 26/10/2005).

28 McNeill, 'Interview', 9.

29 Raymond Williams, 'Culture is Ordinary', in Ann Gray and Jim McGuigan (eds), *Studying Culture: An Introductory Reader* (London: Edward Arnold, 1993), 6.

30 See Martin Heidegger, *Ontology – The Hermeneutics of Facticity* [1923], trans. John van Buren (Bloomington and Indianapolis: Indiana University Press, 1999), 11–27 and Jean-Paul Sartre, *Being and Nothingness: An Essay on Phenomenological Ontology* [1943], trans. Hazel E. Barnes (London and New York: Routledge Classics, 2003), 503–11.

31 Dorothea Frede, 'The Question of Being: Heidegger's Project', in Charles Guignon (ed.), *The Cambridge Companion to Heidegger* (Cambridge: Cambridge University Press, 1993), 53.

32 Kelman was a mature student at the University of Strathclyde from 1975 to 1978. He claims to have left after three years without graduating. See H. Gustav Klaus, *James Kelman* (Tavistock: Northcote House and British Council, 2004), vii and Kirsty McNeill, 'Interview', 2.

33 James Kelman (ed.), *An East End Anthology* (Glasgow: Clydeside Press, 1988), 1.

34 See Dorothy McMillan, 'Constructed Out of Bewilderment: Stories of Scotland', in Ian A. Bell (ed.), *Peripheral Visions: Images of Nationhood in Contemporary British Fiction* (Cardiff: University of Wales Press, 1995), 80–99.

35 An excellent historical summary is provided by David Cannadine, *The Rise and Fall of Class in Britain* (New York: Columbia University Press, 1999), 167–94.

36 J. Campbell, 'An interview with John Fowles', *Contemporary Literature* 17:4 (1976), 462, quoted in Stuart Laing, *Representations of Working-Class Life, 1957–1964* (Basingstoke: Macmillan, 1986), 78.

37 McNeill, 'Interview', 4.

38 George Blake, *The Shipbuilders* (Edinburgh: B&W Publishing, 1993), 8.

39 See Tony Crowley, *The Politics of Discourse: The Standard Language Question in British Cultural Debates* (Basingstoke: Macmillan, 1989), 91–124. Crowley follows work by Raymond Williams, *The Long Revolution* (London: Chatto & Windus, 1961) and *Keywords: A Vocabulary of Culture and Society* (London: Fontana, 1976), and by Roy Harris, *The Language Machine* (London: Duckworth, 1987). Their argument about the ideological implications of linguistic standardisation is squarely opposed by John Honey, *Language is Power: The Story of Standard English and its Enemies* (London: Faber and Faber, 1997), 59–117 and *The Language Trap: Race, Class and the 'Standard English' Issue in British Schools*, Kay-Shuttleworth Papers on Education, 3 (Kenton: National Council for Educational Standards, 1983).

40 *OED* online: http://dictionary.oed.com/ (accessed 18/10/2005).

41 Cairns Craig, *The Modern Scottish Novel: Narrative and the National Imagination* (Edinburgh University Press, 1999), 65.

42 Much earlier, columnist W. D. Latto was pioneering the use of Scots for both narrative and direct speech. See John Corbett, *Language and Scottish Literature* (Edinburgh University Press, 1997), 144–7.

43 Klaus, *James Kelman*, 2.

44 Robert Tressell, *The Ragged Trousered Philanthropists* [1918] (London: Harper Perennial, 2005); Edward Gaitens, *Dance of the Apprentices* (Glasgow: W. MacLellan, 1948); Alan Silitoe, *Saturday Night and Sunday Morning* [1958] (London: W. H. Allen, 1973); William McIlvanney, *Docherty* [1975] (London: Hodder & Stoughton, 1985).

45 See Kelman's marginal gloss to *Bleak House* in Alasdair Gray (ed.), *The Book of Prefaces* (London and New York: Bloomsbury, 2002), 540–2.

46 Charles Dickens, *Bleak House* [1853] (London: Everyman, 1994), 573.

47 McIlvanney, *Docherty*, 39.

48 McIlvanney, *Docherty*, 177–8.

49 'Plato in a Boiler Suit: William McIlvanney', in Isobel Murray (ed.), *Scottish Writers Talking* (East Linton: Tuckwell Press, 1996), 137.

50 McIlvanney, *Docherty*, 23.

51 McIlvanney, *Docherty*, 24.

52 Ray Ryan reads McIlvanney's narrative eloquence as productive of a sensitive humanising of the working-class world he represents, concluding that Kelman's 'absence of narrative voice reflects the lack of volition in characters' lives'. *Ireland and Scotland: Literature and Culture, State and Nation, 1966–2000* (Oxford: Oxford University Press, 2002), 48.

53 McIlvanney, *Docherty*, 232.

54 Sartre takes 'human reality' from Heidegger. Sartre writes: 'Atheistic existentialism, of which I am a representative, declares with greater consistency that if God does not exist there is at least one being whose existence comes before its essence, a being which exists before it can be defined by any conception of it. That being is man or, as Heidegger has it, the human reality.' Jean-Paul Sartre, *Existentialism and Humanism*, trans. Philip Mairet (London: Methuen, 1948), 27–8.

55 Catherine Lockerbie, 'Lighting up Kelman', *Scotsman*, 'Weekend', 19 March 1994, 3.

56 The clearest and most authoritative analysis of Kelman's narrative voices is presented by John Corbett, *Language and Scottish Literature* (Edinburgh: Edinburgh University Press, 1997), 149–61.

57 Laurence Nicoll, ' "This Is Not A Nationalist Position": James Kelman's Existential Voice', *Edinburgh Review*, 103 (2000), 80.

58 Typed draft of *A Chancer*, 'Chancer 3' [box], Mitchell, 775038 SR89, 308.

59 Examples of the importance of butter to the French working-class diet appear in *Germinal*, trans. Havelock Ellis (London: Dent, 1946), 13 and 15.

60 Potted history of margarine gleaned from J. H. van Stuyvenberg (ed.), *Margarine: an Economic and Social History, 1869–1969* (Liverpool: Liverpool University Press, 1969).

61 Information on fat consumption in Scotland taken from the following online sources: 'Changing patterns in the consumption of foods at home, 1971–2000: Social Trends 32' [Anon.] (London: National Statistics, 2002), http://statistics.gov.uk/StatBase/ssdataset.asp?vlnk=5234&More=Y; Sally Mcintyre, 'Socio-economic inequalities in health in Scotland', *Social Justice Annual Report Scotland 2001* (Edinburgh: Scottish Executive Department of Health, 2001), http://scotland.gov.uk/library3/social/sjar-41.asp; Andrew Shaw, Anne McMunn and Julia Field (eds), *The Scottish Health Survey 1998*, Vol. 1 (Edinburgh: Scottish Executive Department

of Health, 2000) http://show.scot.nhs.uk/scottishhealthsurvey/ (all accessed 15/10/2005).

62 Macdonald Daly, 'Politics and the Scottish Language', *Hard Times* (Berlin), 64/65 (1998), 21–6, http://nottingham.ac.uk/critical-theory/papers/Daly.pdf (accessed 21/11/2005). Daly sets out to debunk what he sees as the myth of Kelman's realism. Kelman's rendition of Glasgow speech infuriates Daly because of 'an overall lack of consistency'. Edwin Morgan, however, sees much value in Kelman's variations: 'Glasgow Speech in Recent Scottish Literature', in *Crossing the Border: Essays on Scottish Literature* (Manchester: Carcanet, 1990), 317.

63 See Mitchell Library [box] 'CHANCER: Novel Drafts and Play Drafts', ref. 775038 SR89, [no pagination].

64 Other than the re-balancing of the margins of the text on the page, I can find no evidence of any textual adjustments in the Dent edition: it looks as if it is exactly the same setting as the Polygon original.

65 Tom Leonard, 'Honest', *Three Glasgow Writers: A Collection of Writing by Alex.Hamilton, James Kelman, Tom Leonard* (Glasgow: Molendinar Press, 1976), 47. Introducing a recording of 'Honest', Leonard says this 'was a thing written I think it was 1970'. *Nora's Place and Other Poems, 1965–1995.* Audio CD. (Edinburgh: AK Press Audio; 1997). 'Honest', track 7.

66 Gilles Deleuze and Felix Guattari, *A Thousand Plateaus: Capitalism and Schizophrenia,* [1980] trans. Brian Massumi (London and New York: Continuum, 2004), 112.

67 Laing is discussed by Deleuze and Guattari; Guattari was Laing's French counterpart in radical anti-psychiatry. See *Anti-Oedipus: Capitalism and Schizophrenia* [1972], trans. Robert Hurley, Mark Seem, and Helen R. Lane (London and New York: Continuum, 2004), 143.

68 Tom Leonard, [untitled essay], in Bob Mullan (ed.), *R. D. Laing: Creative Destroyer* (London: Cassell, 1997), 90.

69 Gilles Deleuze and Felix Guattari, *Kafka: Toward a Minor Literature,* trans. Dana Polan (Minneapolis: University of Minnesota Press, 1986).

70 Deleuze and Guattari, *A Thousand Plateaus,* 111–14.

71 Deleuze and Guattari, *Kafka,* 28.

72 Ronald Bogue, *Deleuze on Literature* (New York and London: Routledge, 2003), 109.

73 Deleuze and Guattari, *Kafka,* 16.

74 Deleuze and Guattari, *Kafka,* 19.

75 'A lot of the stuff that has been written about my work before *Translated Accounts,* or even before *How Late It Was, How Late,* doesn't know the body of my work at all, it makes sweeping judgements without knowing the short stories for example, or without knowing the other novels, or the plays, and generally doesn't want to know.' Gardiner, 'James Kelman Interviewed', 102–3.

2

The Busconductor Hines (1984)

The busconductor: an endangered species

The Busconductor Hines was at least ten years in the making. Drafted
as early as 1973,[1] and published in 1984, its title prompts two simple
questions which this chapter will consider at length: why choose a
busconductor as the subject of the first novel? And why put Hines
on Glasgow buses? The blunt biographical answer would be that
Kelman himself had been a busconductor in Glasgow, indeed it was
when he was 'a bus conductor, [that] he attended writing evening
classes'[2] for the first time. But Kelman had many other occupations
from his own experience from which to choose, as a 1983 *Herald*
article details:

> James Kelman has been an apprentice printer, maker of shoes, potato
> picker, bus conductor, asbestos worker, hospital storeman, and shop
> salesman of natty gent's suits.
>
> He dug spuds on the Channel Isles. "We picked potatoes and lived
> in a tent. It was good," he says. He also enjoyed selling clothes in a
> Glasgow shop because there was a snooker hall in the next street.
>
> Apart from cannoning off the Channel Isles, jobs have put him in
> London off Manchester, and the other way about, several times.
>
> Much of the time between jobs his main employment has been
> unemployment. Because they best filled waits in social security offices,
> he has read a lot of big books, bumper with much fiction.[3]

Kelman himself provides an account of the importance of keeping
the subject matter of his writing as close to his life as possible:

> When I started to write stories I was twenty-two and naturally enough
> I thought to use my own background and experience. I wanted to write
> as one of my own people, I wanted to write and remain a member of

my own community. That advice you get in the early days of writing, at any writers' workshop or writers' group, 'Write from your own experience!' Yes, that was what I set out to do, taking it for granted that was how writers began. I soon discovered that this was easier said than done. In fact, as far as I could see, looking around me, it had never been done. (*AJS* 63)

As Tom Leonard suggests in his prose poem 'Honest', why write a book about a Fisherman when you have no idea how a Fisherman lives, other than through other books about Fishermen? Leonard's point is that a book written without an attempted engagement with material reality of some kind, indeed of the writer's own kind, might be in danger of being literature for literature's sake, and so of not being 'honest'. Likewise, Kelman wants to maintain a basis in his 'own background and experience', and to use it as both foundation and subject of his work. Kelman claims he was always alert to the net of tightly politicised, national and class ties restricting and determining what should and should not be deemed fit subject for serious literary treatment. The battleground he stakes out here means that getting right the choice of occupation for his first novel's protagonist was vital. If restricting himself to choosing fit subject from 'experience' narrowed his choices somewhat, the author still had numerous jobs and places in his personal experience from which to select, many diverse 'realities' on which to base his 'realism'. Paradoxically, *Hines* was also to be liberated from readings which confined it to 'the actual city of Glasgow', as we shall see soon. This paradox might undermine this chapter: while trying to contextualise *Hines* in relation to historical accounts of Glasgow, this chapter concludes by exploring the possibility that the city in *Hines* might not be 'the actual city of Glasgow' at all. This is a paradoxical tension at the heart of Kelman's realism.

Many of the situations, localities and jobs listed in the *Herald* article quoted above, provided the engines for the early short stories, his first publications. The stories of *An Old Pub Near the Angel* (1973) – Kelman's first collection and his first book-length publication – use settings, subjects and working environments which range from bus driving in Glasgow, to pub life in London, a fruit-pickers' campsite in Jersey, a Scottish tenant's argument with his Polish landlord in London, an encounter with an Irish man in a dole queue, an old man's paper round in the West End of Glasgow, the tyrannical officiousness of shop-floor trades unions, the tyrannical officiousness of government bureaucracy and, endemically, the ravages of unemployment and economic destitution. Identifiably Glaswegian the dominant narratorial voice might well be, but these collected stories confirm that from the start of his writing career Kelman's fictional ambitions took him far beyond buses, Glasgow and even Scotland.

Still, there is more to be said in response to the initial question: why choose a busconductor? Even in the 1960s when Kelman was a young man, it looked like the manned conducting of buses was on its way out. New technologies combined with drives for efficiency and with perennial shortages of drivers, meant that as early as 1964 the Glasgow Corporation (city council) ran buses which were available, if need be, for 'omo' – that is, 'one man operation'.[4] In the 1970s, when Kelman was writing *Bussing About* or *Bussed* – early titles of the novel – there was, as bus historian Stuart Little points out, an established 'mix of one-man-operated ('omo') and conductor buses, some buses having reversible boards with "Please Pay Driver" on one side, "Conductor" on the other'.[5] In 1977 and 1978, trials were being run of 'autofare' machines, which automated ticket delivery, taking the process out of the hands of both the drivers and the conductors. *Hines* reflects these developments in the bus industry, and Hines himself reflects upon the future of his bussing life: the novel is peppered with references to his failing as yet to secure a job as a driver, and to conductors being doomed. The increasingly defunct nature of the job means that unless Hines can knuckle down and qualify for re-training as a driver, thus earning both more money and more job security, he will be out of a job soon. That is, if he neither quits again nor gets sacked for repeatedly infringing rules – and both of these possibilities seem likely. Insecurity of current employment and inevitable future redundancy therefore combine to unsettle the entire narrative.

Kelman might also have chosen the bus service as a setting because the public largely held it in contempt. Another Glasgow bus historian, A. Millar, published the following account a year after the publication of *Hines*, in 1985:

> Glaswegians, feeling oppressed by whatever instrument of officialdom offends their dignity, can often be heard to dismiss the whole nightmare with the words: 'Och, they couldn'ae run a minodge.' The literal translation is 'They could not run a menage' and it is the local equivalent of the English put-down of people's inability to organise a booze up in a brewery. As often as not, 'they' means 'the Corporation', and if the

exasperated cry was not aimed at the latest failure of the council housing department, it was aimed at the city bus service.

This sums up the average citizen's view of the buses. While the trams were an integral and well-loved part of the daily social fabric, the buses were not. They may have formed the backbone of the public transport system, but they were viewed widely as over-priced, unreliable, unfriendly and scruffy substitutes for a high quality if latterly unfashionable tram service.[6]

That Millar feels he has to explain a Glaswegian expression with delicate 'English' ('booze' should really be 'piss') suggests that the intended audience is not Glaswegian or working-class, nor perhaps is the readership meant to be exclusively Scottish either. Millar does not explain the full meaning of a 'menage' (or 'menodge') which is a traditional communal savings club, from which members can borrow money. Millar's distance from this Scottish working-class urban custom, suggests that he is explaining the feelings of the 'average citizen' to others who are implied I think to be 'more than average'. There is the faintest whiff of contempt from Millar in his possibly ironic reference to Glaswegians' ruffled 'dignity' and in his conflation of their ongoing impatience with council provision of both housing and transport (the reason for my analysis of this style of Glasgow social history will become clear soon). For all these concerns, Millar's account is supported by a chatting bus queue in a story by one of Kelman's close writing comrades, Agnes Owens:

> 'Ah hope that bus comes soon,' said the other woman to her companion, who replied, 'The time you have to wait would sicken ye if you've jist missed one.'
> 'I wonder something is not done about it,' said the well-dressed woman sharply, turning back to them.
> 'Folks hiv been complainin' for years,' was the cheerful reply, 'but naebody cares. Sometimes they don't come this way at all, but go straight through by the main road. It's always the same for folk like us. If it was wan o' these high-class districts like Milngavie or Bearsden they wid soon smarten their ideas.'[7]

Also published in 1985, this story suggests that public resentment stems from a perception that working-class areas are not as well appointed in bus-service terms as middle-class areas, like the two mentioned here. If this is even partly true, it is odd to say the least: why would middle-class areas with higher rates of private car ownership require a better transport system than those areas where the population is much more dependent on buses? Perhaps Owens' bus-queue critic is highlighting the illogicality of exactly this sort of social neglect (a confirmation of localised rather than governmental neglect concludes Owens' story: the bus arrives, a boy is stabbed and left behind by a conductorless bus driven away by a resentful driver). There is historical evidence that official transport policy was not appropriate for social need: in the 1960s, Glasgow had a very low rate of car ownership relative to the rest of the UK. For economists and sociologists, car ownership is a key indicator of an area's overall wealth, though when applied to Glasgow such statistics do not seem to take into account the remarkably high density of population in the city due to the dominance of tenement and other types of multi-storey domestic accommodation across the social spectrum. But whatever the reason for it, low car ownership means that Glasgow and its network of new satellite towns were far more dependent on public transport than other areas in the UK. Oddly though, its local and national government was in league to build one of 'the most ambitious' urban motorway systems in Britain.[8] It is important to recognise that while he is of course pulling all the strings and making all the decisions, Kelman is not constructing a miserable fictional transport world out of thin air, to render the urban context deliberately bleak with no justification in the reality he holds so dear. If the bus service of the early 1980s is portrayed as a degraded industry in *Hines*, Kelman seems to have been justified in doing so. So for example, when the uniformed Hines is recognised as an off-duty busconductor and harangued by a 'crabbit wee red face shouting on about timetables' (*BH* 122), we should perhaps acknowledge that it was generally accepted in the 1970s and 80s that the bus service was indeed failing areas of acute need.

Let's move on now from broad national and urban contexts and climb aboard the tighter confines of the inside of a bus. The bus service is resented from the inside by Hines, and from without by its fare-paying public. But there is little mutual sympathy extended between Hines and his customers because the conductor has the only customer-facing role in the bus service. His is the only human face of an otherwise anonymous transport system. If that system is widely seen to be failing, the uniformed conductor is singled out for continual criticism and hostility, even when off-duty. Hines might be unfulfilled and bored in his job, but for the novelist, the environment of the Glasgow bus is ripe with possibilities for interpersonal friction. A bus packs people in: the resultant physical proximity necessitates either interaction, or otherwise it heightens the awkwardness of avoiding communication at close quarters. Of course in his uniform, the conductor could become a leader of a temporary and physically intimate social group, a genial host of a travelling party like Chaucer's Harry Bailly, coaxing, cajoling and policing behaviour *en route*. Hines performs none of these tasks comfortably, though he is comically performative on occasion (e.g. *BH* 65–6); by his own account he 'can make cunts laugh more or less at will' (*BH* 137). One of the markers of the state of his relationship with Sandra is that he 'used to make her laugh' but not so much now (*BH* 147). If he does show comedic confidence with family and friends, he rarely uses this talent with the travellers on his bus. More often than not, amidst the smoky, 'extraordinary smells' (*BH* 152) of the bus fug, Hines' encounters with the public are cabined conflicts, as in the following example:

> Out my road . . . He squeezed between them and clumped down the stairs. The lower deck was mobbed. A large alsatian dog wagged its tail at the spot next to the luggage-compartment. Hines scratched his head and moved to the cabin but the newdriver was gripping the steering wheel with one hand while reaching to switch on the indicator with the other. Hines stepped back and turned to manoeuvre past the alsatian but the footbrake was applied and he staggered forwards and grabbed for the wrist of the animal's owner. The man took the pressure and pushed to aid Hines' recovery.
>
> The bus stopped, the doors opened, the queue crushed up onto the platform. He dashed forwards. Full up we're full up come on, down, off the fucking bus. He waved his arms till the platform was clear and turned to the newdriver. Come on, get moving.
>
> The newdriver gestured at the doors and Hines glanced round. A middle-aged woman was now aboard and holding onto the safety rail at the front window.
>
> Sorry mrs you'll have to get off.
>
> Dont give me that, I've been standing since half-past one waiting on you.
>
> Come on, off the bloody bus.
>
> The woman snorted.
>
> Fuck sake.
>
> I beg your pardon – dont you dare use that kind of language with me.

> Hines sighed. From upstairs feet were stamping, voices rising; a
> song: Why Are We Waiting. The newdriver was looking at him. Hines
> nodded and took out his tobacco tin, and began rolling a cigarette.
> (*BH* 26–7)

Here the packed claustrophobia of the bus interior dominates the
dynamics. Inevitably the confined decks and stairwell model the
increasingly crowded mental space in which we watch Hines
suffocating, being pushed around by people, being thrown around
by the movement of the bus, being told what to do, being told what
language to use. Here we see him at his most physically active:
stumbling, dashing about, gesticulating, commanding, and finally
resorting to playing a waiting game with the middle-aged woman,
using his fag-rolling as a rare assertion of cool control. Conflicts with
the public on the bus are mirrored by career-limiting encounters with
the real policemen of the buses, the Inspectors, who, like the
Inspectors in Kafka's *The Trial*, Kelman gives an initial capital 'I'.
Officious Deskclerk's get a capital 'D' (*BH* 153). The busdrivers,
newdrivers and busconductors always remain lower case, and lower
caste. Hines is reprimanded and booked by Inspectors for various
breaches of proper conduct: for not wearing a hat, for getting off the
bus to buy tissues, for sitting down on the bus and putting his shoes
on the seats, for letting the bus be early or late, and for generally
taking 'the effing piss' as one Inspector describes it (*BH* 77). This
particular Inspector evidently feels it is necessary for someone in his
position to change 'fucking' to 'effing', something Hines simply will
not do, as his middle-aged female passenger finds out above. The
implication arises that the Inspector, having ascended the bus
company's promotional ladder a little, is now suppressing his culture's
language use, a secular sin in Kelman's eyes, perhaps in Hines' too.
In summary, Inspectors and public conspire to oppress Hines in
the sardine can of the bus, always with pressure generated by time,
always with the friction of language clashes, all compounded with
the constant threat of a busdriver falling 'deep in reverie' while driving
(*BH* 155).

The enervating frictions generated by other tight spaces of this
novel are both psychological and political. The three main corners
of Hines' world – bus, tenement, and bothy[9] – are constructed by
others for efficiency. The cheap confines of all three of these spaces
are designed by managerial powers to get as much functionality –
be it transport, housing, accommodation for workers – out of the

lowest possible investment. As Hines is a voluble agitator for change, and a hopeful prophet of progress – if not an active generator of either – these spaces are narratorially politicised. In their study of Kafka, Deleuze and Guattari offer a political interpretation of space in 'minor literature':

> its cramped space forces each individual intrigue to connect immediately to politics. The individual concern thus becomes all the more necessary, indispensable, magnified, because a whole other story is vibrating within it. In this way, the family triangle connects to other triangles – commercial, economic, bureaucratic, juridical – that determine its values . . .[10]

Hines, Sandra and their four-and-half-years-old boy Paul, form a familial triangle – a compact, fragile unit which is strained, stretched and squeezed by other triangles of relationship: bus – tenement – bothy in Hines' case. While it would be daft to press on with the mapping of exclusively triangular patterns of relationship in the novel, it is evident that Hines conceives of the world (space, time, interpersonal relationships) through geometric shapes, lines and curves: lines of time, lines of relation, lines of territory, lines of possibility, lines of flight and lines of retreat. For example, ostensibly discussing his lack of 'connection' with music and books, he complains that the 'lines had snapped. Lines extend from sound to point' (*BH* 101). A page later, the lines are outlining the frayed nature of his mind, life and, possibly, of future directions:

> This is no longer something that Hines is finding; and what is said – all of it – all that is said, of that, of what is going on the fucking shite going through him ear to ear a sickener, he has been sickened. That's it. The lines split and the curves tailed off. A pile of lines left lying about. Each being there for the taking. What you do is choose one – like Hines. Hines has chosen 1 and this 1 leads maybe as far as the sky and that point up there, the point is somewhere up there you see and there is no lurch backwards because the line is always curved, the choice is being made; either you fucking go or do not fucking go. Understand the position. Hines has been having a think. The curve has been perceived. What he is doing is becoming the curve that the way is forwards only, there being no backsliding nor turnoffs nor tangents of any kind; the 1 way forward, and it can even be a charge; and from this charge the 1 fell swoop delivered, the pure on the pure the red on the white; staged in an absent square; one clear stretch for one fell swoop, the sweet implementation of a rightful strategem, ah, good on you Mr Malthuse, the fresh air and the green pastures. (*BH* 102)

Hines uses the line to model time, action and, in the specific shape of the curve, differing rates of change over time. Lines also represent different choices, parallel and divergent future universes for Hines. His conceptualising of future life as a chosen line seems to be conceived of as a one-way linear equation which will prevent his going 'backwards', the plotting of the line being determined by time, the 'I way forward'. Hines' focus here is on his own line of future determination, his individual path, the graphic line in the emblematic upwards-thrusting 'I', becoming commitment to one line. The line plots a graph of future purpose. But the nod to political economist Thomas Malthus undermines the graph and any reliance Hines might have upon mathematical purity of purpose for the management of his economically-threatened livelihoods. Malthus's *Essay on the Principle of Population* (1798) suggested that population expands by 'geometric ratio' and so will always outstrip expansion of food production, which can only increase by 'arithmetic ratio'.[11] Therefore, Malthus argued, the natural, God-given 'checks' on population – such as war, famine and disease – should not be resisted by laws which keep the poor alive, as resultant overpopulation will devour 'the fresh air and the green pastures'. Through this ironical genuflection to Malthus, Hines undermines his own preceding play with geometrical control of his human messiness; 'Malthuse' is derailed immediately by its odd, possibly phonetic, certainly European, spelling. Hines' increasingly abstract, imagistic and even coloured patterning of thought is interrupted, possibly critiqued, by Paul 'yawning and staring about the place'. Hines has been lost in personal reverie, the line of relation and responsibility between himself and his son temporarily suspended. If his busdrivers threaten Hines' safe passage with their distracting reveries while driving, likewise Hines might be threatening the stability of his familial relationships through extended indulgence in playful philosophical musings.

Deleuze and Guattari suggest that relationships in minor literature are connected 'immediately to politics'. Lines of relation are clearly drawn in *Hines*, especially between job and home, between individual and state. The doomed nature of the job of conducting, its confined spaces and the role of the local council in the bus service, come together to forge a palpable political link to that other doomed material aspect of Hines' life, the single-room council tenement flat in which he and his family live.[12] There are thus convergent lines of pressure on Hines to get a new job and a new home, before both are made things of the past by council policy. The quality of life, past, present and future, for Hines' family, is entirely determined by its inescapable relationship with an anonymous local government body. The influence of Franz Kafka's maddening world of unaccountable, mysterious bureaucracies of a state leviathan in, for example, *The Trial*, is as evident in Kelman's work as it is in Gray's *Lanark*.[13] The influence is signalled explicitly in an unpublished version of *Hines* which includes a title-page epigraph quotation from Kafka's *Diaries*.[14] The cost of an imbalanced relationship wherein an enormous bureaucratic entity holds complete dominion over the fortunes of an impoverished family, is something with which Kelman first tussled in his first short story collection, *An Old Pub Near the Angel* (1973). In 'Nice to be Nice' (*OP* 97) a mother of four children, Moira, is threatened with eviction by the Glasgow Corporation. The focus of the story, Stan, is extremely angry at this news, but suffers a stroke when he confronts the Corporation's officials. At the news of Stan's stroke his son (or tenant) Tony in turn gets enraged, physically confronts the same Corporation housing official, and is arrested. For all the heroism of Stan and Tony the Corporation wins out. Kelman will return again and again to anonymous, compromised and dehumanising powers in the governance of workplaces, unions, council offices, police stations, health establishments and educational institutions, both in his fiction, and in his political activism. But few of his protagonists will come close to the brave, if rather naïve, heroism (or blundering machismo) of Stan and Tony. Where both this short story and *Hines* offer ostensible frameworks of a dependent and supportive family, increasingly in subsequent work the state will be represented as having an isolating power over individuals, as the protagonists become more separated, more alienated, from a comforting social network or familial triangle. In his most recent novel *You Have To Be Careful in the Land of the Free*, an itinerant individual of the near future is labelled and monitored by the paranoid state as an outsider when deemed politically and religiously non-conformist. In his extended essay on Kafka's novels, Kelman writes that 'Kafka's central characters are in conflict with any authority which seeks to impose itself on individuals by appealing to necessity in the face of what cannot be recognised as true' (*AJS* 332). Much the same could be said of Kelman's entire *œuvre*.

'Holy Dustbins': meditations and time

Timetabled and highly pre-determined though it is, the job of bus-conductor allows some space in between stops, or when the bus is empty, for what Kelman in his draft notes calls 'Medit' sections: stream-of-consciousness 'meditations' wherein Hines ruminates internally and monologically at length, and which are punctuated by bursts of frenetic activity when the bus stops and by the occasional poor driving of his various colleagues at the front of the bus. To a degree the busconductor assumes a passive role on the journey of the bus: compared to the driver he has no direct control over where the bus is going. As he says himself, in mocking summary: 'It has never been necessary to think. Hines can board the bus and all will transpire.' (*BH* 154) The passive aspect of working on the buses has obvious metaphorical connotations for Hines' life more generally: he has no control, no agency, no determined direction. If the word 'conductor' primarily suggests someone who directs or manages, conjoined with Hines it becomes ironic and shifts to its other meaning of a transmitter, of a passive conveyer. On its own 'conductor' is rarely used in the novel, most often it occurs within the epony-mous conflation 'busconductor', likewise 'busdriver', 'Newdriver' and 'Deskclerk'. H. Gustav Klaus points out that this conflating device 'indicates the rigid fixity of Hines' condition'[15] but as this is something Kelman does extensively elsewhere, with other job titles and even countries – 'machinesetter', 'carassembleyman', 'Northamerica' and 'Greatbritish' for example (*D* 115, 123, 135 and 140) – the intentions are perhaps more numerous, diffuse, poetic and stylistic than merely to signify existential or employed 'fixity', though clearly Klaus does have a point.

Though someone who drives might well be more in control than someone who 'conducts', in work-a-day factuality neither buscon-ductor nor busdriver is in total control of where or when they go: the time, motion and direction of their working lives are controlled by timetabled routes. Personal lives are to be relegated by timetabling: as an admonitory Deskclerk tells Hines, 'that's what diaries were invented for; so folk can mark in their timetables!' (*BH* 153). Driver and conductor operate as part of a machine, and are continually checked by Inspectors and corralled by Deskclerks to ensure they are functioning according to the exacting instructions and directions of the timetable. Flexibility is not permitted. Mechanical time therefore controls everything in the job. 'To be on time' is one of the primary requirements of the industry. The busconductor is supposed to be the timetable's functionary, as Cairns Craig points out:

> The Busconductor Hines is a modern Charon whose passengers do not cross to the other side, but simply cross and recross the empty and meaningless spaces of the city. The busconductor is the timekeeper of the world's journeys, but he himself journeys nowhere, travelling out only to come back, travelling forward only to reach a terminus which is no conclusion.[16]

Charon is never mentioned in the novel. Kelman studiously avoids the sort of allusion which excites literary or historical explication (the 'Malthuse' reference discussed above is an isolated exception). Craig brings his own allusion to a novel which tries to elude the allusive game. If Hines is Charon, the Glasgow setting of the novel becomes Hades. Material conditions are frequently grim in the novel: but is this world hell on earth? The river across which Charon ferries the dead, for a fee, is neither 'empty' nor 'meaningless', but is Acheron, the river of woe. Craig's subsequent assessment of Hines as 'timekeeper of the world's journeys' loses grip only through its excess, in elevating Hines to a global role which is nothing like as reduced as the conducting of local buses. Of course, here Craig is reading the novel allegorically, and as a work of internationally-significant literary literature, so perhaps he should be applauded for moments of allusive and metaphorical flourish. But how distant does such figurative and classical commentary take us from Hines' discourse, and does the novel support its implication that the Glasgow of the novel is hell? Hell is horrible, but it is never meaningless, nor, unfortunately, is it ever empty. The hell that Hines crosses and re-crosses is not Glasgow, but his own apocalyptic mind which can set the most mundane of scenes alight. Here, for example, he looks around a pub one afternoon off work with a drunken, sickly eye:

> Amazing to see them sit there in that eternal manner, fixed in their places, the lives assumed on the strength of it, the sitting, while all around them the fires fucking burning and the stench of it engulfing every fucking thing under the sun, the cries and the screams of the cunts being tortured, the bellies, of the fucking weans there and their grandparents, their fucking ribs for christ sake look at their ribs, jutting out. (*BH* 146)

This vision of human torture is imposed upon old men playing dominoes in a pub. Hines, feeling physically sick, drunk, and guilty that he has taken an unscheduled day off, and contemplating that he 'may have gone mad' (*BH* 144) decides to cast himself and all around him into hell: a hell not of meaningless travel, but of people 'being fixed in their places', a hell of no progression, of stasis, a torture of eternal repetition, a hell of stolid economic deprivation, starving stomachs framed by 'ribs, jutting out'. This is as visceral, as prophet-like, as fire-and-brimstone, as Hines gets, and it is the closest he comes to seeing Glasgow as a hell on earth. But still, if Hines is not quite Charon, Craig is quite right to note the significance of Hines' function in relation to time. The managing of time, for Hines, is undoubtedly a living hell.

Throughout the novel, Hines considers time. Time is to be controlled, the future managed better than the past, the past not to seep into the future; these are temporal aspirations Hines has. Along with and in relation to architectural shapes and forms, time is the other major system by which he constructs and conceptualises his life. From draft plans for the novel, in which Kelman goes over again and again the ordering of scenes and events, it is evident that the job structures the life Hines is to lead. In manuscript plans, sketched in the late 1970s, Kelman makes clear that the supreme overarching structure of the novel is determined by the pattern of the shifts Hines is working. The rationale is obvious: the high-stress points on Hines' life, and on the lives of Sandra and Paul, are very much determined by the different work schedules by which he and Sandra have to work. Sandra works part-time in an office, with the pressing possibility that she will work full-time 'after the New Year perhaps' (*BH* 147). Hines however, flits between an 'early shift' and a 'backshift'. Unsurprisingly, early shifts start very early in the morning – Hines sets his alarm for 4.45am if he is on an early (*BH* 110) – and so there are many scenes set in the discomposing pre-dawn world of Hines' rush to work. Backshifts start in the afternoon and finish late at night. There is also a nightshift, which is manned by the 'blacksquad' (*BH* 115) but Hines manages to avoid it for the duration of the novel at least. A sad irony is that if it was available to him, Hines would be working as much over-time as he could, squeezing his family time into even tighter timetabled slots; in the present time of the novel, no 'O.T.' is on offer (*BH* 24), which is why the family is increasingly dependent on Sandra's income. Much of the emotive force of entrapment which dominates the lives of Hines, Sandra and the unwitting Paul is the result of the rigid framework of their very separate working and nursery timetables. With the manuscript plans throwing clarifying light on the foundational structure of the novel, we might go as far as suggesting that the shift pattern, the timetable of work, is the insensitive, dumb, omniscient, structural and narra-torial author; author of a godless existential 'clockwork universe' that benumbs the world of Hines. The timetable is an enforced imposition within whose constraints Hines finds it difficult to live, and which he finds impossible to ignore or forget:

> Smoking helped him to get out of bed on bad mornings. Without that to look forward to he would be an even worse timekeeper. And yet he wasnt the worst of timekeepers because the worst of timekeepers had already got the boot [. . .]
>
> Take the clockwork universe: aye, just pick it up and set the wheels in motion; tick tock etcetera; just lay it down, aye, that's correct, the broad shoulders will attend to such a burden. (*BH* 112)

Time is a burden for Hines because it is exterior, it measures and orders the universe but he cannot get the measure of it, highly conscious of it though he is. There are two basic 'flows' of time in Hines, and they are readily made available to us through Henri Bergson's splitting of time into 'duration' and 'mechanical' types of time. Bergson defines the time of consciousness, or duration, which he regards as being internal and something quite different from the external, physical, mechanical time we might parcel, measure and count with a clock. For Bergson, 'measurement of time'

> expresses our inability to translate time itself, our need to replace it, in order to measure it, by simultaneities which we count. These simul-taneities are instantaneities; they do not partake of the nature of real time; they do not endure. They are purely mental views that stake out conscious duration and real motion with virtual stops, using for this purpose the mathematical point that has been carried over from space to time.[17]

The texture of *Hines* is dominated by interior monologues, which enact long pauses of mechanical time for the durational time of Hines' thoughts. His existential anguish is generated by the respon-sibility he has to display over time management. The manuscript plans suggest that exterior time forms an overall structure for the novel, and for Hines' exterior, mechanised experience. Hines seems to be falling through the abrasive but widening gap between these two types of time, and he is fully aware of his lack of control, and of the distance between his meditative interior life and his control of the dynamic exterior world. Often, strategies for his management of future time form 'purely mental views', are entirely abstracted and show little or no engagement with the persistent material realities overloading his life.

In manuscript plans, Kelman abbreviates 'meditation' to 'medit'. One of the most significant 'medit' sections Kelman labels 'Holy Dustbins'[18] (BH 79–81). The next few pages propose a reading of this key section. This meditation starts with a, by now familiar, quasi-objective stance – the comically cod-scientific language of the diagrammatic analysis of the shape, the architecture, of the tenement midden arrangements. The perspective assumed is parodic of the architectural or sociological historian. To set up a context for the close analysis of the 'Holy Dustbins' passage, let us consider a 'straight' account of similar waste problems on a real 1970s Govan scheme, by Seán Damer, a Marxist social historian:

> There was a considerable amount of rubbish blowing about the streets, which were covered with broken glass. Much of this mess was due to the fact that the 'midgies', or open concrete bin shelters, in the back-courts were totally inadequate. They each contained three bins for a close of six houses, and these bins were permanently overflowing, with contents strewn around the courts; as there was frequently an accumulation of old bed-springs and an astonishing collection of broken-down furniture as well, the general picture was of a shambles. These bin-shelters provided informal adventure playgrounds for the local children, whose rummagings contributed to the spread of the junk.[19]

The Glasgow bin problem described here, seems to have been widespread in both old tenements like Hines' (like Duncan Thaw's in Lanark too[20]), and sadly enough in the new schemes meant to replace and improve upon them. In Hines' 'Holy Dustbins' medit., he is the man-child, mordantly 'rummaging' around in both the reality and the symbolic suggestiveness of the bin. The historian Damer likewise strategically, polemically deploys the graphic potency of uncontrolled rubbish and bins. Damer continues at length in his omniscient narration about the 'visually very depressing' scheme in Govan [his emphasis], noting that the 'only person in SEGS [socio-economic groups] 1–4', was himself, 'living in the scheme for the purposes of research'[21]. This fact does not hinder him from commenting in critical detail on the people and culture around him, from his omniscient, loftily academic perspective, looking down from higher knowledge, a higher SEG, with precisely the sort of eye Hines will only parody. Damer says that 'older women tended to be somewhat shabbily dressed'; teenagers were 'very friendly, but, as is to be expected in a working-class scheme, extremely boisterous', and the 'Glaswegian tone was also clear from the empty wine-bottles on Monday morning's bins'[22] Lest we think Damer is in any way prejudiced against the inhabitants of this scheme, he prefaces his research with a defensive assertion:

> Let me make it crystal clear that I do not subscribe to the view that the tenants of this scheme are all winos, lumpenproletarians, criminals, junkies, or anything else of a nasty nature. This is not to say that the place is devoid of unpleasant people, but they exist everywhere, even in academe.[23]

Even in academe? Can this be? Hines' parody of this style of 'academic' omniscient account, and of the style of Millar's bus history I discuss above – like Damer, somewhat distant from the 'the average citizen' – is fragmentary and momentary, though the pseudo-scientific register is one he continually returns to for sourly playful and political purposes.

The 'Holy Dustbins' passage (*BH* 79–81) contains a generalised account of the communal use of a tenement midden with some seemingly detailed mathematical, architectural calculations.[24] The use of the generic impersonal second-person pronoun 'you' creates a general and inclusive perspective; but where the 'you' pronoun is maintained even into the discussion of the family, the job, the future, time, and back into the rubbish, the debris, its general applicability seems somehow unconvincing and desperate. Hines' use of 'you' is a hollow attempt to distance the material facts from his singular subject position – to push it away from him (singular) to you (plural). But all the material of the passage relates directly to himself. If however he is addressing himself – if 'you' is singular and meant to be himself – then 'you' is actually *not* impersonal or generic at all. Here as elsewhere, it is hard to tell whether Hines is vocalising these words or not; the one explicit address to his son suggests little Paul could be a silent auditor, as he often is in the novel, trapped like a rabbit in the glare of his father's full-beam monologues. One of the many awkward interfaces of language use in the novel occurs in the recurring fact that Hines does not talk four-year-old language to his quiet boy. Here then, Paul, in some ways the unspoken moral heart of the novel, could be the silent recipient of a vocalised 'Holy Dustbin' meditation. In Hines' eyes, Paul is not 'extrovert, the withdrawn side maybe allowing him to survive that bit more easily' (*BH* 148). Although Hines persistently worries about the effects upon Paul of the material conditions in which the family live, he rarely concerns himself with the impact upon Paul of his own tendencies to be 'a bit quick to strike at times, bad tempered on occasion, and probably inconsistent' (*BH* 149). For a father with a full-time job Hines spends a lot of time with Paul, ferrying him to nursery, cooking for him, bathing him, meaning the novel as a whole fights against the gendered stereotype of exclusively female management of domestic and parental responsibilities: Hines mucks in a good deal. Perhaps ironically, many of his activities with Paul are enabled by the odd times of his shift pattern, and inversely they are necessitated by Sandra's working times. While Hines often entertains his son, either Paul rarely speaks or else his words are neglected by the free indirect narrative which centres exclusively on Hines.

But whether Hines' 'Holy Dustbin' monologue is spoken or silent, the content compounds Hines' private thoughts with a performative, non-personalising 'you' form which together confirm a detachment – comic, intentional, acerbic, sardonic though it may be – of Hines from his own circumstances. Detachment opens up in the final few lines, as Hines admits an inability to do anything but watch and wait, and even then, concedes he is unable to do so 'properly'. This passage is one of a number of pivotal moments where Hines admits, seemingly to himself, that he is not in control of the material circumstances of his life, a general characteristic of Kelman's male protagonists. Here we get a sense that Hines has put himself out of reach of the possibility of control by not playing the game at work. There is no sense of anger in this passage, at least not with the rules or the rule-enforcers; instead he exhibits an existential realisation of the impossibility of positive action or activation of new futures. The comic gestures at mathematically taking control – the measurements of the tenement middens, the closing and confusing playfulness with counting time – are futile number games which emulate a controlling, rationalising, scientific discourse but are productive of a brittle two-dimensionality, of flat despair, of formulae for the alchemy of emptiness. In this, Hines is like Yevgeny Zamyatin's hero D-503 in

We, who likewise attempts to pour the 'cold water' of 'logic' onto the overheating machine of his life which is slipping out of control; D-503 fumbles to develop a formula for love, to take mathematical control of it.[25]

Hines' life is so fraught and pressured, that love has been squeezed out of his family's schedule. His scrabbling with numerals adds to the burgeoning evidence that he cannot play the number games: he cannot manage the numbers of a clock face to help him live time according to that most rigorously, though often laughably, timetabled of industries – bus transport. The bus timetable is a form of crude, in-your-clock-face ideological apparatus with which Hines clearly has systemic problems: he has a personality clash with clocking on, a depressive's love of sleeping on the couch, and more seriously he displays an anarchic individualist's desire for liberty. In this passage, the numerology of time is presented as someone else's system, and it is a system which is to be ignored. The work timetable could be regarded as the structure which, as the abstract other half of a double-act with the concrete failures of the tenement building, continually presses in upon Hines' relationship with Sandra. But it is precisely his flouting, neglecting, even abhorring, of the bus timetable system which has made him '[fail] to make a go of things' (*BH* 80). Measuring, parcelling, managing of time is rendered into a ridiculous, meaningless futility by the final paragraph of this passage.

The attempted reassurance in the flagging repetition of versions of 'you just go along' in the 'Holy Dustbins' meditation does not last long. What follows is 'the house coming on top of the job': unmanageable, untimely, hugely significant problems are piling up, which tumble through Hines' retreating passivity, and breach his blank, recursive defence of 'just going along'. All the packed double-decker buses of Hines' problems are coming along at once, at a frenetic, asphyxiating, uncontrollable pace. And so Hines clears the space, clears the crumbling edifices of his anxieties, carrying them away with the ease of a wheelbarrow, dismissing them into the midden, into someone else's hands, from the private into a communal space, into the plural 'you'. But the bin he is emptying all this 'debris' into, is a 'holey dustbin': he is fully 'aware of how light it feels and then to be finding all the rubbish lying in a heap on the fucking floor' (*BH* 79). The mental processes he is engaging with here are 'light': he is not engaging with the detail of the problems of his three-headed family. His hands, his wallet, his thoughts cannot between them contain, cannot hold, so cannot control, the problems. So the holy holey dustbin is of course that comic, publicly performative, perforated, porous, recursive brain of his; full of stuff but not functional, not properly doing the job which is its lot. The midden is somewhere in there, in his 'wide head', in a backcourt area which is festering with all these problems heaped on top of each other, becoming food for the rodents of his own febrile anxiety, a grotesque private space which is impossible to clear. It is from this mental midden that Hines has finally, though temporarily, to turn away; he cannot 'look properly' at it. And in that turning away is the beginning of Hines' most significant problem of all: his breakdown, what he calls his 'cracking up' (*BH* 108).

Glasgow and *Hines*: 'real stories'

Even the most sensitive critics are unquestioning in their belief that Kelman's world is uncomplicatedly Glasgow. Here Ben Knights, a non-Glaswegian critic, worries about his distance from that locatable world:

> Kelman has made a speciality of devising a literary notation for Glasgow working-class speech, and any account of his fiction that overlooked Glasgow, that behaved as though this richly coded context could be simply transposed elsewhere, would be a travesty. His linguistic construction of Glasgow is as much a part of the fiction as Grassic Gibbon's Kincardineshire is of his. This provenance presents problems to the middle-class English teacher critic . . .[26]

Knights is by no means the only self-reflective critic of Kelman, but he is the most self-critical. The anxiety about the social and cultural distance between himself and the origins of Kelman's writing is something I share. What I want to focus on here is Knights' assertion that to deny Kelman's fiction its locality, its specific rootedness, 'would be a travesty'. For Knights, the Kelman critic has a moral responsibility to ensure he/she does not forget *for a moment* the locus of the text, and the geographic origins of the language. And I think this is an assumption of almost all critics of Kelman, no matter what the text: at no point in the critical process is Glasgow to be forgotten. While it might be entirely justifiable from a reading of Kelman's published version of his origins as a writer, this is yet a version of moralised critical necessity which does not tally with Kelman's own unpublished account of what *Hines* is about. In fact the world of *Hines* was not simply to be Glasgow, or rather, not *just* Glasgow. In an undated draft of the novel, which included Kelman's typed frontispiece mock-ups, he incorporates a brief, single-paragraph 'Foreword':

> That which you are about to read is a work of fiction. Thus the "city of Glasgow" referred to by the author is not the actual city of Glasgow which is situated on the west coast of central Scotland, it is simply a part of the fiction. This applies to other geographical locations as well as to individual characters and the rest of the named detail.[27]

As a foreword this sounds formal, stiff and perhaps could be characterised as legalistically defensive, and perhaps it is no wonder it did not appear in the final published version of the novel. Kelman does not want to allow any reader to think that they are implied directly as being represented in the novel, a standard device of any creative work based on 'real life': such a deflective statement secures the novelist and publisher from being sued for defamation. What is more significant to this discussion, however, is the distance forced between textual Glasgow and 'actual Glasgow'. Here we have two Glasgows conceptualised, a splitting of fictional from actual which might remind us of Unthank and Glasgow, Lanark and Thaw, in Gray's *Lanark*. *Lanark* had an unparalleled impact on Scottish culture in 1981. It provided a context for the publication of *Hines* in 1984 which deliberately bifurcated Glasgow into 'real' re-imagined city and previously unthinkable Unthank. Through Philip Hobsbaum's creative writing group in Glasgow, Kelman was an early reader of and influence upon Gray's first novel.[28] We might therefore wonder why Kelman thought it necessary to include the defensive assertion that 'the "city of Glasgow" referred to by the author is not the actual city of Glasgow', even if only temporarily in an earlier draft of the novel. But in *Lanark* the reality is that neither represented world is 'real' at all, even if Thaw's Glasgow-based narrative seems more realistic, attends to recognisable conventions and techniques of literary realism, and is founded in identifiable places, we still read Unthank as analogous to real Glasgow, so Unthank is just as 'real' as the Glasgow explicitly mentioned in the novel. Differently fictionalised though they may be, both Unthank and Glasgow are fictionalised representations of *real* Glasgow, and are equally and textually distant from it, even if one makes play with the space between text and reality, while the other tries to diminish its presence.

All of Kelman's characters tell stories of some kind; but the female subject of a short story entitled 'Real Stories' is worth consideration because she constructs fantasy stories 'with outcomes different from real life' (*TB* 157). She defends her stories from 'criticism', and she knows clearly their relationship to actual reality:

> She always knew them for what they were so so what is what she said to herself as soon as the criticism started, they're my own stories and nobody else's so why should I worry about them being true or no, just to suit other people. (*TB* 157)

The 'criticism' seems to come mostly from her husband, who, with possibly gender-determined 'rationality', assumes these fantasies are designed 'to keep the real ones secret. He thought there were "real stories" she was keeping secret from him' (*TB* 158). Ben Knights reads the typical Kelman hero in a parallel way: '[t]he isolated man acts out imaginary roles before an interior audience'.[29] The word 'imaginary' is always key to understanding the narratives weaved by Kelman's protagonists. The woman in 'Real Stories' has an intrusive, bullying husband as an exterior audience who forces his way in, and the stories out. The woman's tragedy is that she is not allowed to keep her stories to herself. Her story can serve as a gendered model for the nature of Kelman's own 'real stories' and their reception among real critics who assume that his fictional world is really and only Glasgow and serves uncomplicatedly to document 'real life', often a yardstick held up against Kelman's work. As we shall see, later novels much more obviously problematise this assumption by removing concrete contexts or by including contextual suggestions of a futuristic world (*TA* and *YH*). From the deleted 'Foreword' to *Hines* though, it appears it was always Kelman's intention to make readers aware that the novel presents something other than 'actual Glasgow', an intention rendered latent in the published version of the novel. However there are strategies of nomenclature with which Hines himself plays, and which support the probable intention of the omitted 'Foreword'.

One such strategy is Hines' partial avoidance of concrete nouns and specific reference to recognisable places. The 'District of D' (*BH* 80) is Drumchapel, 'the Drum' (*BH* 110), which is named as the place where Hines grew up (*BH* 102) and where Hines' family still lives now (*BH* 45 and 149); while 'Zone K' by contrast is possibly Knightswood (for Neil McMillan at least[30]), where Sandra's wealthier family reside, both suburban Knightswood and the satellite town Drumchapel lying north-west of Glasgow city centre. Douglas Gifford is confident that the Hines' tenement is in Maryhill[31] though this is not made explicit in the novel. For all this identifiable specificity, when reduced to the abrupt denotation of a single initial these areas become anywhere, become types, are rendered nameless, abstracted, anonymous; to a degree they are emptied of identifiable character. At the same time the renaming or, rather, *denaming*, is playfully alliterative, suggestive of centralised town planning and state control and possibly in this regard it is allusive to the abbreviated surname of Kafka's Joseph K – what Nathalie Sarraute calls 'but a slender prop' and a 'frail envelope'[32] – or to Zamyatin's dystopian hero D-503. Whatever the possible allusion, Hines curtails whole areas of his life to blunt consonants:

> At times like the present 1 or 2 items cannot be dwelt upon. Especially when cutting through from Y to D because of the route taking on to the outer skirts of High Amenity Zone K. (*BH* 119)

In playfully digressive passages such as this, the regionality of the traditional working-class novel, with all its concrete proper nouns, with all its locatedness in recognisable proper-name factuality, is dismissed by coldly mathematical-sounding formulae. Locality becomes anonymity while local organic character becomes planner's rationalising urban and suburban scheme. Shocking though this might sound, especially to the more territorially-inclined Scottish critics, it simply doesn't matter where Y or D or Zone K are meant to be: what matters is that they do not matter, to town planner, to council policy-maker and to some degree to Hines. They are letters marking a meaninglessness which is imposed from above. Paradoxically they are letters that give the 'Glasgow novel', if this is what *Hines* is – and most commentators would have it so – a more immediately and abstractedly universal significance. Kelman's fictional Glasgow becomes any city, any town: a sprawling, confusing urban stage-set for the studying of the human condition, and for the 'zoning' management of town planners, of social engineers. Dorothy McMillan successfully proposes that Kelman charts the space between managed zones:

> The invention of suburbia supported by blue trains and motor cars worked to protect the managerial and professional classes from too-disturbing proximity to urban degradation. But the *coup de grâce* to

the notion of the readable city comes with the development of outer-city schemes: it is no longer necessary to by-pass the others, their existence need scarcely be recognised at all. For why would anyone go to Drumchapel, Easterhouse, Castlemilk and so on unless they lived there or knew someone who did, knew personally that is, the powerless and the dispossessed. It is in the gap between the inner city and this undiscovered territory of the periphery that James Kelman imagines his Glasgow.[33]

For McMillan, the zones demarcate and separate classes, and Kelman is a pioneer, charting liminal areas written out of Glasgow's self-presentation. I would like to argue that, just as his world focuses on the 'gap between the inner city and this undiscovered territory of the periphery', Kelman also opens up for inspection and consideration the gulf between textuality and actuality. Expressed predominantly in the negative though it is, it may have been a shame that the Foreword did not make it in to *Hines*, as from the start of his novel-writing, it would have complicated and textualised his reception which is too often reductively contextualised in the straightjacket of a realism interpreted through authorial autobiography rather than narrative form. When positioned next to Kelman's repeated and foundational declarations that he always intended to write about and from within his specific culture, so much so that it almost becomes the *raison d'être* for his choice of form, the assertion that the world of Hines 'is not the actual city of Glasgow' is problematic to say the least. It is especially so when positioned alongside his oft-quoted opening declaration in *Three Glasgow Writers* (1976), which in its entirety reads as follows:

> I was born and bred in Glasgow
> I have lived most of my life in Glasgow
> It is the place I know best
> My language is English
> I write
> In my writings the accent is in Glasgow
> I am always from Glasgow and I speak English always
> Always with this Glasgow accent
>
> This is right enough[34]

As Douglas Gifford has noted, this pithy declaration is 'probably the closest to poetry Kelman has ever attempted'.[35] Poetical it certainly is in its tensions generated by the brevity of form, and by repetition within that confining, irregular shape. The tensions are apparent between the repeated dominant proper nouns: 'Glasgow' (repeated five times) and 'English' (two times). The written Glasgow 'accent' only emerges in the form of an expression in the final line: 'right enough' is a recognisable Glaswegian expression. It forges a bridge to a poem by Tom Leonard, which starts:

> right inuff
> ma language is disgraceful

And which ends:

> ach well
> all livin language is sacred
> fuck thi lohta thim[36]

The speaker of this poem fights his way through repeated condemnation from all quarters towards the concluding assertion of his right to own and to express his language in the way he sees fit. In Kelman's poem, 'right enough' is likewise a declaration of moral certitude, though the 'enough', on the page at least, serves to soften the assertiveness of the phrase with a slight inflection of sufficiency; 'enough' seems to infer a qualification that what has been said is 'right enough *for now*'. 'Enough' is more directly an expression of closure and sufficiency. Kelman's Glasgow accent might indeed be 'right enough' as a starting point, but it does not account for the complexities of his relationship to English, which language is said to be possessed by the speaker. The contrast with Leonard's use of the differently spelt 'inuff' displays exactly how 'English' Kelman's spelling is: Leonard's spelling enacts the phonetic difference they are both asserting. Kelman's claim that his 'language is English' opens up a number of possible interpretations: the language is to be English, not Scots; Glasgow-accented English is a valid, living variety; the Glasgow-accented writer 'owns' English as much as anyone else; when it comes to language, there are no margins, no peripheries, indeed, no 'dialects', just English with an 'accent'; therefore, every variety of English is a variation with an 'accent': even standard English. Scotland, Scottishness, the Scots tongue, a Scottish accent: none of these possible derivations of Kelman's national location are included. This poem, if that is what it is, might well repeat 'Glasgow' frequently in a short space, but not as many times as the first-person pronoun, a rare enough occurrence in Kelman's work. Here, 'I' appears six times and the possessive 'my' three times: nine assertions of the first person in nine lines means that this poem is as much about the individual identity of the author as we could find anywhere in Kelman's commentaries on his own work. And that identity, the identity which we encounter through language on the page, is to be emphasised and shaped by Glasgow, and by English. But in its purpose, in its situation as the introduction to an early and formative anthology of his work, an anthology which is likewise defined by its Glasgow-ness, by the Glasgow-ness of its Glaswegian writers who all write, albeit variously, with a 'Glasgow accent', this poem becomes a performance of identity, a shop window, a sandwich board; it is also an essentialising gesture towards an ideal. 'Glasgow is to be being maintained throughout this work', it seems to be saying.

The unpublished foreword to *Hines* is likewise a performance, but it forms an opposite game of warning for the readership not to fall into the trap of assuming that Glasgow simply means Glasgow, that this fiction is simply equable with reality, with factuality. We are to be careful, but we are also to be free to take this novel where we want; indeed we are enjoined to relegate the significance of Glasgow to being just 'simply part of the fiction'. Hines himself plays with the same relationship when he fashions the 'District of D': this is and is not Drumchapel; 'High Amenity Zone K' is and is not Knightswood or Kelvinside. Of course, because it is text we are dealing with, materially it is only Kelman's textualising of Drumchapel that we can ever experience through this text, not its actuality. Hines makes us aware not only of his own deliberate distancing from his reality when he abbreviates places to initials: he makes us aware of our own distance from the real place, whether we have been there in reality or not. If it is the case that *Hines* is not only about Glasgow, if this was Kelman's intention, the English middle-class critic Ben Knights is partly wrong to be so fully anxious over his distance from Glasgow culture, and so he, and many of the rest of us, can rest a little easier. If a paradoxical tension remains, it is between Kelman's fictional realism – in commitments to the local, to the particular, to 'his' culture, to facticity – and his political idealism – in anarchic rejection of nationalism or regionalism, which surfaces most graphically in the supranational worlds of *Translated Accounts* (2001) and *You Have to be Careful in the Land of the Free* (2004). Discussing *A Disaffection* in 1989, Kelman claimed an infinitely broad canvas for his art, painting himself out of the autobiographical corner this chapter started out in: 'I can write about anything. I don't have to have direct personal experience myself'.[37]

Notes

1 When Kelman organised the manuscripts for deposit in the Mitchell Library, Glasgow, he remained vague as to when he had first drafted the novel that was to become *Hines*. On one pack of drafts he has written: 'Various early Bussed Drafts pre 1975 & maybe 73'. Mitchell Library MSS, 775039 SR89 [almost all Kelman MSS carry this reference number, many sheets not being numbered, making references to specific pages difficult].

2 Nicholas Wroe, 'Glasgow kith', *Guardian* 'Review', 2 June 2001, 20–3. See subheading, at 20.

3 William Hunter, 'A voice of Glasgow with a withering effect on apostrophes', *Glasgow Herald,* 12 February 1983, 8. See Kelman's account of working conditions and 'army' style of bus-station management and ineffectuality of the union in 'Say Hello to John La Rose', *AJS*, 220–2. Talking of the circumstances which led Kelman to study at university, he says: 'I was no longer able to drive a bus; I'd been in the job too often, so I was basically barred out of the three bus companies at that time – Alexander's, SMT, and the Corporation of Glasgow.' Michael Gardiner, 'James Kelman interviewed', *Scottish Studies Review*, 5:1 (2004), 108.

4 Stuart Little, *Glasgow Buses* (Glossop: Transport Publishing Co. Ltd. and Scottish Tramway and Transport Society, 1990), 48.

5 Little, *Glasgow Buses*, 55.

6 A. Millar, *Strathclyde. British PTEs: 1* (London: Ian Allan, 1985), 57. My thanks to Dorothy McMillan for explaining the full Glaswegian significance of 'menodge'.

7 Agnes Owens, 'Bus Queue', *Lean Tales*, with James Kelman and Alasdair Gray (London: Jonathan Cape, 1985), 120–1.

8 'In 1966 Glasgow had only 1 car to 11 people, compared with 1 to 4 in Surrey, yet the city's urban motorway plans were among the most ambitious in Britain', Chistopher Harvie, *No Gods and Precious Few Heroes: Scotland 1914–1980* (London: Edward Arnold, 1981), 145.

9 'Bothy' has widespread use in Scotland as a dwelling for workmen, but the *OED* skews that meaning in an interesting direction: 'hut or cottage; *spec.* a building consisting of one room in which the unmarried men servants on a farm are lodged together, or in which masons, quarrymen, etc. lodge together'.

10 Gilles Deleuze and Felix Guattari, *Kafka: Toward a Minor Literature* [1975], trans. Dana Polan (Minneapolis: University of Minnesota Press, 1986), 17. For a dismissal of their work on Kafka see Pascale Casanova,

The World Republic of Letters [1999], trans. M. B. DeBevoise (Cambridge, MA: Harvard University Press, 2004), 203.

11 Thomas Malthus, *An Essay on the Principle of Population* [1798], ed. Geoffrey Gilbert (Oxford: Oxford University Press, 1993).

12 The Hines family is 'typical' of the majority of Glasgow residents in living in council-owned and managed accommodation. At 64%, the proportion of people living in public housing in greater Glasgow is much higher in 1990 than both Scottish and UK averages (54% and 32% respectively). See Miles Horsey, *Tenements & Towers: Glasgow Working-Class Housing, 1890–1990* (Edinburgh: The Royal Commission on the Ancient and Historical Monuments of Scotland, 1990), 69. For Horsey, writing his exhibition-based booklet 'as a contribution to Glasgow's year as European City of Culture' (ix), this percentage indicates success on the part of the Corporation.

13 In *Lanark*'s 'Tailpiece' Alasdair Gray seems to owe everything to Kafka:

Q But where did *Lanark* come from?

A From Franz Kafka. I had read *The Trial* and *The Castle* and *Amerika* by then, and an introduction by Edwin Muir explaining these books were like modern Pilgrim's Progresses. The cities in them seemed very like 1950s Glasgow, and old industrial city with a smoke-laden grey sky that often seemed to rest like a lid on the north and south ranges of hills and shut out the stars at night. *Lanark* (Edinburgh: Canongate, 2002), 569–70.

14 After the manuscript 'Foreword' discussed later in this chapter, the following quotation is included and referred to as shown: ' "Don't you want to join us?" I was asked recently by an acquaintance when he ran across me alone after midnight in a coffee-house that was already almost deserted. "No, I don't," I said.' (Kafka's DIARIES).

15 H. Gustav Klaus, *James Kelman* (Tavistock: Northcote House and British Council, 2004), 35. Klaus notes that George Friel's *Mr Alfred M.A.* features many of these same compound words, 98, n. 5.

16 Cairns Craig, *The Modern Scottish Novel: Narrative and the National Imagination* (Edinburgh: Edinburgh University Press, 1999), 103.

17 'Concerning the Nature of Time', in Keith Ansell Pearson and John Mullarkey (eds), *Henri Bergson: Key Writings* (New York and London: Continuum, 2002), 215. See also 'The Idea of Duration', 49–77.

18 Heading, section of *Hines* from Kelman manuscripts, [Kodak Box], Mitchell Library, Kelman MSS 775039 SR89, 116.

19 Seán Damer, *From Moorepark to 'Wine Alley': The Rise and Fall of a Glasgow Housing Scheme* (Edinburgh: Edinburgh University Press, 1989), 129.

20 Gray, *Lanark*, 122–9. Here, lower middle-class boy Thaw encounters working-class 'midden-rakers' for the first time.

21 Damer, *From Moorepark to 'Wine Alley'*, 131.'

22 Damer, *From Moorepark to 'Wine Alley'*, 134–6.

23 Damer, *From Moorepark to 'Wine Alley'*, viii.

24 Hines delineates and counts sections within other sections on the front of the tenement's gas fire, which is typical of the internal process of geometric mapping and counting he undertakes for various parts of his territory: 'For each of the 3 sections there are 24 miniscule rectangles concealing hundreds and hundreds of toty wee pointed items of the colour white' (*BH* 150).

25 Yevgeny Zamyatin, *We* [1922], trans. Mirra Ginsburg (New York: Avon, 1972), 135.

26 Ben Knights, *Writing Masculinities: Male Narratives in Twentieth-Century Fiction* (Basingstoke: Macmillan, 1999), 180.

27 Mitchell 775039 SR89, [Kodak Box, no pagination].

28 In the playful 'Epilogue' to *Lanark* Gray, or rather, Gray's version of the 'author' of the novel, admits that he 'received from James Kelman critical advice which enabled him to make smoother prose of the crucial first chapter' (*Lanark*, 499, n. 13). For Kelman's discussion of their mutual influence, see Tom Toremans, 'An interview with Alasdair Gray and James Kelman', *Contemporary Literature*, 44:4 (Winter 2003), 585. For a full account of Kelman and Gray in Hobsbaum's group, see 'Postscript' to *Lean Tales*, James Kelman, Agnes Owens, Alasdair Gray [1985] (London: Vintage, 1995), 283–7. See also Philip Hobsbaum, 'The Glasgow Group: An Experience of Writing', *Edinburgh Review*, 80:1 (1988), 58–63.

29 Knights, *Writing Masculinities*, 190.

30 Neil McMillan, 'Wilting, or the "Poor Wee Boy Syndrome": Kelman and Masculinity', *Edinburgh Review*, 108 (2001), 48. Could 'K' also suggest the prosperous Kelvinside, which is near Knightswood? In contrast to Knightswood, Drumchapel in the 1980s was becoming a 'problem', which definition is itself problematic (see Damer, *From Moorepark to 'Wine Alley'*, 169). Drumchapel was the product of the 1946 Housing Act, as Damer outlines: 'In many cities, "perimeter estates" were developed on virgin sites at the edges of the urban development or even well beyond them. Some of these were massive, bigger in population size than small towns: Glasgow's four perimeter estates, Castlemilk, Easterhouse, Drumchapel and Pollok, were to house between 40,000 to 50,000 each. From the late 1950s, wholesale slum clearance, or 'comprehensive redevelopment' as it was called, resulted in the emigration of large numbers of inner-city dwellers to these outlying estates' (Damer, *From Moorepark to 'Wine Alley'*, 51). Born the same year as Bevan's Housing Act, Kelman with his family followed the same trajectory: from Govan tenements, near Elder Park, to Drumchapel.

31 Douglas Gifford, 'Scottish Fiction Since 1945 I', in Douglas Gifford, Sarah Dunnigan and Alan MacGillivray (eds), *Scottish Literature: In English and Scots* (Edinburgh: Edinburgh University Press, 2002), 879.

32 Nathalie Sarraute, *The Age of Suspicion* [1956], in *Tropisms and The Age of Suspicion*, trans. Maria Jolas (London: John Clader, 1963), 77.

33 Dorothy McMillan Porter, 'Imagining a City', *Chapman*, 63 (Spring 1991), 47. This article is discussed by Willy Maley, 'Denizens, Citizens, Tourists, and Others: Marginality and Mobility in the Writings of James Kelman and Irvine Welsh', in David Bell and Azzedine Haddour (eds), *City Visions* (Harlow: Pearson, 2000), 60–72.

34 *Three Glasgow Writers: A Collection of Writing by Alex.Hamilton, James Kelman, Tom Leonard* (Glasgow: Molendinar Press, 1976), 51.

35 Gifford, 'Scottish Fiction Since 1945 I', 873.

36 Tom Leonard, *Ghostie Men* (Newcastle: Galloping Dog Press, 1980), untitled poem, no pagination. Reproduced in *Intimate Voices* (Buckfastleigh: Etruscan Books, 2003), 134. For a linguistic account of the language of this poem, see John Corbett, *Language and Scottish Literature* (Edinburgh: Edinburgh University Press, 1997), 13–14.

37 Alasdair Marshall, 'Hot tip for the top', *Evening Times*, 27 September 1989, 10.

3

A Chancer (1985)

Withdrawal and reticence

Tammas, the twenty-year-old man who is the focus of Kelman's second published novel, *A Chancer* (1985), is defined by two actions: he habitually gambles and he habitually leaves. He gambles in card games at work, on dominoes in pubs, at bookmakers, at greyhound races, at horse races, on games of snooker and in casinos. He leaves social situations of all sorts: a date with a girlfriend, a football game, employment, nights out with friends, a wedding, the living room if his sister and her husband are about to enter and, perhaps most bleakly, he splits off from a party of his friends just before they leave Glasgow for a fun weekend in Blackpool (*C* 39, 13, 63, 118, 227, 193, 56 respectively). Inevitably all social get-togethers are left by all participants at some point, so Tammas' repeated leaving would be no peculiar characteristic at all, were it not for the fact that his departures are either abrupt and supplied with only the most minimal, often fabricated, of excuses; or else his departures are silent, and happen without notice, without warning, without explanation or expressed rationalisation.

Sometimes, the magnetism of gambling lures him away from social gatherings, and occasionally gambling has a palpably isolating effect: a clear instance occurs when Tammas misses the team selection for a football game because of placing a bet on horses at the bookmakers. Missing the selection means that he ends up as an unused substitute, which in turn leads to his decision to leave the game after half-time, becoming, as Donnie describes him, a 'vanishing substitute' (*C* 10–13). But it would be simplistic, and judgemental, to assume that gambling is the sole reason for Tammas' frequent social withdrawals. Some types of gambling as they appear in this novel are inherently social: Tammas has strong, reliable bonds with experienced gamblers such as Phil, Deefy and Joe, and is himself regarded with clear esteem by gambling friends less seriously committed than himself, such as John and Billy (e.g. *C* 166–8). Studies of the psychology of gambling have emphasised that gambling 'does not take place in isolation' and that 'the main reward for gambling was recognition by others in the group of their courage and strength in the face of great risks'.[1] For Tammas, gambling is as much a source of rich sociability as it is an excuse for retreat. Nevertheless, his leaving and extended absences are the subject of much teasing discussion among his acquaintances – 'Ya sneaky bastard ye where've ye been hiding!' (*C* 296) is how Billy jokingly greets him after a protracted, unexplained absence from their usual social haunts. Fall-out because of his unannounced social and communicative withdrawals can also cause serious friction with those who depend on him. When combined with the effect of Tammas' verbal reticence, these departures mean that he seems semi-detached, reluctant to engage. At the same time he is, paradoxically, highly sociable.

If this lead male's partial social withdrawal is perplexing and paradoxical, his personality is rendered yet more unreachable by a narrative which is pared down to the thinnest of frames. John Corbett rightly points out that the 'reflector' narrative style of *A Chancer*, in which a neutral third-person narrator is fused with the perspective of an individual character, largely maintains itself in a 'language of categorical assertion and physical description without positive or negative shading' and exhibits a 'concentration on physical detail, and the privileging of external, observable states rather than internal states'.[2] Therefore, actions must speak louder than words if we are to begin to know Tammas at all.

This novel is Kelman's purist and most determined realisation of his double-edged ambition to 'obliterate the narrator, get rid of the artist'.[3] The narrator of the first novel is embedded within Hines and follows exactly Hines' thoughts without providing access to anyone else's unspoken thoughts, and so provides nothing which Hines himself could not know. *A Chancer* is a more puritanical text in a sense, and is at the extreme end of the spectrum of Kelman's realist project in its desire to present an untrammelled 'facticity'. It does not allow obvious artifice into the narrative form: it is evidently intent on resisting a narrative process which it regards as untenable because

unbelievable, discredited because corrupting. Tammas is the protagonist, in the sense that we follow his moves, his actions, we hear
his words, and in the governing sense that no scene exists without
him. Yet we follow his perspective externally, so there can be no
omniscience, no knowledge of anything else but Tammas' actions
and the tight, local milieu in which they occur. In the absence of an
overt narrator to set a scene, to pull away or digress, the narrative
sticks to the lead male like glue, predominantly being granted access
only to his material exterior. For the most part, Tammas is a closed
book, other than through reported speech. Though H. Gustav Klaus
is quite right to point out that there is a 'much larger amount' of
dialogue in this novel than in Hines,[4] it tends to happen around the
still centre that is Tammas, because he himself does not say much.
Tammas is regarded as 'the quiet man' in the workplace (C 30); his
silence renders his relationship with Vi unstable (e.g. C 179), and
irritates his sister Margaret who is frustrated that he does not tell
her anything of substance: 'you never say a word' she says to him
during a confrontation which is closed, typically enough, by Tammas'
frowning retreat to his bedroom (C 82).

As indicated in Chapter 1 (Introduction), the combination of the
withdrawn narrator who provides almost no access to Tammas'
thoughts, with a socially reticent and retreating Tammas, means that
this novel demands interpretation of the most fundamental kind,
even if it is only to work out what Tammas' motivations and intentions
might be. This could be defined as a psychologically realistic novel,
in terms of the dynamics of characters' interactions, but it is never
psychologically explicit: we might know that Tammas has a nightmare
for instance, but we never know what that nightmare is. After the
nightmare, he wakes up and posts 'a short note to Vi', but we are
never to know what it contains either (C 212). Does it respond to the
nightmare? Does the nightmare indicate a troubled conscience? More
generally, what does Tammas worry about? What are the psychological
impacts of gambling losses and wins, for example? The narrative
style ensures that interpretation of this most basic sort is necessary,
difficult and at times, impossible.

The narrative perspective follows and watches Tammas, but this
watching and following is itself fictional and unbelievable, for how
can any novel provide access to an individual's actions without a
reliance on the suspension of disbelief at a structural level, at the
level of the act of reading? The narrative's perspective on Tammas

comes from a somewhere which is a textual nowhere: the position of the narrative voice does not exist in Tammas' world, because the voice is not embodied, and apparently has no subject position; it is outwith subjectivity. In fact, minimal Glaswegian inflections and lexis aside, the narrative is not a 'voice' at all: it is text and does not have an imaginable mouth, or a locus of oral delivery. It perceives with Tammas, but deliberately, systemically it makes no attempt to understand him, to interpret him, to judge him or account for him: in short, it has no mind. The blank, quotation-mark-free style presents a semblance not just of narratorial withdrawal into an effaced merging with Tammas' position, but also of authorial disengagement. Both effects are stylistic processes rather than textual facts, because of course both narrator and author are as present and as absent, respectively, in this text as in any other: without either, the text ceases to be. They just do a good job of keeping off stage, keeping their voices and techniques hushed and diminished, adverbs and adjectives minimised, the language pared down to a bare minimum redolent of the styles of American authors such as Ernest Hemingway and Sherwood Anderson, both of whom Kelman acknowledges as formative influences (*AJS*, 226).

At times though, this general description does not fit what the narrative does. While it is dominantly the case that the style seems to present a diminished status for the narrative voice – at once levelled with and external to the protagonist – actually there *are* moments in which the narrative adopts an interiorised position, and seems to have merged with and to be expressive of Tammas' thoughts. Such moments might outline a complex processing of unspoken calculations during a gambling situation or, much more rarely, might suggest his feelings when watching his lover Vi, as in the following scene:

> When he awakened he felt really stiff, his shoulders and neck and legs all cramped. And he had been lying on his cigarette packet. He leaned to turn off the electric fire, sitting until the bars stopped glowing. He lifted the half cigarette from the ashtray and found his matches on the floor. He did not smoke it. He knelt on the floor and stared across at the bed. Vi's shape was easily recognisable though he could not hear her breathing. He stood up.
>
> She was on her back, and the shape of her breasts, rise falling pause, rise falling pause. She lay close in to the wall. After a moment he returned to between the fire and the settee and he took off his clothes but left on his underpants. At the bedside he raised the blankets and

the sheet very carefully, very slowly, until there was enough space for
him to climb inside. He lay on his back close to the edge without
moving for a period, gradually inclining his head in her direction,
becoming more aware of her warmth, a smell of perfume or soap. Then
he turned a little, to touch her shoulder with his left hand, the material
of her nightdress nudging his forefingernail.

   He watched her and listened but except for her breathing there was
neither sound nor movement. She was asleep. He kept on watching
her. (*C* 152)

And the novel keeps on watching him watching. The stiffness he is
said to have 'felt' here is a sensation neither emotional nor intellectual,
and could probably be determined by watching the expression and
movement of Tammas as he wakes, therefore it is neither fully nor
only internally readable by the narrative. The unarticulated sensation
of cramp would only be experienced by Tammas, so an observer
would not 'see' it necessarily; to access the cramp here necessitates
access to his mind. Subsequent to this waking everything else provided
in the description of Tammas is mechanical, focused on actions, and
his responses to interpretations of his material surroundings – 'Vi's
shape' especially. The moment the narrative might be effecting a
change of position is in the rhythmic repetition of 'rise falling pause',
which is a metrical, even onomatopoeic, literary device. It is a
description of physical action, but it is also a moment of delicate and
sensual poetry. Entirely appropriate for this male subject watching
his lover it may be, but is this free indirect intervention into Tammas's
thoughts, or is it blank description of the mechanics of a human
body sleeping: is it plainly just what Tammas sees? Is it what he
would say, is it how he would express it, indeed, is this the way he
conceives of the breathing of his lover? Is this poetic phrase his
interior articulation of the sight? Because of its quite affected, and
effective, poetic economy, the narrative at this instance seems to
be implying that this is indeed both what Tammas sees and how he
reads the movement and rhythm of her body as she breathes. The
male eye is the active source of this poetry; the female 'shape' is the
passive stimulus, the bodily muse, we might even say, the territory
of the male explorer. And our access to the aroused male eye seems
to be momentarily interior and psychological.

   The remainder of the passage relates the scenario and Tammas'
actions in standard English, grammatically and orthographically
speaking, until the compound 'forefingernail', a technique Kelman

uses extensively in *Hines* and elsewhere (see Chapter 2). The elision of spaces between the constituent words of this compound makes the touching more connective somehow, the nail closer to the finger, more attached to the body, more firm and to the 'fore' as a link, as a channel of nudge. The intimacy of this passage is peculiarly heightened by these two moments of linguistic strangeness, moments of material description consistent with the overall narrative position, but which are somehow suggestive of much more than merely breathing or physical proximity. The detail of watching and the care which Tammas takes when moving, are all the product of a committed, interested, lustful love, a love which is otherwise barely articulated by Tammas, remaining mostly left to the reader's and Vi's faltering interpretations. The repeated phrase and the compound both seem to do much more than merely delineate an exterior action, and delicately, momentarily re-focalise the narrative towards an internal, reflective position.

Much more frequently, extended passages of access to Tammas' mind occur during his gambling, and the technique Kelman uses is more redolent of a free indirect style, as in the following passage:

> Collecting his jerkin from the locker-area he raced on to the exit and right out and up the road to the betting shop. The boardman was marking up the results of the race his third runner was in, its name being marked up, into the first position, 9 to 1. His third runner had won at 9 to 1. Nine to one. Tammas closed his eyelids. 20's 16's and 9's; 50 to 20 was 10 plus the 50 is 10.50 at 16's; 10.50 at 16's. He walked to the counter and got a pencil and a betting slip and went to one of the wall ledges to check the figures. As far as he reckoned he had £178 alone for the treble, £178 going on to his fourth and final runner, £178. That was a lot of money, it was fine, good money, plus the doubles, even if it lost, the fourth runner. Tammas nodded. It was good money – plus the three doubles, the 20's and 16's and the other two. Win lose or draw he had £178 plus three doubles – about another thirty or forty quid. Two hundred quid minimum. He opened the cigarette packet, put one in his mouth and looked for his matches, he did not have them, he must have left them on the oil drum or someplace. He walked to the counter and asked the woman cashier for a loan of her lighter. She pushed it beneath the grille to him. A sweetish taste in his mouth. He examined the betting slip once again and dragged on the cigarette. The taste had been there all day, to do with the heat probably, and the copper bars. The fourth runner was forecast favourite and favourites always had a favourite's chance, the most fancied horse

> in the race, the best fancied horse in the race, the horse with the best
> chance of winning – the horse that always let you down. It did not
> always let you down. Sometimes it won. Just not often.
>
>   He walked across to one of the walls where the formpages were
> tacked up but he stopped. He knew the betting forecast on the race,
> the favourite being reckoned an even money chance. There was nothing
> else he needed to know. Not now. He had backed it and that was that,
> the money was running on and there was nothing he could do about
> it, either the horse would win or it would lose. There was not anything
> in between. (*C* 253)

This is not the only scene where Tammas races from work to a betting
shop, but this occasion is distinctive in that he has just resigned
his job at the copper works during his first day in part because he
hears he is winning his 'comedy' bet (a bet in which winnings from
the first race are placed on the next race and so on – also known as
an 'accumulator', *C* 251). The potential winnings could amount to 'a
thousand quid' (*C* 254), so this is a moment of truly great expectations.
The merging of the third-person narrative with Tammas' own
thoughts is deliberately indistinct, but is shown initially through
the inconsistent repetition '9 to 1. Nine to one.' This repetition is a
technique used elsewhere in the novel, to suggest a thought being
processed and chewed over, a significant fact being taken in. Moving
from numerals to letters is a graphic representation of an expansion
of contemplation as Tammas slows down to digest the implications
of these odds. Towards the end of this passage he considers the
chances of the favourite winning: 'the most fancied horse in the race,
the best fancied horse in the race'. Such moments of repetition are
representative of a mind in process, not blankly descriptive narration:
these are Tammas' thoughts. We are granted access to his silent
calculations after he 'closed his eyelids'. He shuts out the visual to
focus his mind on calculations, which is a move also calculated
to enable the narrative access to his mind in action, without resort
to a blunt narratorial direction such as 'he thought'. Tammas thinks
his own language of numbers, and the result of his complex
calculations is that the fifty pence outlay now stands at £178. Again
Kelman uses the repetition of '£178' to suggest Tammas' mental
accommodation of a large sum of money being tackled from various
angles, while all the time allowing the narrator to externally show
what Tammas and people around him are doing in the third person:
'Tammas nodded', 'He walked', 'She pushed', 'He examined'. Not

resorting to the first person means that Kelman can segue his third-person descriptors into the train of thought, without recourse to traditional invasive markers of boundaries between voices. The lack of boundary markers also means Kelman can stylistically maintain pace and tension without entering into commentary such as 'Tammas was excited': it is remarkable that his narrator never resorts to such commentary here, though clearly that is exactly what Tammas is. His excitement is reproduced through sentences such as: 'That was a lot of money, it was fine, good money, plus the doubles, even if it lost, the fourth runner.' Here the terse quasi-paratactic syntactical units, the clipped jerking rhythm enacted by commas and the variety of monosyllabic adjectives applied to the money ('a lot', 'fine', 'good') effect tension and stuttering excitement, without any overt guidance from the narrator. This is not a rhythm of speech, but of recursive, frequentative, churning and quickly shifting thought. The thoughts also seem to be in process because they work against each other: 'the horse that always let you down. It did not always let you down'. Deployed commonly and comically in *Hines*, this technique presenting internal debate – of a dialectic tussle between contradictory propositions with no sure conclusion – is much rarer in *A Chancer*, and appears only when he is gambling. At the end of the quoted passage, Tammas seems to admonish himself for all this fervid engagement with possibilities and relinquishes the locus of control, admitting that there can be only a positive or a negative outcome for the fourth and final race, as for all gambles. The horse in the final race falls, but Tammas still walks away with 'two hundred quid minimum'.

Tammas' balancing of possible books is presented for a number of reasons: it demonstrates that, far from being a passive gambler who arbitrarily slaps money down on random chances, Tammas is a prospector, hunting the elusive gold, but with a mind-mapping of figures and calculations which is dextrously managed and adapted to the rolling, shifting figures and results, probabilities and possibilities which mathematically determine and conceptualise multiple outcomes. In *A Chancer*, gambling is not a mere metaphorical device for revealing the melancholic ironies of working-class life lacking control, or a sentimental tool to expose the fragility and fatalistic passivity of working-class life. In fact, if working-class passivity is anywhere in this novel, it is at work. Gambling by contrast is an arena for the active managing of risk. It is determined by the free choice of the individual to operate within a justifying and considerably cohesive set of interpersonal relations. Both lack and presence of money are means to forging and reinvigorating social bonds, mutual loyalties and dependencies, rivalries and conflicts. I do not mean to read this world anthropologically or analogically: as this novel presents it, gambling does not need to be a microcosm of anything else. It defines itself and is structured through the ongoing dynamics of relation between individual and chance. Chance is neither god, nor, as Cairns Craig reads it, absence. For Craig, the form of the novel means there is thought neither in gambling nor in Tammas:

> Immediate action and event are the only realities because the inner world of thought is nothing. In Tammas, Kelman has constructed his own version of Camus's Meursault: he is the outsider, whose consciousness of the existential condition means that he must live in entire dislocation with the ordinary human world and its emotions; he is the negater of all the values which chain us to our social world as though it were the ultimate reality.[5]

What Craig misses here is that we are provided only with an outsider's view of Tammas' world. It is not Tammas who is the outsider to his own experience, but the reader. Unless the reader happens to be well-versed and so necessarily well-experienced in the gambling culture of Glasgow, they will need explanations, and this novel offers none: clarifications of its mathematics, its calculations, or its gambling terminology are absent. The novel offers no explanations because this is not a guide to gambling which offers a way in: instead the novel is a blank assertion of what Kelman calls 'facticity'. The withdrawal of a narrative voice as guide means that the reader is left outside of the experience: watching, alienated, neither acknowledged nor involved. Kelman constructs alienation as a necessary subsequence in the reading and interpretative process, not as the dominant characteristic of Tammas' mind – or at least, not necessarily so. Craig is interpreting not what Tammas is thinking (as he cannot know, can only guess), but what the text's form means to him as a literary thinker: the blanks which Kelman leaves are filled in by Craig's horror.[6] The narrative withdrawal is read as discombobulating negation, not as creating free space in which to fulfil the unexpressed riches of Tammas' possible mind. Craig's reading of Tammas' 'entire dislocation' fills blanks not with questions, but with a retreat, with a critical withdrawal to match the narrative withdrawal. To read

Tammas as 'negater' is, ironically, to negate him: it is to deny his assertions of will and independence, to deny the qualities which others see in him which we are not permitted to see. As Sarah Engledow rejoinders, 'just because we are denied internal access to Tammas's qualities, including the quality of intelligent evaluation of his situation, it does not follow that he is without them'.[7] Similarly H. Gustav Klaus authoritatively summarises that 'poverty of condition in Kelman never means poverty of mind'.[8]

Freedom and facticity

The gambling passage from *A Chancer* quoted above can serve as a useful case study to determine why Kelman chooses to allow extended access to Tammas' mind only during gambling episodes. The answer lays in the opening to this passage: the winning of an accumulating bet, which Tammas relevantly calls a 'comedy', provokes him to leave a job he has only just started and which he does not like at all. Gambling encourages and enables Tammas to be free of a job he did not want to have. Gambling is freedom from wage slavery: not just in the winning of money, but in active participation. I do not mean this metaphorically: gambling actualises freedom. Kelman regards the narrative style likewise to be enacting a sort of freedom for his subjects:

> Getting rid of that standard third party narrative voice is getting rid of a whole value system. You have to start examining every term. The example I would use is the term 'beautiful', or 'pretty', or 'handsome', or 'ugly'. There is no possibility of using such a term in my work, not in the standard narrative, it's not a possibility. I can't even say 'fat' or 'thin' because to do that would be to assume a whole value system. None of my work will have any of that in it whatsoever. This is an extreme example of the kind of formal problems you might have to get through; in a way to begin a story from nothing. In a sense I think the jump is similar to the *nouveau roman*, a similar type of thing, trying for a value free text, total objectivity. Writers like Robbe-Grillet, Nathalie Sarraute. Let's just go for the factual reality here. Any colouring that's going on to try and get rid of. Whether it's from a feminist point, a heterosexual male point, a middle-class point, any point at all. Get rid of it. So that nobody else is going to be oppressed or colonised by it. And that's what I was trying to do in *A Chancer* – to get something that was "Let me state a fact here". So nobody can say that's your opinion because you're working class or middle class. It had to be something

that is so cold, so straight black and white that no-one can deny it as
fact. So in a sense, getting rid of the narrative voice is trying to get
down to that level of pure objectivity. This is *the* reality here, within
this culture. Facticity, or something like that.[9]

Kelman's plan is to reduce the narratorial mediation of his subjects
as much as possible, to attain what he calls 'factual reality'. The
inherent problem with Kelman's position, as Alan Freeman points
out, is that: 'Stories cannot be judged to be either true or false; they
are not factually verifiable.'[10] But it is all a question of degree: for
Kelman, the packaging of the subject by the voice of a narrator means
fiction becomes an exercise in the control of the subject by a 'value
system'. In application to a life like Tammas', such a value system
could only distort the authenticity of what is being represented. In
this passage, 'fact' can not mean something that actually happened
to a 'real' Tammas, for example, but is instead the representation of
a figure in an authentic historical context, without a traditional,
prejudicial, framing and constructing voice. Kelman's construction
of his creation of a 'story from nothing' is of course also impossible
because the novel enters the pre-existing meaning system of a
language which it uses even if it resists some of its standard practices.
But the aspiration is to clear the authorial mind, to attain a position
which is sufficiently primordial that the remaining narrative voice
appears free of any preconceptions, any prejudgement, of what the
character is, or where he and his world are going. The narrative voice
is to know and evaluate nothing, just to convey, without *apparent*
mediation. Following the example of the French *nouveau roman*
writers and theorists Robbe-Grillet and Sarraute, Kelman's narrator
does not *characterise* Tammas so much as present an individual in
society free of psychological essentializing. More broadly, this novel
inherits the *nouveau roman*'s 'drastic reduction in the scope of
what is represented by the fiction'.[11]

Kelman's recourse to the word 'facticity' means that there is a
phenomenological basis for his understanding of what he is doing
in his fiction.[12] Martin Heidegger uses the term to encapsulate a
philosophical approach which centres itself on 'being-in-the-world',
the 'present-everyday', 'everydayness, absorption, into the world,
speaking from out of and on the basis of it, concern.' Relevantly,
Heidegger offers a steer away from two potential routes of 'fundamental misunderstanding' of facticity: the first would be to assume
facticity could be followed through 'entertaining *portraits* of the

so-called "most interesting tendencies" of the present'. The second erroneous route of understanding facticity would be one 'fixated on vacantly *brooding* over an isolated ego-like self'.[13] Each of these routes can be considered through available fictional choices: firstly, narratives of extremes, of overt plotting, rather than narratives of the ordinary, the everyday, the quotidian; secondly, use of a first-person voice, focus on the 'I' of an author or narrator. We could characterise Kelman as avoiding the 'most interesting tendencies' of the contemporary moment, instead making great play of the neglected ordinary, the avoided common. While he is interested in isolated, alienated individuals, he determinedly avoids the first-person singular, and '*brooding* over an isolated ego-like self'. In choosing facticity as a guiding principle for *A Chancer*, Kelman is making a bid for narratological freedom, emancipation even, for the ordinary subject. For Jean-Paul Sartre, facticity is the determinant of freedom:

> We are condemned to freedom, as we said earlier, thrown into freedom or, as Heidegger says, "abandoned." And we can see that this abandonment has no other origin than the very existence of freedom. If, therefore, freedom is defined as escape from the given, from fact, then there is a fact of escape from fact. This is the facticity of freedom.[14]

We can directly apply Sartre's model to *A Chancer*, and to the context of the gambling scene above particularly. Tammas is the abandoned subject: his parents do not appear, and are never mentioned, in this novel. It is a 'given' in working-class life that the subject must work to live. Tammas rejects that model of existence, and gambling is set up in contradistinction to the imprisonment, the suffering and boredom, of work. Gambling money *immediately* that same money is acquired by the working subject – the race to the betting shop – is an act which 'determines itself by its very upsurge as a "doing"', as Sartre conceives of freedom. Gambling, like Sartre's freedom, is a 'nihilation of a given'. Tammas certainly annihilates his wages, and his relation to the structure which provided him with the precious money, the labour which makes that money precious. Tammas negates his labour through gambling, and in the act of gambling, frees himself of the determining necessity of labour. And he manages this, not through winning, but through the very act of gambling. Success is not the point, though of course it is a motivation: the act itself is resistance to an order, is the embodiment of a freedom. This is not to relegate the significance of winning large sums of money for Tammas who is so abjectly poor, but it does go some way to account for Kelman's choice of gambling as a forum for the investigation of facticity. He allows a degree of narrative interiority to deliver the psychological excitement of the gamble because he wants to show how much activity, how much engaged and complex thought, is involved in the skilful achievements of the gambler. Gambling is activity, not passivity, and it is in that action that freedom pertains. For Sartre, freedom is not wish-fulfilment:

> In addition it is necessary to point out against 'common sense' that the formula 'to be free' does not mean 'to obtain what one has wished' but rather 'by oneself to determine oneself to wish' (in the broad sense of choosing). In other words success is not important to freedom. The discussion which opposes common sense to philosophers stems here from a misunderstanding: the empirical and popular concept of 'freedom' which has been produced by historical, political, and moral circumstances is equivalent to 'the ability to obtain the ends chosen.' The technical and philosophical concept of freedom, the only one which we are considering here, means only the autonomy of choice.[15]

Tammas resolutely determines his own autonomy of choice in the act of gambling. As we shall see, the act of leaving is similarly determined by autonomous choice.

'nothing is more active than flight':[16] leaving Glasgow

> There was a brief silence. John turned to Tammas: Ever thought about emigrating?
> Emigrating? Course.
> Whereabouts?
> Any fucking place! (C 15–16)

The desire to move away that persistently pressures *The Busconductor Hines*, never results in Rab Hines actually leaving his tenement or his job permanently. The same is true of Kelman's third novel *A Disaffection*, in which Patrick Doyle considers heading south for good. Neither Hines nor Doyle enact their desire to move away. But *A Chancer* is closed by Tammas autonomously leaving Glasgow and heading south; heading south is also the action which closes 1994's *How late it was, how late*. Tammas has various possibilities and paths open to him, all of which encourage his quitting Glasgow. In his home city, there seem to be few attractive opportunities available for his consideration. People in Tammas' social circle who want to make a change to their lives, do so by leaving Glasgow. No other route of change is made available. On hearing tales of people leaving, the Glaswegians often celebrate with exclamations such as 'Aw great – that's smashing! Get him away from this place, eh!' (*C* 149). Glasgow is somewhere to leave. It would be hard to over-emphasise just how frequent the leaving of Glasgow is a conversational subject, in this archetypal 'Glasgow novel'. Tammas' first girlfriend, Betty, has been told by an aunt that 'there was plenty of jobs in England'. She talks of 'packing my bags and going away, going away from here altogether' (*C* 9 and 95). Tammas' close friends Rab, Donnie and John, separately leave Glasgow during the course of the novel: Donnie to New Zealand with his emigrating family, Rab to be a professional footballer for Hull City and John to look for work in Manchester (first mentions of these places: *C* 16, 115, 99). His remaining close friend and perennially unlucky gambling partner Billy is also attracted to the idea of moving to Manchester to get work in one of the 'stack of factories and industrial estates' (*C* 163). As it is presented in this novel, Glasgow is an emptying vessel, losing its population at an alarming rate.

Together with the drag of this contextual current around him, direct pressure is applied to Tammas to think about leaving too. John, who is 'fucking fed up with it here' (*C* 99), asks Tammas to go with him to Manchester (*C* 163), while acquaintance Brian McCann asks Tammas to go to Peterhead. The latter, a north-east Scottish fishing port, experienced considerable industrial expansion after deep-sea oil was discovered in 1970 one hundred miles off the coast. McCann, an unemployed electrician almost always referred to by surname (unlike Tammas, whose surname we never know), intends to take Tammas with him to find well-paid work in more building projects which he claims are about to be confirmed in the Peterhead area: 'it's a really big fucking job' (*C* 203). McCann also puts pressure on Tammas to do a burglary with him, which, through doubt and prevarication, he effectively turns down, never having 'done anything like that before' (*C* 240). This is an important moral decision on Tammas' part, marking him out as gently heroic. The job centre Tammas and his peers visit only seems to offer employment in distant locations: Welwyn Garden City and the Channel Islands, for example, some 400 and 500 miles south of Glasgow respectively (*C* 80 and 236). Through these advertisements, the United Kingdom's stark imbalance of economic opportunity becomes officially sanctioned. In its own subtle way the state is promoting economic migration out of Scotland to the economically-booming south. The novel provides no evidence whatsoever of inward investment or industrial development in Glasgow.

However, the novel does in fact provide some limited employment opportunities for Tammas in the Glasgow area, if not a job that interests or stimulates. Tammas leaves his first job because, he says, it is 'boring' (*C* 63 and 115). A more complex psychological reason is probable though not made available: this first resignation follows the awkward avoidance of a social trip to Blackpool and heavy losses incurred in gambling on greyhounds the same weekend, both events isolating Tammas utterly. Alone he watches his friends depart for Blackpool; alone and anonymous in a crowd of punters he watches dogs run away with his money (*C* 56; 58–63). The anonymous factory, in the process of cutting back on overtime, reducing shifts and inexorably threatening redundancies (*C* 2, 35 and 50), has so little work for the machinists that, when not playing cards, Tammas and a colleague Ralphie have to collect and burn rubbish to keep themselves occupied. It is evident to his older colleagues that clock-watching Tammas is impatient with this sort of work (*C* 25). As we have seen above, Tammas leaves his next job in a copper mill on his first day partly because he wins a large accumulator bet on the horses which takes him momentarily out of dependence on a wage (*C* 252), but also because he is not provided with basic safety equipment[17] and more generally, more aspirationally, because he does not 'really want to work in factories any more' (*C* 273). He is heavily criticised by older men for expecting to get something other than factory work (*C* 115 and 274). Interpreting his actions, and the way he is treated (typically he says next to nothing on this topic himself) we might conclude that Tammas does not believe that a miserable, even life-threatening, work environment is better than unemployment. The classic Scottish working-class, masculine work ethic, embodied so manfully by Tam the miner in William McIlvanney's paean to collective working-class identity *Docherty*,[18] seems irrelevant to the needs and desires of Tammas and his generation. And indeed while masculinity is much explored by Kelman, traditional 'masculinist workerism'[19] will prove largely irrelevant to all of Kelman's heroes. It is possible that the security and community of that collective workers' impulse is also something he keeps away from deliberately, and is redolent of an ideology from which Tammas wishes to flee entirely. Unions are always problematic in Kelman's opinion, because while he is committed to collective activity and the improvement of workers' rights, his experience tells him their management compromises unions' independence and their ability to fully represent the membership's interests (see *AJS*, 222–5). For example in the early story 'New Business' union discussion about the 'Bill' is stymied by the Chairman as '*ultra vires*' and by the 'Acting Secretary' as 'just politics anyway', and muddied by a discussion over the adequacy of toilet paper (*OP* 81–8). But this 'Bill' must be the Industrial Relations Act of 1971, designed by the Conservative government, as Campbell Balfour summarises, to 'strengthen official trade unionism by giving it more power over the militant work groups on the shop floor. This would in turn weaken the force of the lightning strike as a wage lever and slow down the pace and volume of wage demands'.[20] In the short story, the local union management do not want the 'Bill' discussed by the membership, modelling exactly the government's decision not to consult UK unions in framing the Act.[21] The Act initiated an irreversible decline in the power and status of unions. This power suffered its death-throes in the miners' strike of 1984–85 (in which as much as 94% of Scottish miners participated[22]). *A Chancer* was published at the height of that same strike in January 1985, yet for Tammas, unions and a sense of collective purpose in the workplace are simply not relevant at all.

While Tammas has father figures in Joe Erskine and Phil, his actual mother and father are absent from his life, and are not once mentioned in this novel; he visits his frail grandmother once and she says five functional words to him (*C* 233). His relationship with his sister Margaret in whose house he lives is solid, but muted. If Tammas finds a wider sense of community at all, it is in the honour-bound world of gambling and gaming, at dog tracks, in casinos, in snooker halls and occasionally on a football pitch – all of these spaces being predominantly, but not exclusively, male (he meets Vi at the Ayr horse races [*C* 122]). The masculine work ethic is irretrievably dwindling to irrelevancy because the heavy industries which produced it are no longer dependable. Work is not at the centre of Tammas' identity; perhaps the 'deep play'[23] of gambling serves as a meaningful and occasionally fruitful stop-gap, enabling a support to social status and self-esteem which work does not provide.

As the novel progresses, social networks around Tammas shift and fragment through divergent channels of emigration. Tammas lives with his sister Margaret and her husband Robert, the latter gradually increasing pressure on him to leave home. Perhaps predictably Tammas begins to discuss his own future move away from the city with other people: with Rab's father, with his grandmother, with his second girlfriend Vi and with his sister Margaret (*C* 220, 234, 268 and 275). To all of them, he suggests a move to Peterhead is a far more concrete and imminent possibility than it actually is. While Tammas is almost certainly serious about wanting to make Peterhead a reality ('I really fancy it – I do' he says to Billy, *C* 298), it is a source of dramatic irony that the Peterhead jobs actually exist only as a tenuous repeated suggestion in conversations with the unpredictable McCann, who turns out to be the only character in the novel who is unstable to the point of violence (*C* 304).

The manner in which Tammas uses the Peterhead possibility in his relationship with Vi is worth investigation, precisely because we know nothing of Tammas' intentions. He tells her he is going to Peterhead initially as a way of drawing her interest back to him after a falling out (*C* 268). Having succeeded in repairing the faltering relationship, he asks her to move with him to Peterhead. This invitation comes during a hesitant conversation about her imprisoned, violent husband, who has threatened to 'get' her. Tammas offers a move with him to Peterhead as a way to free herself of this threat. She agrees to consider the invitation (*C* 289–92). The history of Vi's previous domestic situation is not made clear, though portentous traces of it are discovered by Tammas in scars on her baby daughter Kirsty's stomach. On this subject Vi silently resists any inquiry (*C* 157 and 215). With the weight of Vi's maternal responsibility and the threat of a return of masculine violence, a move to Peterhead cannot be decided upon in a fickle or impulsive manner. It is no coincidence that in this same conversation Vi mentions that Tammas has been labelled a 'chancer' by her friend Milly (*C* 286): Vi would be taking a tremendous chance with her own and her daughter's future. Characteristically the narrative provides no clues as to Tammas' rationale for an invitation with such serious implications. Typically, perhaps problematically, Tammas does not tell any of his friends or his sister about Vi and Kirsty. Our position is the same as Vi's: we can have no idea how serious Tammas is in his proposition to Vi.

If Tammas does not give full voice to his reasons for leaving Glasgow, the entire novel and the social context it constructs, point to Tammas' final departure, to his individual assertion of change. He follows a trend which has broken up families, torn social groups apart, leaving mothers red-faced with grief (*C* 222), and departing Glaswegians bereft: Rab because he could never get a football career in Glasgow (*C* 198), Donnie because he simply does not want to leave at all (*C* 131). The only mention Tammas makes of his heart in the entire novel is in conversation with Donnie, during his leaving party: 'Ah Donnie Donnie Donnie, it'll break my heart to see you away. Tammas pursed his lips and sighed: New Zealand by fuck! That's terrible, terrible.' (*C* 131) This is Tammas' most emotionally expressive moment in the time-frame of the novel, and its implications cannot be underestimated. Is Tammas grieving from this moment on for a friend who could not have moved further away geographically? Tammas' is a community in the process of fragmentation, and logically enough, at the end of the novel the young man becomes just another isolated fragment of the Scottish diaspora. Historical statistical evidence reveals that Kelman's portrayal of a city losing its population is no exaggeration. *A Chancer* was begun in the early 1970s, before *The Busconductor Hines*. Throughout this period emigration was having a huge impact on Scotland's population: between 1976 and 1986 152,000 people emigrated. The strangest statistic appears if we focus attention on the population of Strathclyde (the regional council area which Glasgow dominates): between 1976 and 1986 the net loss was 172,360 people.[24] During the writing of *A Chancer*, more people left the Glasgow region than left Scotland altogether. As for every year but one of the twentieth century, Scotland was in migration deficit in the 1970s and 1980s (losing more people to emigration than it gained by immigration) but this trend was particularly fierce in Glasgow.[25] *A Chancer* is produced with a raw sense of this historical context and reflects a complex of currents of people moving out of Glasgow, out of Scotland, and out of the UK, moving on their own, as couples or as whole families.

Industrial jobs in Glasgow declined dramatically during the period of the writing of this novel – from 35% in 1971 to 24% in 1983[26] – and Kelman reflects the resultant insecurities for industrial workers from the opening page. *A Chancer* is a localised study of the intertwining of economic insecurity and the circulation of stories of improvement through emigration. Tammas is not the only chancer in this novel. Because life is deemed to be elsewhere, many of his friends take huge gambles with their lives, throwing their futures upon the shaky barks of stories of betterment: better living conditions, better pay, better possibilities and opportunities, or as Tammas alliteratively puts it, 'lying on a beach all day, big blondes and bottles of bacardi' (*C* 131). Rooted in Glasgow, the narrative watches over Tammas' shoulder as the region is debilitated.

An example of the possible problems caused by the compact silence between narrator and protagonist comes at the end of the novel when, alone, Tammas hitches out of Glasgow in the hush of dawn. Other than the words written on a note to his sister – which remains a blank to us – Tammas leaves without telling Vi or any of his friends, without warning, without a voiced explanation of any kind. What he is thinking, we simply cannot know. An explanation is provided implicitly through the context of the preceding narrative of course, which forms multiple lines of flight away from Glasgow as detailed above.[27] But interpreting the manner in which Tammas departs is key to the reception of the novel as a whole. Hitching out of Glasgow, and out of the novel, Tammas climbs into a lorry without asking where it is heading. Once it is in motion Tammas asks the driver how far he is going: the driver replies 'Me Jock? London' (*C* 309), Tammas has already become a foreigner, an archetypal Scot (Kelman's early short stories often illustrate the displacement of the protagonist through similar use of the word 'Jock' [e.g. 'A Roll for Joe', *OP* 15 –21]). Reading through the lens of Tammas' gambling, critic Cairns Craig cites this unexplained departure as evidence that Tammas confirms 'the accidental nature of all existence'. For Craig, Tammas 'disappears into a future defined by the chance of where the lorry is going'.[28] Because Tammas is a habitual gambler, this might seem to be a logical point. But Craig's argument omits the fact that the place from which Tammas chooses to hitch determinedly marks his unspoken intentionality, his agency, his purposefulness. To a degree, hitching is always a gamble: such is the lot of those who cannot afford the cost of public or private transport. They do not have the money to control their circumstances fully, so they have no choice but to take chances. For Tammas 'everything's got a chance' (*C* 166) of enabling him to increase control of own his life, be it through gambling, hitching or emigrating. Apart from the odd windfall of money from gambling wins, Tammas is basically broke for the duration of this novel (he cyclically pawns and redeems his most valuable possession, a suit [*C* 42, 53, 56, 103, 203], and at times has to resort to buying 'singles' – individual cigarettes [e.g. *C* 33]). But, like so many behaviours in his world which are determined by economic necessity, the odds for success in hitching can be improved with skill. The outcome of hitching, though including an element of risk, is determined by some controllable elements. This is the attraction of gambling for Tammas: that he can at times, with skill, manoeuvre himself into a position of seeming control, make the odds better, outwith the sacrifices of work in the labour market. For Sarah Engledow Tammas' gambling forms a 'site of liberation from the capitalist system and other ideologies' and 'makes a mockery of the legitimate economy'.[29] The sophisticated management of chance independent of an orthodox relationship to capital, is modelled in hitching, which likewise relies on skill to end in success for the traveller. In hitching, Tammas has to decide where to stand, a determining choice which Craig ignores. The famous 'Auchenshuggle terminus' which is mentioned as the place near which Tammas is hitching (*C* 309), was the end-point of many old tram routes, and marks a commonly-known boundary to the city, just as it marks the terminus to this novel. This Auchenshuggle terminus is on London Road, not mentioned here, in the east end of Glasgow. London Road is the A74, the main west-coast route south to England, and the road *A Disaffection*'s Patrick Doyle takes on his aborted trip south (*D* 69).

That Tammas wants out of the city on a road named after its own terminus, London, means that his destination is not accidental at all: his departure is positively determined, only not in dialogue with anyone, nor through the narrative. As we can have no idea what his note to his sister contains, likewise we can have little idea what Tammas is thinking. Could he explain if he wanted to, if he had someone to talk to? Does he apologise to his sister in the note? In the absence of any expressed intention on Tammas's part, of any rationale, and because of the sudden shock of Tammas's departure – a shock morally heightened by the departure following so rapidly on the heels of the invitation to Vi – Craig reads accident, chance, negation of social relation and abdication of social responsibility. He assumes that because the novel provides no explanation, there is no possibility of there being one at all. Craig's reading suggests that there is no thought engineering Tammas' actions, and that this is the point of the novel. For Craig, the novel asserts humanity as accident, as absence of thought or intention.

Craig is not to be condemned for this: the critical pitfall of this novel, which is also its formal daring, lies in the fact that the reader is given so little access to Tammas' thoughts, and barely any guidance by a narrator. This narrative structure leaves the world of the novel narratologically blank, and horrifically so if the critic is in pursuit of explanation, a narrative of coherency, of social unity. The narrative structure seems neutralised and functional: is this the same thing as meaning that the world presented is negated? Is the critic respond-ing to the world of *A Chancer*, its structure, or through a buried critical preconception of what a novel should do, of what it ought to provide? Does this novel provide less than the bare minimum? For Craig, absence of the accustomed comfort of narrative – grand, unifying, omniscient, first-person or otherwise – effects vertiginous critical horror. Kelman's intention was to create a space for the liberated subject, but Craig equates the obliterated narrator with an obliterated psychological landscape, as if the manner in which the novel were told is itself commentary upon Tammas' mind; indeed, as if the narrative *were* Tammas' mind. This might be logical, were it not for the fact that all of Kelman's accounts of his desire to remove a 'value system' by withdrawing the overt interference of a narratorial voice suggest the opposite: that the narratorial voice is meant to be unreadable, blank, disappeared, not in order to construct or negate the material or psychological universe it presents, but to liberate the subject and his world from anybody's manipulating judgement. If Craig is right, Kelman has failed.

The novel closes as a future opens which will be defined by Tammas alone, as an individual subject free of known contexts. In leaving, Tammas rejects the contexts, behaviours and perhaps even the ideologies of a native Glasgow which is itself fragmenting. As the novel breaks off into unwritten futurity beyond the remit of the novel, so Tammas leaves a note and his absence behind him. It is of key importance that on his way to his hitching pitch, we see him 'passing the turnoff to Shawfield' (*C* 309). The mention of this proper noun should alert us to the possibility that Tammas is leaving not just Glasgow but also his gambling life behind him. Shawfield is a greyhound racing track in Rutherglen, a town bordering Glasgow, and a symbolically important place for Tammas to be walking past. Just before the start of the time-frame of the novel, Tammas has been a regular at Shawfield for Saturday night races (*C* 15) and still goes on occasion (*C* 58–63 and 227). His 'passing the turnoff' could be a marker of a new direction and determination in his life, not just geographically, but also habitually. But then, because it is Tammas, we can never be certain, and we are forced to be chancers in our own interpretations.

Notes

1 Summarised in Michael B. Walker, *The Psychology of Gambling* (Oxford: Pergamon Press, 1992), 127.

2 John Corbett, *Language and Scottish Literature; Scottish Language and Literature* (Edinburgh: Edinburgh University Press, 1997), 158–62.

3 Duncan McLean, 'James Kelman interviewed', *Edinburgh Review*, 71 (1985), 80.

4 H. Gustav Klaus, *James Kelman* (Tavistock: Northcote House and British Council, 2004), 39.

5 Cairns Craig, 'Resisting Arrest: James Kelman', in Gavin Wallace and Randall Stevenson (eds), *The Scottish Novel Since the Seventies* (Edinburgh: Edinburgh University Press, 1993), 108.

6 Craig is not alone: summarising Kelman's work, Ray Ryan asserts that: 'Commentary disappears, because existences as arbitrary as any greyhound race defy interpretation. So instead of narrative development there is repetition', *Ireland and Scotland: Literature and Culture, State and Nation, 1966–2000* (Oxford: Oxford University Press, 2002), 48.

7 Sarah Engledow, 'Studying Form: The Off-the-Page Politics of *A Chancer*', *Edinburgh Review*, 108 (2001), 74.

8 Klaus, *James Kelman*, 91.

9 Kirsty McNeill, 'Interview with James Kelman', *Chapman*, 57 (Summer 1989), 4–5.

10 Alan Freeman, 'The Humanist's Dilemma: A Polemic Against Kelman's Polemics', *Edinburgh Review*, 108 (2001), 29.

11 Ann Jefferson, *The Nouveau Roman and the Poetics of Fiction* (Cambridge: Cambridge University Press, 1980), 2.

12 Heading for different conclusions, Cairns Craig uses the existentialist concept of 'thrownness' to launch his analysis of *A Chancer* (Craig, 'Resisting Arrest', 106–8).

13 Martin Heidegger, *Ontology – The Hermeneutics of Facticity* [1923], trans. John van Buren (Bloomington and Indianapolis: Indiana University Press, 1999), 24–5.

14 Jean-Paul Sartre, *Being and Nothingness: An Essay on Phenomenological Ontology* [1943], trans. Hazel E. Barnes (London and New York: Routledge Classics, 2003), 506. For a broadly positive reading of Sartrean freedom in Kelman, see Laurence Nicoll, ' "This Is Not A Nationalist Position": James Kelman's Existential Voice', *Edinburgh Review*, 103 (2000), 79–84.

15 Sartre, *Being and Nothingness*, 505.

16 Gilles Deleuze and Claire Parnet, *Dialogues II*, trans. Hugh Tomlinson and Barbara Habberjam (London and New York: Continuum, 2002), 36.

17 Tammas' shoe is set alight by the hot metal. For Kelman, jobs like this are often about avoiding serious injury, for which the employer makes no provision. Tammas' situation in the factory is based directly on Kelman's own experience: 'I was in this situation where my foot went

on fire because a metal bar touched it, a copper bar. That means I wasn't doing the job properly, you know! Every hour I worked I had to avoid going on fire. And I've worked in many jobs like that, never mind asbestos.' Pat Kane, 'Underclass, under-what? Fictions and realities from Glasgow to Prague: an interview with James Kelman', *Regenerating Cities*, 7 (1995), 20. For the most succinct presentation of industrial danger, see the short story 'Acid' (*NN* 115).

18 William McIlvanney, *Docherty* [1975] (London: Hodder & Stoughton, 1985).

19 Willy Maley, 'Denizens, Citizens, Tourists, and Others: Marginality and Mobility in the Writings of James Kelman and Irvine Welsh', in David Bell and Azzedine Haddour (eds), *City Visions* (Harlow: Pearson, 2000), 60.

20 Campbell Balfour, *Unions and the Law* (Farnborough, Hants and Lexington, MA: Saxon House & Lexington Books, 1973), 41.

21 Michael Moran, *The Politics of Industrial Relations: The Origins, Life and Death of the 1971 Industrial Relations Act* (London and Basingstoke: Macmillan, 1977), 93.

22 Andrew J. Richards, *Miners on Strike: Class Solidarity and Division in Britain* (Oxford and New York: Berg, 1996), 109.

23 Clifford Geertz reads the social complexes of cockfight gambling in Bali as 'deep play' (a term borrowed from Jeremy Bentham) wherein 'much more is at stake than material gain: namely, esteem, honor, dignity, respect – in a word ... status.' 'Deep Play: Notes on the Balinese Cockfight', in Rachel Adams and David Savran (eds), *The Masculinity Studies Reader* (Oxford: Blackwell, 2002), 87.

24 Isobel Lindsay, 'Migration and Motivation: A Twentieth-Century Perspective', in T. M. Devine (ed.), *Scottish Emigration and Scottish Society: Proceedings of the Scottish Historical Studies Seminar, University of Strathclyde, 1990–91* (Edinburgh: John Donald, 1992), 158.

25 Lindsay, 'Migration and Motivation', 155.

26 Seán Damer, *Glasgow: Going for a Song* (London: Lawrence & Wishart, 1990), 204.

27 'Lines of flight' is a term Deleuze and Guattari's use to emphasise things in connective process, rather than the stasis of existence. As Tamsin Lorraine explains: 'A "line of flight" is a path of mutation precipitated through the actualisation of connections among bodies that were previously only implicit (or "virtual") that releases new powers in the capacities of those bodies to act.' Adrian Parr (ed.), *The Deleuze Dictionary* (Edinburgh: Edinburgh University Press, 2005), 145. *A Chancer* leaves us with a question: will Tammas 'release new powers' on his flight from Glasgow?

28 Craig, 'Resisting Arrest', 106.

29 Engledow, 'Studying Form', 73 and 77.

4

A Disaffection (1989)

Class and classrooms

Though the men in all three of Kelman's first novels could loosely be described as having a working-class background, only Patrick Doyle of *A Disaffection* attends university. Of the three, Doyle is the only car-owner and the only one who lives on his own. With his degree and his postgraduate teaching certificate from what he refers to as 'teacher trainers', Doyle is professionally qualified which means his work as a secondary-school teacher is solidly-paid and we might even say his occupation, if not his troubled identity, is middle class.[1] Doyle condemns his job as being supportive of the state, productive of an ideology which is in conflict with his own, and so he repeatedly distinguishes his job from his identity. On this basis he refuses to identify himself as being of the class in which the teaching profession can squarely be placed, and it is clear that he maintains an allegiance with working-class culture. In 1989, the year that *A Disaffection* was published, Kelman put some political and experiential distance between his protagonist and himself:

> Doyle is like a lot of people who come through university without any experience of working class jobs. They think and the educational process teaches them to think – that they can change the system from within. I think Doyle has only become aware of his own knowledge of the futility of things quite recently. He's led a fairly normal existence in the working-class-boy-goes-to-uni routine. I think his elder brother and sister-in-law are much more worldly than he is.[2]

Kelman goes on to say that Doyle is 'a naive character', and that his own political leanings 'are to the left of Doyle's'. Kelman here forces a political distinction between himself and Doyle, and Doyle does a similar thing in demarcating a clear boundary between his own cultural identity and the education system which led him into the teaching profession. After considering an estranged English university friend, Doyle attacks 'them' with a blunderbuss:

> They were all like that, these middle-class bastards, lying fuckers, so absolutely hypocritical it was a way of being, they never even bothered reflecting on it, all these lecturers and students, so smugly satisfied and content to let you say what you wanted to say and do what you wanted to do, just so long as it didnt threaten what they possessed, and what did they possess why fucking everything, the best of health and the best of fucking everything else. (*D* 53)

The anger here is directed at voracious, mendacious, avaricious materialism, and relies on the blunt politicking of 'us' and 'them' which is evident in Kelman's own understanding of class issues in education. Doyle is at pains to keep himself separate from those he dismisses. He isolates himself, making a political point out of cultural disillusionment and educational misanthropy. Throughout the novel he takes great pains to set himself apart from the educational class in which he now works, and from which he repeatedly considers resigning. Doyle blames his parents and his older brother Gavin for encouraging him to go to university (*D* 53). We can assume that Gavin must be aware how sensitive Doyle is over the core issue of being set apart from his family by his job. Yet Gavin makes a point of salting his younger brother's open wound of class guilt. In so doing, Gavin fulfils the stereotypical cruel older brother role but, then again, in the time-frame of the novel, both are grown men so perhaps should have moved on from such limiting role-play. Doyle is twenty-nine and Gavin is between thirty-two and thirty-three years old (*D* 35). Unlike Doyle, Gavin is married with children, and unemployed. If class is only about what job you do and what things you own – which it clearly is not to Doyle – Gavin is unproblematically working class, with all the entailing economic problems. To Doyle he says:

> All your teachers and all your fucking students and pupils and all your fucking headmasters and your cronies from the fucking staffroom. Fucking middle-class bunch of wankers ya cunt! Gavin sat back on the chair and drew his feet up onto it, sitting on his heels, and he swallowed the whisky in a gulp and put the tumbler up onto the mantelpiece. He got his packet of fags open and stuck one in his mouth, then threw the packet to Davie a moment later. He glanced at Patrick briefly: I'll be glad to see you finished with it, dont worry about that.

What do you mean middle-class wankers? Said Pat.
Gavin shook his head. He replied, I didni mean them all.
You fucking said it.
I know I fucking said it.
Well ye fucking must've meant something.
Aye, I meant something, I meant middle-class wankers; middle-class
wankers, that's what I meant. Okay? Middle-class wankers.
Who exactly?
Whoever you fucking like brother.
Do you mean me? Are you fucking calling me a middle-class wanker?
Gavin laughed and snapped the spent match into two pieces, dumped
them in the ashtray. He stopped laughing, but continued to look at
Patrick until Patrick felt he wouldnt be able to stop himself laughing
he was going to burst out laughing, right in Gavin's face [. . .] (D 281–2)

All of Doyle's relationships are fraught, that with his family most of
all, and that with his brother especially so. Through Doyle's entirely
dominant focalised perspective, Gavin is introduced as someone who
'didni say things' (D 19), and the outburst quoted above is indeed
relatively long for him. Just before this excerpt, Doyle confesses that
he seeks Gavin's 'blessing' for quitting his job, therefore exposing
himself deliberately in a passive and junior position relative to his
brother. Still Gavin attacks him. The manner in which he does so is
not all that far removed from Doyle's own tirades about schools and
the staff who inhabit them: Kelman effectively displays how similar
these brothers are, even during outright conflict. Patrick agrees that
teachers are 'middle-class wankers', but he cannot see himself as one
of 'them'. This is the root source of his irritable lack of comfort with
his role and function: he cannot accommodate the class politics, as
he interprets them, of his own profession within his understanding
of himself. He will not identify himself as middle class to any degree,
which means his understanding of class has little to do with job or
money, and much to do with personal cultural allegiance, familial
background and politics, and, as I shall argue, masculinity. All of
which make Doyle's understanding of class commensurate with
Kelman's own.

The source of the drizzling ironic pathos which saturates the whole
novel, is that for all his passionate avoidance and condemnation of
middle-classness, there is no sense whatsoever of Doyle being closely
tied to a sense or experience of working-class community. Doyle is
a depressed individual caught between two worlds of his own delineation, each of which he continually defines against the other. The

demarcation of the two worlds is drawn with sour rejection of one, not with passion or hope for communal comfort within the other.

Kelman ensures that the various possible meanings of 'disaffection' meet in Doyle: generally he displays a 'spirit of disloyalty to the government or existing authority', 'political alienation or discontent', outright 'dislike' of and 'hostility' towards his profession, and 'alienation' from his own family and his own class (all *OED*). As with *A Chancer*, the indefinite article suggests this is to be read as one disaffection among many, one alienated individual among millions. The title of the novel is fully justified. Published in 1989, ten years after the rejection of a referendum to give Scotland more independence, *A Disaffection* must be read as part of the response of the Scottish 'libertarian socialist, anarchist'[3] Kelman to ten years of Margaret Thatcher's unchallenged Conservative government. Thatcher is never mentioned in the novel, but her absence only serves to increase the distance between Tory Westminster and non-Tory Scotland. Kelman's device of not explicitly mentioning the proper nouns of late 1980s politics further estranges Doyle's world from the contemporary political landscape, and shows just how irrelevant it is to him. Even if Doyle says he stands forever in 'defiance of central authority' (*D* 104), his rebelliousness is always at a remove, negotiated through the local, diminished by isolation. Critics of 1980s Scottish politics and culture always point out that by the late 1980s Scotland was being run by a government which did not represent it, so threadbare had Scottish Tory support become by this point. As James Mitchell points out, the Prime Minister might not have been bothered:

> Margaret Thatcher seemed unwilling to make any effort to appease the Scots, appearing to be oblivious to the damage done to her party north of the border. From her perspective the Conservative position in Scotland mattered little so long as the party won majorities in England that would secure its position across Britain.[4]

Disaffection, alienation, discontentment: Doyle's characteristics can be generally applied to the political and economic state of Scotland in the late 1980s, and to its relationship with unrepresentative and uninterested English power. When the Tories under John Major retained power in the 1992 election, Kelman, shocked by the fact that: 'Seventy five per cent of those who voted [in Scotland] rejected the Tory national government' concluded that Scotland remained 'subordinate to an imperial power' (*SRA* 85–6).

Nation, faith and masculinity

If Doyle is representative of an alienated Scotland, Gavin can be read likewise as just one of millions who were unemployed across the UK in the 1980s. This historicising of Gavin's aggression towards his brother over his occupation accounts for some of its vitriol. There is also a sexual dimension to the accusation Gavin levels at Doyle which is equally worth consideration. The word 'wanker' is of course idiomatically used by Gavin, but its literal meaning of 'someone who masturbates' – usually, but not exclusively, 'wanker' is used in reference to male masturbation – suggests that he is attacking the masculinity of his brother. Doyle is literally a wanker: we see him considering masturbation at various instances, and admitting to himself that he is 'sick of wanking' (D 55). If with a measured delicacy typical of Kelman with regard to sexual activity, the door is shut on any masturbatory scenes in this novel, masturbation still merits frequent contemplation. One such contemplation results in a dismissal of it as a possibility for familial reasons:

> Masturbation could never be a possibility here in the home of his parents. That was one thing about P. Doyle. That was one tried and true thing about him. This is how come he's the man you see today. What the fuck does that mean. It just means that eh etcetera. (D 109)

Critic Neil McMillan – politely correcting Doyle's Latinate 'masturbation' with his own, rarer Hebraic 'onanism' – is in danger of over-reading the avoidance of wanking when he claims it might be the result of a '*crushing* sense of sexual repression'[5] (my emphasis). But he has a point: there is some relation between his stopping himself and his being inside the womb of his parents' bath. McMillan might be right in claiming that a characteristic of Doyle's past family life, which is now continuing in adulthood, is sexual repression. We might speculate further and consider that the repression is now manifesting itself in adult life as social awkwardness, sexual anxiety and an edgy, faltering approach to the opposite sex. Both Patrick Doyle's forename and surname are clearly of Irish origin and would be noted as such in sectarian Glasgow, but as Doyle never extends analysis of his sexual problems into an assessment of the impact of a specifically Roman Catholic background – if that is what he has – perhaps we should not speculate.

When Doyle does engage with the religious politics of Glasgow, it is unsurprisingly through football. He recalls his teaching colleague

Joe Cairns telling him about a match wherein Rangers 'got their usual last minute Loyalist handshake of a penalty', which Doyle repeats, is 'typical' (*D* 102). This isolated moment implies Doyle's probable allegiance to the opposing Celtic, though as he never confirms this, it is important to note it is conjecture. Although we see him relishing a low-division Saturday game (*D* 99 ff.), Doyle does not think about or mention football that much, and certainly never talks about Celtic as if it were his team. An allegiance to Irish Catholic culture as opposed to Protestant Unionist culture might for Doyle be as political as it is familial. In her analysis of Irvine Welsh's *Trainspotting*, Patricia Horton concludes that characters 'identify with Ireland on the basis of a shared sense of oppression, grounded in sentimental nationalism and inflected by Catholicism and working-class affiliations'[6]. Unlike the republican young men in *Trainspotting* however, Doyle does not sing Irish songs, nor does he provide any sense or explicit history of individual or shared faith. Nor indeed is Doyle a nationalist – Scottish, Irish or otherwise – even if he does have a complex resentment of the oppressions of the state and uses idiomatic expressions like the 'Auld Enemy' for England (e.g. *D* 70).

The headmaster 'Old Milne' embodies the policing of state-authorised ideology, and is the coalface at which Doyle nurtures his political resistance. Milne is condemned as a 'protestant' (*D* 27), an 'Edwardian aristocrat' (*D* 30), a 'congregationalist' (*D* 104), 'a right-wing fucking shite' (*D* 151) and more playfully, a 'capital A R S E arse' (*D* 168). When parodied by Doyle, Milne's voice clearly has an antiquated English register, including comedic idioms which are not matched by anything we hear in Milne's direct speech. For example, Doyle fantasises that Milne will be perplexed at Doyle's absence: 'Confound the fellow, where can he be! How on earth can he have forgotten!!' (*D* 50). Milne comes to stand for English power, for Empire, Queen and Country – and unsurprisingly perhaps, Doyle fantasises about killing him (*D* 116) and threatening him with 'a trusty Dobermann Pinscher and a big fucking double-barrelled shotgun' (*D* 167), a route parallel to Hines' equally fantastic if less directed determination to get a gun (*BH* 84–5 and 169). Generally, Doyle is passionate about not wanting to be a building block in the ideological wall defending and defining the status quo. Milne is the manager and representative of that status quo in Doyle's life and, unawares, bears the brunt of Doyle's resentment not only at what he himself is doing as a teacher, but also the resentment he feels as a disenfranchised and politically sidelined citizen of a stateless nation. Whether Milne is actually English or not, for Doyle he is a tool of the government and so might as well be.

Doyle also defends his relationship with Milne over the territory of ownership of his labour: when Milne asks him how his father is, Doyle says 'Ye dont own my da' (*D* 181). He reads Milne as a state-sanctioned capitalist and ideologue and himself as exploited, beleaguered labour; he may have sold his labour, and so his integrity to the state, but he will not have that power relationship arrogate his family. His family, particularly the patriarch, is to be defended, kept separate from the inveigling tentacles of an establishment figure, another senior male, to whom Doyle owes a debt of labour. The defence is based on a construction of Doyle's relationship to his work which criticises it as a partial betrayal of his culture, his class, his family. Douglas Gifford notes the prevalence of a 'Judas motif' in the novel, concluding that Doyle is 'self-deceiving, a self-betrayer of what he most believes in.'[7]

While Doyle makes a meal out of Milne's autocratic Englishness, the novel actually does not reinforce the classroom clash between Scots and English that contemporary Scottish novels often portray. Because the Scottish teaching of English in the classroom is effectively the arena where majoritarian standard English is legitimised and vernacular Scots is demoted and minorised, as a context educa-tion has had a significant role in Scottish fiction.[8] In allowing and promoting not only Scots and dialect usage in his classroom but also irreverent profanity, Doyle is an idiosyncratically freethinking teacher, with more of a socialist than a nationalist impulse underlying his rebellion (it would be interesting to see how Doyle marks his students' work – the battleground where the teacher notes the 'incorrect' language of his charge). Yet *A Disaffection* still rests quite comfortably in a tradition of Scottish literature which critiques the politics of education in a parallel way. Alasdair Gray's *Lanark* (1981) cyclically portrays the intimidation, fear and institutionalising mechanisms of schooling, the militaristic marshalling of free beings into order in school rooms and colleges. The splitting of subject which structures *Lanark* and which, for many critics, is prevalent throughout Scottish literature (classic examples being Hogg's *Confessions* and Stevenson's *Jekyll and Hyde*), is managed by a school culture which divides classes between those who will do Latin and go to University, and those who will do modern languages and will not[9] (in the parallel fantasy world, patients in the Institute are 'treated' with classics, in the medium of music, until they die, and then are consumed by members of the Institute). For Gray, school classes are directly productive of social classes. This is one of the perceived intentions of the education system that Doyle is trying to undermine, from within. Gray's later novel *1982 Janine* (1984) focuses upon the warped sexual development of a man beaten repeatedly by a masochistic schoolteacher. William McIlvanney's novel *Docherty* (1975) features a key scene in which young Conn is beaten for using Scots and is told by the teacher to 'translate' his sentence 'into the mother-tongue'. This results in Conn rejecting the value of education entirely, precisely because he 'despaired of English'.[10] In summary, *Docherty*'s omniscient narrator takes an even harder line: school determined 'that the vivid spontaneity of his natural speech was something he was supposed to be ashamed of'.[11] Though written in the early 1970s, *Docherty* is set in the early decades of the twentieth century, and its version of the use of language in and for education can be supported to a degree by a real contemporary of the period in question, James Joyce. A similar if less violent encounter between an English teacher and an Irish student occurs in *A Portrait of the Artist as a Young Man* (1916). Their separate linguistic lives centre on the Irish word 'tundish'. Student Stephen Dedalus concludes:

> The language in which we are speaking is his before it is mine. How different are the words *home, Christ, ale, master,* on his lips and on mine! I cannot speak or write these words without unrest of spirit. His language, so familiar and so foreign, will always be for me an acquired speech. I have not made or accepted its words. My voice holds them at bay. My soul frets in the shadow of his language.[12]

Here Dedalus realises who can confidently claim ownership of the English language, and who cannot; and which accent, register and lexis is the accepted manner of expression for the powerful, and which is not. English is all-pervasive and yet remote; the language of a colonising power which can never be, *should* never be, fully acquired by the colonised culture. The language is not to be fully 'accepted'. The language of education, of literature, of authority, of rule, of an enforced and superiorised culture, is alienating for this Irish subject of British rule.

For Doyle in *A Disaffection*, England remains a colonial power to be resisted. As a result, Scotland is touchy and insecure about its status:

Probably the whole of Scotland is huffy. That is why their history is so shitey. The English are not huffy, just fucking imperialist bastards. Which ones? Quite right. And that applies to the Northamericans as well. Imperialists cannot be huffy: it would be a contradiction. (*D* 116–17)

When red, white and blue Rangers get 'their usual last minute Loyalist handshake of a penalty' the football club so described becomes a tool in the corrupt imperialist project for Doyle, and he seems as sure about this murky state of affairs as he does that god does not exist. Doyle is a self-avowed atheist, and understands himself to have cleared his mind of any trace of superstition, since the age of twelve (*D* 249). The religious superstition of his childhood has been replaced by febrile paranoia in adulthood: he worries, when at the football match for example, that he is being watched by an agent of the CIA or MI5 (*D* 101), or that there are 'stormtroopers, shadowy dark figures' in his flat when he takes a bath (*D* 107). In the place of angels and demons, Doyle puts state-sponsored chimeras, none of them real. Pointedly, worries over such improbable figures do not surface when Doyle is in his parents' bath, so perhaps it is indeed a comforting 'womb' in a way that his own bath never could be, no matter what obsessive-compulsive 'rituals' he carries out to keep himself safe (*D* 107). For all his stress and boredom when with his parents, Doyle derives much security from knowing they, rather than 'stormtroopers', are outside the bathroom door. His own analysis of his sexual repression in his parents' bath is semi-serious but coyly abbreviated by a stifling, teasing 'eh etcetera', suggesting that he withdraws from relaxing fully on his own psychoanalyst's chair. While he is willing to condemn his family for encouraging his path into higher education, he does not blame them for his sexual problems (if that is what he has) and self-censors any delving into the history of his early sexual development, though he does give some detail on his adult experiences and condemns them for being limited and in the distant past (*D* 7). He considers that girls at the school in which he now teaches might think he is 'homosexual' because he is 'not married' (*D* 7) but also that the same pubescent girls of '[t]welve or thirteen' have sexual 'stirrings' towards him (*D* 28). He asserts his heterosexuality to himself by, perhaps stereotypically, considering women to exhibit 'contradictory behaviour' (*D* 13), which is of course perfectly descriptive of his own sexual awkwardness. Nicola, the sister-in-law who Doyle places on a pedestal of admiration, is quite clear about the root cause of Doyle's problems with women: 'I think you've got a glamourised view of women which is wrong, it really is wrong.' (*D* 315) Kelman says in the interview quoted above that Nicola and her brother are 'much more worldly than' Doyle. Compared to the sanctified and long-suffering Nicola, Doyle's romantic anxieties over gender and sex do indeed seem restlessly immature and self-pitying.

Doyle is alert to the patriarchy that his classroom is supposed to support: 'how males are aye supposed to win and lassies are aye supposed to come secondbest, and the way the education system colludes entirely' (*D* 288). He thinks he acts, pedagogically, to undermine such a collusion, though his distinguishing of students according to sex seems to run counter to this supposed position, and generates odd tension between males and females in his classroom (D 244–50). Educationally he has policies which attempt to disassemble his male power and teacherly authority (e.g. 'Lassies dont call men sir!', *D* 28), but he simplistically idealises a femininity of 'control' (*D* 147) and a 'sense of peace' (*D* 314). A female student might be regarded as both a 'nice looking lassie' and a 'poor wee lassie' (*D* 28): is his protective sentimentality towards females exaggerated in order that it might counteract his guilt-ridden sexualisation of them? If Nicola's function in the novel is raised high enough to be both confessor and judge – especially in this major scene towards the end of the novel (*D* 258–326) – does this mean that Kelman himself displays 'a glamourised view of women'?

At times Doyle is debilitated by fear of women, sexuality and associated disease. During a lonely evening and a contemplative trawl through Goya's black paintings of dances 'which must end in human sacrifice', which in turn lead towards a serious consideration of suicide, the idea of a prostitute seems a last resort (*D* 78–9). It might not be a serious option for him anyway, but what finally repulses him is 'a succession of pricks'. This 'image' makes him recoil, he rationalises, because of the possibility of AIDS (*D* 79). Often edgily protective of women, Doyle here shows no signs of concern for female exploitation, for the female subject, only for the welfare of his own body, only for protecting himself from an infected object of desire. This is a repugnant nadir: Doyle is desperately lonely and blankly hungry for sex.[13]

With the politics of class, Doyle considers himself on much surer and more publicly-acceptable ground than the murkier world of sexual politics; he is therefore ready to defend himself against Gavin's use of it to attack his masculinity. Perhaps making up for his economic insecurity, Gavin uses his solid platform of a procreative and seemingly sound marriage for his attack on his younger brother's class and sexual success. Gavin implies that Patrick is part of a group which is less sexually successful, less procreatively manly, because it is middle-class: to suggest Doyle is middle class is to attack not just his loyalty to family and culture, but also to attack his masculinity. As Michael Argyle points out in his psychological study of social class, 'working-class speech is associated with greater masculinity'.[14] Working through his own anxieties about working on Kelman, critic Ben Knights rejects the myth that working-class culture is more genuinely masculine than his own middle-class culture:

> A set of inverse snobberies and ignorances seems to lead to a semi-articulated and widespread belief that working-class men – a grouping itself forged in the struggle against oppression – somehow express masculinity in a purer form.[15]

Knights is deftly critical of such 'preposterous' beliefs, and alert to the possibility that Kelman's explorations of the 'vulnerabilities of men' might 'vanish beneath the stereotype' of working-class masculinity.[16] Part of Kelman's artistic project is to reject gender stereotypes, his focus primarily resting on the plight of working-class men. So what are we to make of Doyle attacking, exactly as his brother does, the masculinity of men he regards as properly middle class (i.e. more middle class than him)? Of the headmaster and the assistant head, Doyle says:

> These two males – one hesitates to call them men, if we accept the term as one of merited achievement but is it fuck, it's just a fucking fact. Two men. Things with bollocks and a prick. A pair of rascally fuckers, paid by a sick society, accountable to themselves on behalf of a corrupt government. (D 104–5).

Doyle is dialectic, processing his own immediate responses, politicising what he admits is incontrovertible: that these two people are biological males. The hesitation 'to call them men' says it all: for Doyle, people in such positions of mischievous power have diminished masculinity, are disingenuous, lack the 'merit' of manliness. His hesitation means that he partly buys into the belief that working-class men – like himself – are more masculine, even if he does qualify and analyse it, at the same time as reducing the pair to male genitalia.

Kelman's withdrawn narrators do not guide us to condemn or approve certain behaviours, but parallel events certainly do, all of which are governed by the silent author. If Gavin is hitting his brother with a blunt assumption of 'genuine' working-class masculinity, likewise he is blunt about race; this Doyle finds impossible to stomach. Having worked through his thick haze of rage at Gavin's use of the word 'paki' (*D* 304), Doyle's eventual interpretation is that Gavin is deliberately racist in order to hound him out of his flat. As always at moments of significance, Doyle resorts to Goya's black paintings to encounter the senseless violence of his brother's words: 'There are two blokes in quicksand with cudgels belaying each other' (*D* 305). It is as if Doyle is trying to regain balance, control, through a recollected image of Goya ('The Cudgel Fight' is discussed below). Doyle is aware that Gavin knows exactly what to deal out to enrage his younger brother: masculinity, class, and even racial prejudice. Over the latter issue, Doyle seems unproblematically the more enlightened of the two brothers. Whether his position over the use of what he calls a 'bloody derogatory racist bloody term' (*D* 307) is the product of his middle-class job and his education will remain a moot point. As ever, Kelman is presenting tricky territory here: if the educated Doyle is right over racism and the less educated Gavin is plain wrong, what is the reader to conclude? So dismissive is Kelman of the benefits of structured education, that surely it could *not* be his intention that this novel would confirm that Doyle's advanced education has strengthened his moral fibre and opened his mind in comparison with his brother? If education has nothing to do with this particular issue, why, on hearing his brother say 'paki', does Doyle immediately resort to a complex three-page philosophical and dialectical thought process (*D* 304–7) which includes considerations of Goya and Hölderlin, before he responds vocally? If this tangled web of thoughts is the product of learning, has that learning done him any good at all? Is Doyle suffering *because of* his education?

The anarchist teacher

Education is clearly under critique in this novel, both through its possible effects upon Doyle's prevaricating mind, and through his own response to it as a practitioner. Doyle's lack of comfort as a teacher is muddied further by the fact that his teaching practices are difficult to ascertain and assess. Kelman himself has been associated with various universities and creative writing groups and workshops[17] and, like Doyle, the author has not always found it easy to compromise his intentions within the immovable frameworks of institutional assessment and administration.

In his account of *A Disaffection*, H. Gustav Klaus focuses on Doyle's ironic resistance to ideological indoctrination as he teaches, and interprets some main figures of Doyle's catalogue of references (Goethe, Goya, Hölderlin and Hegel) as being chosen because they evoke the revolutionary age of the late eighteenth century. This interest, Klaus suggests, parallels Kelman's experience of radical resistance and political and social change in Europe in the 1960s.[18] Klaus is convincing on the politics of Doyle's classroom, and on the parallel biographical assessment of Kelman's political growth. He details succinctly the levelling relationship Doyle attempts with his students. Klaus is however quite typical in that he does not mention the fact that we never know for sure what subject Doyle is supposed to be teaching, and what he specifically trained to do. It seems at times to be literature: Doyle moans about novels his students have asked him to read (*D* 170); students in his class bring up *Romeo and Juliet* (apparently re-written as a short story), and Okot p'Bitek and Tolstoy (*D* 244, 245, 249). But the direction of discussion in the albeit rare and elided in-class scenes never points towards a certain text put forward by the teacher. Books he reads at home include many fictional novels (*D* 170), but also books with subjects such as 'the memoirs of an old politician' (*D* 73), 'China and the treatment of cancerous diseases' (*D* 166), or 'geography in a freemarket economy' (*D* 169). Many of the references which feature in Doyle's mental mastication are to European philosophers, mathematicians and artists. He could feasibly be a teacher of geography, politics, art, art history, maths, history, politics, philosophy or economics. If he is an English teacher, the evidence is thin.

As this novel flags itself repeatedly as a realist text, and as we have such kaleidoscopic and bibliographic context-specific detail about the rest of Doyle's intellectual energies, why do we never see him contemplating a lesson plan, a teaching text, a pupil's piece of work? Is he so disaffected that the students' development as determined by school and state is completely outside of his thoughts and so his teaching practice – or does Kelman elide the pragmatics of teaching deliberately? Is Doyle so anarchic that he simply never carries out the day-to-day administrative tasks or give thinking time to the next lesson he is to teach? Does he even *teach*?

His assessment of his own professional ability is clear, and although the following quotation is of Doyle speaking to his paramour, it doesn't seem like false modesty or a ploy to receive compliments: 'Ach, I'm a bad teacher Alison, being honest about it. I get too worked up about everything. Then I get too fucking depressed. I just get too fucking depressed. And the classes all know. They can tell' (*D* 141). Interestingly, Alison does not contradict him, but turns the flow of conversation immediately away from contemplation of Doyle's job and psychological state, to the depression of Balzac: she wants to comment neither on his confession of depression, nor on his professional ability. Her deft manoeuvre away from Doyle as a subject suggests many things, not least that she agrees with him: he *is* a bad teacher, and his colleagues know it.

Doyle's teaching does not 'lead out', a root meaning of 'education'; in contrast, it 'leads in', and attempts to get the students to be continuously self-reflexive and self-critical. What Doyle might well think is politically liberating seems at times to be nothing short of a frivolous and comedic abuse of his power, to do what *he* wants in the classroom, as he knows full well. The novel sets up various scenes which do not throw a necessarily approving light on Doyle's classroom practices. His judgement of what the students need, might not necessarily tally with what they want, and he is in a position of giving them what he wants, indeed what he needs to give them, to salve his guilty conscience: the students protest 'That's no fair' (*D* 186). No matter what his opinions about power in the hierarchies of education, the fact is that he has power invested in him by his job, by his seniority, by his position as the only full-grown adult in the classroom. He does tell the students what to do, provides a narrative of what their lives are about, and points out the limitations on their lives, and their families' lives: at one point he gets them to repeat a mantra: 'We are being fenced in by teachers / at the behest of a dictatorship government / in explicit simulation of our parents the silly bastards / viz. the suppressed poor' (*D* 25). For the children, he is an authority, even if it is an authority on how corrupting authorities are, how trapped the children's parents are, how dangerous this education process is. His undermining of his own status as a teacher is an enactment of his pathological self-loathing, and does not have the liberating impact he desires.

In class, he presents his own life in a comedic fashion to be entertaining and leveling, perhaps enlightening – even joking about his contemplations of suicide (*D* 249). But at every stage, even as a rebellious teacher, he is a failure: the judgement of himself, and implicitly his colleagues and his pupils. The novel does not construct Doyle as a cogent resistor of the powers that control him and inevitably his pupils even more so; nor does he construct for them a path of resistance to compromise which could lead to any practicable or fruitful end: at one point he suggests his pupils should go and 'blow up the DHSS office' (*D* 186). The classroom protests. His disaffection is so complete, that it serves to detach him, and so us, completely from the subject he trained to teach. If Doyle is an English teacher, the purpose of the detachment would be to disassociate his teaching agenda from English hegemony. More broadly, this novel would also be detached from what Kelman criticises as the overall imperial project of the English literary establishment. If the explicit references are anything to go by, the literary tradition to which this novel points is fully international, with English and Scottish writers playing a minor role.

For critic Jürgen Neubauer, Doyle's essential flaw as a teacher is his anger. Neubauer's impressive historicised survey of representations of teaching in Scottish literature praises Doyle's dialogic democratisation of the classroom, but condemns the advocacy of 'a pedagogy of rage, in which positions confront each other without having to reach any preordained conclusions'.[19] Neubauer goes on to criticise Doyle's failure 'to provide social and political languages for education', because his 'pedagogy' is 'based on anger' and is 'not accompanied by a larger political perspective'.[20] This condemnation assumes that Doyle should not be angry, should have a wider sense of his own position, and should always have preordained learning outcomes in mind; it implies that Doyle's worldview is narrow, that he is incapable of controlling his passions, thought by Neubauer to be necessarily bad for the classroom. But Neubauer misses just how anarchic are Doyle's intentions, how his lack of pedagogical direction, his ignoring of 'preordained conclusions' might be the product of a clear political intention. To have a conclusion, a teaching destination, in mind, is to be in favour of preordained closure, of managing the end product of the learning experience in a manner which is the antithesis of what Doyle is about, as a teacher, as a thinker. Ineffectual he may be, but Doyle wants to be an agent who deliberately flouts convention through impassioned argument where it is not expected, indeed, where and when it is not desired, even if this can be personally intimidating and professionally frustrating for himself. After the confrontation with his brother and the suggestion that all teachers are 'middle-class', Doyle turns to his sister-in-law Nicola. Here Doyle reveals what Neubauer terms a 'pedagogy of rage':

> What I try and do, he said, in the classroom I mean, is just make the weans angry. And other folk as well; I try and make them angry. That includes relations!
>
> Nicola was still saying nothing.
>
> Because making them angry's a start. That's something. Even just making them angry. I was trying to make big Arthur angry earlier on. I didni really succeed. I have a lot of failures. My failure rate is quite high. I get reminders about it at school. I get subtle tellings off.
> (*D* 320)

In exchanges with his colleagues, with Milne, with his brother, with his school children, Doyle is an awkward provocateur, and deliberately so. It seems he does not mind if he is disliked, as long as he stimulates people into some sort of defence which he hopes will lead to critical awareness. Neubauer quotes this passage as evidence of Doyle's lack of understanding of the politics of both classroom and class, and his blinkered and personalised limitations as a theorist of teaching (implicitly the personal and the professional are mutually exclusive in his critique). But there is a self-aware and passionate seriousness in Doyle's acknowledgement of his own anger which suggests that while he might be ineffectual against 'the system', Doyle is at least consistent in his commitment to flouting usual codes of conduct in education, just as he is socially. And if he tries to stimulate self-reflexive criticism in his pupils, he is not hypocritical, as he acknowledges both his frequent 'failures' and that he is not free to do as he chooses simultaneously with an admittance of his deliberate provocation of anger in others. Doyle's rage is directed at social predetermination, which is why he cannot and will not predetermine the 'learning outcomes' of his lessons. There is a logic to his affirmative anarchy. His ideals mean he will not be a god, or tyrant as he would see it, in the classroom; he will not organise or dictate the outcomes for his society of students from above, which is a corollary of Kelman's decision to reject narrative omniscience. Like Kelman in narrative, Doyle in the classroom refuses to be a petit bourgeois organising subject of a mass of working-class objects. He will not sentimentalise and he will not dictate from above. Where Kelman attempts to cut the strings of narratorial omniscience, Doyle denies the inherent power relationship between teacher and pupil. The problem is, novelist and teacher are still in control of their arenas, no matter how often they attack the rationale for that power, and no matter how much the style of their delivery suggests they have no authority.

Art and control

Doyle frequently alludes to his inability to control his world in ways that suggest that, for him, control is desirable. The person he desires most, his married colleague Alison Houston, is repeatedly described in terms of the facility with which she asserts control: 'she would be in control, he would be in her power' (*D* 18); 'Alison was fine. Much more in control of the world' (*D* 98); '[s]he was so totally in control' (*D* 147). If Alison is a role model for control, the dominant symbol of Doyle's own developing control, and the symbolic engine through which he will practice it, is the pair of pipes. His discovery of the pipes opens the novel; the pipes generate a story, a possibility, outwith the job of school. Initially they are likened to a 'pet', a 'surrogate child' or a 'wife' (*D* 4). But, lest we misinterpret them, 'these pipes have got fuck all to do with Scotland' (*D* 24). They do however, have much to do with Doyle's disaffection for the workplace, as they may offer him a new direction of interest, and of creative, free-playing, aspiration: 'he was about to resign from school in order to play the pipes. Play the fucking pipes!' (*D* 39). Doyle laughs at his own naïvety at times, but it is clear that Kelman wants us to think of Doyle as a frustrated artist, as someone who thinks he might have painted murals like Goya's black paintings. We might speculate further that Doyle is like the doomed Duncan Thaw of *Lanark*, or like the real Alasdair Gray, who has bedecked Scottish churches, pubs, restaurants and heritage centres with his work.[21] Doyle's 'secret hankering was to be a painter, doing fairly large murals' (*D* 1). Could this introductory aspect of Doyle's mostly frustrated artistic aspiration be Kelman's subtle homage to Gray?

In the novel, Doyle paints the pipes, in enamel colours 'silver, red and black' (*D* 8), and subsequently questions the purpose of the painting which he concludes is to show that his use of them is to be 'regulated, thought to the fore' (*D* 9). The pipes are all about artistic control, nothing rushed, everything measured and carefully prepared:

the slow, methodical build towards a moment of playing. Doyle reads his own pipe playing sexually, as both phallic control and as artistic agency, and there is no doubt that the realisation of his playing is a momentary expression of individual empowerment. If as a working individual Doyle feels that he is disempowered and ineffectual in the face of the behemoth of a state-maintained ideology, it is at least symbolic that when he first decides to play the pipes, to himself, in his own flat, he is interrupted by a policeman who notifies Doyle about his car's lights having been left on and, more invasively, reminds him that his road-tax is nearly out of date (*D* 59). This blunt, publicly-funded intrusion into Doyle's private thoughts sets him off on his aborted car journey south, wherein he seems most lost, meandering and directionless. The drive away suggests the policeman has destabilised his security at home, and has encouraged thoughts of getting out of town, of leaving Scotland. The novel ends (rather than closes) with a similar scenario: Doyle resentfully walking home, and provoking the interest of passing police officers by shouting a question about buses then running away. He is not certain, but thinks that the policemen are chasing him. Doyle resents 'the sign of guilt' they read in him (*D* 337), just as he resents the *potential* guilt implied by the policeman's mention of the tax disc. In an albeit limited sense, both scenes present Doyle as an individual who is not fully free or fully empowered to do what he wants. The art of playing the pipes offers a freedom for self-expression inadvertently denied by an officer of the state, just as at the novel's end, Doyle does not have full freedom to run in the rain without being judged to be 'suspicious'.

The next time Doyle manages to collect himself sufficiently to play the pipes, the novel's most important – arguably the only – pure moment of catharsis is enabled. Just before the playing, Doyle understands himself as an artist, through self-referential tactility:

> He laid his hand on the pipe. Maybe it was just another aid to the relief of sexual tension. Anything was possible in this life. And playing music has always been medicinal, psychotherapeutic. Maybe this was the key to the entire meaning of art. Of course. Obviously. Soothing the troubled soul. (*D* 82)

Doyle's understanding of art as self-expression, as self-development, as self-help is possibly limited and might seem distant from Kelman's own pronouncements on what art should be, but Kelman does firmly believe in the importance of self-expression, of self-definition,

and we are not led here to think that Doyle is being sentimental or
cloying. Doyle's art is self-justifying because at this point, his audience
is only himself, and he is, by his own measure, fully Cartesian: he
admits to a 'total preoccupation with self. I think therefore I am: and
the thing that I am is all of that which everything else isni' (*D* 249).
As both artist and audience he experiences a blissful, unifying melding
of physical control, intellectual flight and an opening of mental space
which together forms an elevated, transcendent enrichment unparalleled anywhere else in Kelman's world.

> Enter yourself ya bastard. Play the fucker. Before it is too late. Fine.
> What is done is just that Patrick raises the pipe to his lips and closes
> his eyelids; he blows a very long and very deep sound; just one, lips
> compressed, eyelids shut tightly, and tears springing there at the corners,
> like a form of ecstasy, something that has sprung from way out of and
> has relaxed these shoulders and eased that terrible terrible fucking
> tension, just got out from under that pilloriedness, self-pilloriedness,
> self-flagellation, that Goya one, something there maybe to do with the
> flagellants but now away there away there, just there, there, there,
> getting further and further away, not a great distance but a distance,
> definitely a distance, just enough now so that he can open the eyelids,
> the eyes maybe and just blink a bit, and a smile of sorts, looking at the
> pipe and smiling to it, an old friend and a treasure. It was time to walk
> to the windows and peer out at the side of the curtain; and he breathed
> out, a sigh; it was followed by a shiver, a shuddering movement of the
> shoulders, a wee convulsion. Dear dear. Dear dear. The rain falling
> steadily. The halo round the streetlamp. (*D* 82–3)

The first imperative turn here is psychologically inward-looking and
it displays an immediate, momentary exactitude: the moment of art
is, and has to be, now. The presentation of the making of sound here
is fully physical: lips, eyelids, tears, shoulders are all to the fore of
Doyle's consciousness at the moment of playing which becomes a
process of release. The clipped sentences that bookend this passage
surround a long, syntactically complex and repetitive construction.
At the centre of Doyle's thoughts, at the centre of the artful moment,
is 'that Goya one' – again, 'the flagellants', which is probably the
black painting known as 'Duelo A Garrotazos' ('The Cudgel Fight'[22]).
Doyle is 'an authority on Goya' (*D* 258). The artist offers Doyle a
'total honesty of vision' (*D* 61) which he aspires to because his own
sight is, by his own estimation, 'not honest and not steady' (*D* 74).
As I discuss below, Goya's black paintings are crowded with lumped
masses of people, heaped in procession, in ritual, or in reading.

Here Doyle uses the Goya recollection to imagine a pushing away of the crowding of his own life, to enact a pause in his unremitting self-analysis. His affections experience an increase of internal space which here, segue into a peaceful, pitiful communion with the outside world: a de-materialising process which concludes with an elevation of the ordinary streetlamp up to a holy, haloed plane of content clarification. Body, mind and location all seem to be peacefully reconciled in the affectionate, sympathetic heart beats of 'Dear dear. Dear dear.' Such peace is as rare in Doyle's life as it is in Kelman's oeuvre. When Doyle finally plays the pipes to his fantasy audience-come-true, Alison, the playing is repeatedly said to be an enactment of 'control' which allows 'an easing of the spirit' (*D* 153). It is as if Doyle is asserting his masculinity, his individuality and his artistic agency all through the control of the phallic pipes. That the result is less satisfactory than when he first played the pipes to himself, indicates the inherent problems he has in courting the attentions of this married woman, but also how inhibited he can be in communication with another: he has, he thinks, 'objections to doing most things in company' (*D* 159).

If his own artistic expression is problematic for Doyle, full and repeated engagements with the art of others is essential to his way of understanding, interpreting and managing experience. Goya is referred to by Doyle more than any other proper noun, from the first page of the novel onwards in fact. The black paintings of Goya show how artistically minded and visually alert Doyle can be, but they also have a relevant political dimension which is worth exploring. The black paintings were produced between 1820 and 1823 in Spain, after Goya had recovered from a life-threatening illness, and during Spanish monarch Fernando VII's repression of an uprising of militant liberals. The reinstatement of Fernando's tyranny, together with the re-establishment of the position of the Church and its Inquisition, signalled the end of a liberal constitution. This process coincides with Goya's painting of the inside walls of his house, the Quinta del Sordo, on the outskirts of Madrid. Goya left the paintings behind him when, as a result of Fernando's continuing repression of liberals, he left Spain for France in May 1824 and, as it turned out, for good. The paintings are therefore a response to political terror of the worst kind: the loss of liberal ideals to a tyrannical, violently repressive monarch. They might also be autobiographically responding to Goya's near-fatal illness, his realisation of his own mortality.

The paintings were domestic and interior: painted directly onto the plaster walls of his home, ostensibly for private viewing only, rooted to home, to be looked at from within, inward looking, inwardly viewed. Their mystery emanates not only from their obscure purpose, but also the mystic nature of what is represented. As Robert Hughes points out, Goya's Black Paintings are of 'surpassing pessimism'.[23] They include images of a lonely dog, cannibalism, superstitious ritual, witchery, violence, and mobs of garish, ghoulish human processions, all rendered in dark and bruised tones of brown and black, contrasted with pale flesh, obscured but exaggerated features, and often flecked with dirty blood. Robert Hughes describes one of the paintings, *Pilgrimage of San Isidro*, as follows:

> No earlier artist had conveyed the irrationality of the mob, especially the mob inflamed by a common vision – religious, political, it makes no difference – with such unsentimental power. What is more, the expressive roughness of the paint, the urgency with which it is applied, and the theater of expression on the crowd's individual faces – angry, stupefied, cunning, close to madness – amount to an assault on silence. (Hughes, 2004, 18)

Hughes's key descriptive term here is 'unsentimental': Doyle is attracted to Goya for precisely this quality. Goya's interests were often to portray, when he was able, lives and habits of ordinary folk; in the black paintings his vision of that same mass becomes threatening, terrifying even. Doyle repeatedly condemns himself for a tendency to display 'sentimental maudlinity' (*D* 83), or 'unspeakable sentimentality' (*D* 186). This is something Kelman also resists: to be sentimental about the poor is to patronise, to romanticise and to be distanced from experience. Even of Doyle, Kelman says: 'I don't think he feels beat. Maybe to say that would be to risk sentimentalising the character'.[24] Doyle's imagination churns over Goya's unsentimental, menacing human scenarios, nursing itself on irrationality, madness and, in one painting in particular, the loneliness of a dog (*D* 170). The paintings threaten to overwhelm, to drag down and suffocate Doyle in a quicksand of suffering.

One such instance is a dream so bad it wakes him up; the figures in the dream – 'sixteenth-century peasants', approaching him with 'staves or hoes' – could be lifted straight from Goya, but also from Pieter Bruegel or Hieronymus Bosch, painters who revel in, and often find horrors in, ordinary village life, in the masses. In coping with the dream, Doyle has recourse to the self-reflexive panic of an isolated Dostoevsky hero. In Doyle, we can hear the relentless self-questioning of *Crime and Punishment*'s Raskolnikov or the spiteful self-flagellation of the speaker of *Notes From Underground*: unable to determine what is real and what is dream, Doyle begs 'what is to become of me now? Is this the end of my sanity?' (*D* 121). Less frantic and destructive than Dostoevsky's protagonists,[25] but more politically energised than Camus' Meursault, Doyle is middling modern man: alienated from family, detached from community, spiteful towards social hierarchy, ineffectually enraged, without hope, tragedy, direction or calling. Doyle is an existential archetype with only his own intellectualised anguish to serve as an unreliable measure of existence. To describe him thus is not to judge him: if the novel has any structural progression at all, it is in Doyle's increasing sense that 'bitterness would engulf him completely' (*D* 334).

The community of references and critical sympathy

Goya, Dostoevsky and Camus are mentioned in *A Disaffection*. As are other famous proper-noun names: fictional characters like Bob Cratchit, Gregor Samsa, Wringhim, Joseph K, Oblomov, Scrooge, Werther and Zeus; classical authors like Cicero, Empedocles and Heraclitus; philosophers and scientists such as Copernicus, Descartes, Gödel, Hegel, Kierkegaard, Schopenhauer and Wittgenstein; writers such as Balzac, Okot p'Bitek, Boswell and Johnson, Burns, Goethe, Hogg, Hölderlin, Kafka, Joyce, Flannery O'Connor, Scott, Schiller, Tolstoy and Wordsworth; musicians and artists like Eubie Blake, Picasso and Renoir. Each mention is worthy of individual examination (for which this study has neither the room nor the critical wherewithal to attempt); often, Doyle himself does the interpretation for us. Of the lovelorn suicide Werther for example, he considers 'the parallels' with his own life (*D* 80).

Taken as a whole, and as a structural principle, the references form a community of minds for Doyle's discursive dialectical stream of consciousness. Lacking close friends as he does, Doyle ruminates over the lives of intellectual heroes, as much as – if not more than – their ideas. Thus Wittgenstein is mentioned not for his theories on language, on the autonomy of grammar, the importance of acculturation for generation of meaning (all of which are clearly relevant to Kelman if not to Doyle), but because of the biographical fact that three of his brothers committed suicide (*D* 126); Descartes 'used to settle down for the night with his little garret extremely snug' (*D* 98); Hegel 'has a good cheery life as a student' and 'Schopenhauer hated him. Kierkegaard didnt fucking like him either' (*D* 118). Doyle toys with these thinkers as historical people, even as celebrities. Kelman indicates the frivolity of Doyle's mode of engagement with Hegel by the inclusion, on the same page as the discussion of his life, the glitter of 'Fred Astaire and Ginger Rogers, Bing Crosby and Doris Day'. Cairns Craig does an excellent job of making sense of Doyle's relationship to some of these names, for example: 'Hegel and Hölderlin are the ghosts who haunt his imagination: the lucid and ludic system-builder and the poet descending into madness and obsession'.[26] But there are so many names and of such animated diversity that overall it seems as if the novel toys with a roll-call for a fantasy party of famous people, leaving Doyle the stressed-out host.

A Disaffection stands on its own: concrete references to the proper nouns of real historical personages are deliberately omitted in *Hines* and *Chancer*. Both Hines and Tammas are said to be readers; they are described reading frequently and Hines even has discussions about books with his partner Sandra, who we also see reading. The following example is typical of the way books are allowed to function in the first two novels:

> Hines pulled a face at Sandra. As he returned to his chair he glanced back at the book she was reading. Good story that; quite influential in the formative years ... He grinned and sat down, then he reached to the mantelpiece for his tin; he sipped at the tea. It was lukewarm; he set the cup onto the mantelpiece and rolled a cigarette. He glanced at the clock. Well ... I suppose I suppose. He looked to Sandra but she didn't acknowledge him. He lit the cigarette.
>   Five to three I thought you reported? Her gaze had remained on the book.
>   What? Aye. 1457 to be precise. I suppose I can hang on another 10 minutes. A quick coffee maybe.
>   Sandra was still gazing at the book but it was now lying on her lap; and her left hand came to the side of her face, shielding most of it from him. (*BH* 43–4)

Though the book is functional in this scene, put simply it remains an anonymous participant, an object which could contain any text. Hines parodies the self-reflective self-importance of a writer looking back on 'formative years' of reading. His jocularity is not responded

to by Sandra who seems absorbed in the book. The book could be a
serious literary work, but is not necessarily so. Sandra might not be
reading the book at all here: she speaks while continuing to gaze at
it. A little further on it is evident that she is crying. The book is a
shielding screen, like her hand, providing cover so that she does not
have to face Hines, so that she can think privately without discovery,
so that she can turn her thoughts inwards as her son eats his tea.
The book as an object allows her to consider herself, not to be subject
to absorption in a separate textual world. And as we watch her read,
or not read, and as we read Hines' half-sad comedy we too are not
distracted by a name, a novel title, a literary reference. We focus on
the scene without the allusive distraction a book title would bring.
We are not distracted by literariness, which would proclaim itself if
the title was mentioned. A book title would make us think tangentially,
metaphorically, and might make us aware of the narrator, putting
the right book in Sandra's hands to make us think of an explaining,
parallel story. *Hines* as a book would seem suddenly self-aware. So
the absence means any artificial literariness of the scene is kept silent,
the narrator's strings keep invisible, and Kelman's overall intention
to 'obliterate the narrator, get rid of the artist'[27] remains intact.

The omission suggests a great deal as to how the experience of
reading this scene is controlled by Kelman. With or without the title,
the point is still made that books are an integral part of this couple's
life. If the dialogue which Hines tries to initiate about the book does
not get going here, that is surely because Sandra is upset, not because
they never talk about books. Hines is evidently playfully excited by
the prospect of a conversation about the book in question, perhaps
because they talk about books freely and frequently, just not within
the time-frame covered by the novel. That it doesn't happen here
is more evidence of the crisis in their circumstances and their
relationship. Their culture, their class, is fully bookish. But the book
through which we access their bookishness, is blank about other
books. Kelman is fascinatingly candid about his deliberate removal
of literary references from Hines, and the positioning of them front
and centre of Doyle:

> In a sense Doyle's consciousness is much easier because it can *assume*
> a certain further educational level, so the possibility of Doyle knowing
> about what the writer knows about can be taken for granted; whereas
> it can't in *Hines* because that character is just an ordinary working
> class person without a further education. In *Hines* I had to take out

references, say, to Dostoevsky. Camus is implicitly mentioned, implicitly – I had to take out all the references to those writers because it didn't seem to be correct structurally. But only structurally. Most critics and commentators probably would think the reason is the guy's a bus-conductor, and for me to have made such references would have been quite outlandish. That also explains why the formal things haven't been noticed in the novel, because the central character works at an ordinary, so-called unskilled, labouring job – very few contemporary critics ever conceive that a story about a busconductor could be of formal interest to them. It becomes easier when they deal with a character like Doyle because he's a teacher and a professional type of person like themselves and therefore *bound* to know Camus, *bound* to know Dostoevsky. The usual elitism.[28]

Kelman's authorial assumptions about readers' assumptions underpin his strategy: at all costs, readers must not doubt the possibility that what happens in the fiction could happen, does happen. In a sense, Kelman is double-bluffing his conception of literary prejudice: actually he claims that 'structure', not the logic of class, kept Dostoevsky out of *Hines*, and forced Camus beneath the surface. Although he himself was on the buses while reading and writing, he does not expect an audience to accept that an ordinary Hines would be, for 'structural' reasons. What cannot be 'taken for granted' is that latent allusions or explicit references will not distort and distract from the realist project. If we did not know better, saying that Hines is 'just an ordinary working class person' might sound bluntly elitist, but we know that the world of 'ordinary' for this novelist is the focus of attention, the source and mainstay of his project. Kelman says that Doyle's readership would be 'like' Doyle and so would accept a proliferation of reading and a wide range of reference – but is Kelman conceding that his readership is predominantly educated and middle class? Or is he anticipating the appeal of *A Disaffection* to institutions of education? Kelman admits – and to a degree submits – to a division of worlds even at the same time as claiming literature as his right, as the right of all people, no matter what the class or the language.

Even in *A Disaffection* Kelman avoids a conventional game of literary allusion. In no small part, literary tradition consists of, and can be read through, texts in clear dialogue, or that allude to one another, that collude with one another. It has always been a strategy of anxious authors to display and bolster their novels' significance through explicit bridges to other texts, from openly referential devices such as epigraphs, to re-writings of famous passages, to more subtle allusive devices. In fact, most novels attempt some kind of literary allusion, make evident a literary forebear, or have a frictional Oedipal relationship with some parental text (Ian Rankin has a 'rough housing estate called the Kelman' in his Rebus detective novels, for example[29]). Likewise there is an identifiable postmodern take on that same game, turning buried allusion and confirmatory evocation of tradition into playful, undercutting, self-conscious, plagiarising pastiche. Alasdair Gray, for example, famously delineates varieties of plagiarisms to a simultaneously self-aggrandising and self-immolating effect in *Lanark*, and to a lesser extent in the epilogue to *1982 Janine*. If self-aware allusion is a postmodern trait, it is also stimulated by post-structuralist deflation of the romanticising elevation of originality for creative work: 'text is a tissue of quotations drawn from innumerable centres of culture',[30] as Roland Barthes put it, alleviating text from determining author-gods as he did so, of which act Kelman might well approve. While Kelman declares his language to be centred resolutely upon his own culture, actually even in *Hines* there appears to be a complex response to cultural resourcefulness. Hines playfully mixes registers when he parodies and teases English, middle-class, managerial, objective and scientific styles.

As I explained in the introduction, Kelman generally develops an inconsistent version of the major tongue, English, which is an essential ingredient of the minoritarian writer's position for Deleuze and Guattari. If the exteriorised narrative position of *Chancer* maintains an even cultural monotone, *Hines* is notable for its carnivalesque upending of serious styles; Hines style-shifts frequently, drawing lexical items from outwith his own foundational idiolect into play. There is not just one language in Hines, but an intentional and controlled Bakhtinian heteroglossia. Hines himself, draws his language not just from his own immediate points of contact and identification, but from 'innumerable centres of culture' – and some peripheries too. But for all this free play Kelman does not permit us to hear Hines playing with nouns which refer to books or authors of any kind: this is not allowed. The form asserts its authority. Kelman will have no explicit engagement with the used tissues of literary tradition, until they pile into *A Disaffection*. Like Hines, Doyle is similarly playful with a heteroglossic language; but unlike Hines, Kelman allows Doyle and other staff in his school to refer to specific people and named texts, in conversation with one another but more often such references appear in Doyle's unvoiced thoughts.

But why provide such prominent and facile hooks, for readers and critics to hang their responses from, when Kelman's world up to now has been thoroughly and programmatically resistant to exactly this sort of conventional literary flagging? Is Kelman using a middle-class educator to poke fun at the literary critic and educational establishment, having Doyle lay down vacuous red herrings for the critic who is always hungry for a reference to get its teeth into, that it can chase up in a library; is Doyle Kelman's response to Flann O'Brien? Unlike the preceding two novels, the short stories and the plays, *A Disaffection* can be 'fitted' into its displayed network of references, can be explained and accounted for literarily and philosophically, can be placed into a neatly packaged literature course, which it often is. Is Dorothy McMillan right in suggesting that the real middle-class education establishment has had the last laugh because it has welcomed *A Disaffection* with open arms,[31] not least, I would suggest, because it is so explicitly and allusively literary and brazenly intellectual? Does Kelman teasingly give an 'educated' readership what it wants, in bucketloads, but actually is able all the time to push away the 'middle-class wankers' who would appropriate it?

Kelman's strategy might be determined to suggest that tradition, allusion to any part of tradition, carries with it compliance with certain values, with a certain value system, a value system which Doyle, in part at least, subscribes to. Kelman raises a question of literary value: is a novel and the culture it represents only to be valued through its forging of bridges with other texts, with other cultures? If an allusion is recognised ('detected' even) by a reader, some exchange of comfort has taken place, some elevation of cultural value of both text and reader; there is some enriching process not just of the context in which the allusion appears, but also an inducement of comfort, possibly excitement, in the reader. The text displays and confirms knowledge and reading, which a possibly exclusive-feeling set of readers echoes back. Simple literary allusions rely on the readership having read the same books as the author (or rather, narrator), so require a collusive common ground over some sort of 'canon'. Herein lies the powerful economy of a canon of selected texts: if 'we' all point our reading efforts at the same tight group of interrelated texts, we will all get the same references, all be a member of a club of initiates.

Below I follow critic Karl Miller discussing *Hamlet,* and my implicit assumption is that my readers will know who wrote it, because it is so widely canonised; my assumption is that everybody who reads this book has read or seen *Hamlet;* above I make no attempt to explain who Dostoevsky, Camus or Flann O'Brien are. An underlying, usually unquestioned, assumption governs this sort of reference which must be based on a preconceived notion of what I think literate culture consists of, of what 'sort' of reading the 'sort' of person who reads this book will have had already. As such my preconception is prejudiced against those who have not had, or did not want to have, access to such texts. Martin Amis is on similarly canonical ground when he names the focal London pub of *Money* 'The Shakespeare': it is the least risky, the most populist, of allusive literary bets, because the UK's secondary education system guarantees that everyone will know a little Shakespeare. *A Disaffection* on the other hand includes literary references not as embedded allusions, but as the books and authors themselves; if Doyle refers to Shakespeare, Goethe, *Hamlet* or *The Sorrows of Young Werther*, he refers to them as actual writers and texts. In other words, there is still an attempt to avoid literary trickery or device, or any structural, programmatic or coherent allusion to a forebear, such as the eponymous one which frames Joyce's *Ulysses.* Kelman litters Doyle's thinking with mostly familiar references, but the question is, familiar to whom: to me? To everybody? Who is excluded? Do we have to know the published thoughts of every name which Doyle thinks about, to understand the novel?

We should consider what happens when Doyle refers to more obscure names: who is the 'actual painter! Or sculptor!', for example, of whom Doyle asks '[w]hat age was Meurier when he kicked the bucket?' (*D* 93). This is an academic monograph and I should not admit to not knowing who this is; such lacunae are not permitted. I have looked high and low, have asked friends and colleagues and even academic Art Historians: who is this sculptor or painter Meurier? Nobody knows. 'Meurier' suggests that Kelman might not be playing the reference game in as straightforward a manner as it might seem. The risk here is that Meurier might well be someone 'everyone' (everyone else) knows. I may be that one reader who does not know who Meurier is. Or maybe we all are, and that is Kelman's point. To include any literary or 'high culture' reference, to give it import in the structure of the novel, is to exclude someone. Yet again, I would argue, Kelman is making things difficult. Maybe the person he means for us to eventually think of is the Belgian sculptor, Constantin Meunier (1831–1905). To answer Doyle's question, Meunier died just short of his seventy-fourth birthday, having had a lifelong commitment to the portrayal of everyday life in his art (herein lies the relevance). If Doyle gets the name of this sculptor wrong by one letter, Kelman is promoting the instantaneity of his character's recollection, the velocity with which he thinks things through, the instability of story and history. Or maybe this was a genuine mistake Kelman or his typesetters made. Either way, I have fallen into the Flann O'Brien-shaped trap of chasing a semi-bogus reference which, essentially, leads my argument nowhere, other than to the blank horror of academic and critical futility.

To take just one of the plethora of allusions in this novel, as I do with Goya above, might be to read against the complex, vacuum-like inclusivity of the protagonist's mind. Critic Karl Miller takes one reference and runs with it for as long as possible; and because he's a literary man writing a book called *Authors*, pasting the mortar of cohesive tradition between the fragments of contemporary fiction, he reaches for a catch-all multi-signifier, the ubiquitous *Hamlet*.[32] Taking as his springboard a smattering of allusions to the Dane, Miller plays with the interesting similarities with Doyle: they are of a similar age ('the age of Christ at Calvary' Miller portentously asserts[33]), are both loquacious, both have 'charm', as Miller puts it[34]. Both young men have a tendency to soliloquise and perform; both have an artistic bent and are broadly learned. Both experience loneliness, paranoia, flirt with madness and contemplate suicide. But in conjoining these two disparate texts, Miller overreaches: he says that like Hamlet, Doyle 'makes mistakes and causes havoc, in pursuit of the right course'.[35] Here, we can see Miller's usually dextrous fingers falter as he stretches a small Doyle bunnit to fit Hamlet's histrionic head. What 'right course' is Doyle on? While the similarities are clear, they would be too for that other lovelorn, eventually suicidal young man to whom Doyle refers more often and at more length, Goethe's Werther, Hamlet's bastard German son (Hamlet's progeny are everywhere; he could claim part-parentage of Byron's *Manfred* and Freud's Oedipus complex). As he hams-up Doyle so intently – claiming this 'Glasgow Hamlet is the latest in a long line of impersonations'[36] – Miller misses the opportunity to counterbalance his argument with equally revealing dissimilarities. These suggest just how unliterary *A Disaffection* is, even while the mind and modalities of the protagonist are steeped in conventional literary allusions, in which to tell truth Hamlet is but a minor player.

What Miller exemplifies is that because *A Disaffection* beckons a response to the literarily bedecked subject, criticism which takes the bait is markedly different to that provoked by Kelman's other works. In the same way that the Booker prize has distorted criticism of *How late it was, how late*, critical engagements with *A Disaffection* (including the chapter you are reading) are necessarily unlike responses to the first two novels. I am unfairly picking on Miller's essay, which is a fine and well-crafted read, but any essay on Kelman which begins with a portrayal of the monarch's reading of Glasgow, is surely in danger of missing its target. Here is how Miller begins:

> Studying the West Coast of Scotland from the yacht *Britannia*, the Queen is said to have remarked, not long ago, that the people there didn't seem to have much of a life. James Kelman's stories make clear what life is like in Glasgow, and what James Kelman's life is like. They are not going to change the royal mind.[37]

The unfortunate result of considering that the Queen is in any way significant to the world she ignores from afar, is that Miller's own voice gains a monarchical, hierarchical position in relation both to the text and to Kelman; here the author and text are conveniently conflated, just as text and reality are likewise unified. For Miller, Kelman is not a real*ist*, he *is* real, his books are a reality (Miller is certainly not alone in conflating author, text and reality in this way). Miller implies that it is valid to say that 'the people there didn't seem to have much of a life' and Kelman's books prove it. It is as if the Glaswegians aboard the good ship Kelman do not have as much 'value', do not have as much 'life' as people elsewhere; they are lesser beings. But they have less life than who? They are more dead than who? The monarch? Miller? Anyone who has read *Hamlet*? I am picking on Miller's lazy use of idiom here, but it is indicative of an inherent problem of Kelman criticism, and of criticism and reviews of working-class culture in general: sympathy for the lot of the individuals presented so often resorts to the deployment of expressions like 'a drunken, down and out Glaswegian',[38] 'pub-bound, down-and-out',[39] 'dosser',[40] 'alcoholic',[41] 'losers',[42] 'prolier-than-thou beatnik losers',[43] 'aimless life'[44] and Miller's 'not much of a life'. Such phrases reinforce a hierarchy not just of material wealth or crude socio-economic grouping, but of active societal valuation, indeed, of the judging of intrinsic human worth.

These phrases are by no means just simple, innocent descriptors. Douglas Gifford, one of Kelman's earliest, most enthusiastic and sympathetic supporters – indeed one of Scottish literature's most productive critics – condemns *Hines* the novel as a 'portrait of a loser', and Hines the man as 'lazy'; he suggests that Sammy in *How late it was, how late* is 'Kelman's example of human endurance at the lowest level and the lowest ebb'. For Gifford, the latter's world is 'at a lower level of mundane boredom' than Irvine Welsh's *Train-spotting* and Sammy is '[l]ike an old dog'.45 It seems social hierarchies are so embedded in critical discourse that even when we rightly acknowledge, as Gifford is at pains to, that Kelman is successful in convincing us that Sammy 'is a valid human being', there is still a language of quite melodramatic judgement and socially-stratifying reinforcement, which serves to keep Sammy down, render him an animal, into the lowest point criticism can imagine. As Sammy has somewhere to live, a son, associates (some of whom might be called friends), rich memories, musical and critical taste and an actively engaging and articulate mind which powers a storyteller's imagination, this cannot, of course, be true. Bad though things are for him, they could be a lot worse, as Sammy himself would acknowledge. To say Sammy is at our (society's) 'lowest ebb' is to keep him at a safe distance, where we cannot smell him fully, cannot think he is like us. What happens critically is that while one hand of sympathy is being proffered, the other hand is inscribing a language of inherent value judgement, a language to be accessed by worlds other than the one being critically engaged with through Kelman's fiction. Such language reveals sharp, ideological, unconscious prejudices which the stylizations of flocculent critical sympathy cannot fully smother. If a character is a loser, the critic, by happy contrast, is a winner. If a character is 'down and out', the implied critical position is 'up and in'.

Notes

1 Schoolteachers are in the second of six groups in the *Registrar General's Classification of Occupations* (1980), cited in Michael Argyle, *The Psychology of Social Class* (London and New York: Routledge, 1994), 7. Today, teaching is defined as a 'professional occupation' in 'Major Group

2' out of nine in the UK government's occupation classification system. *Standard Occupational Classification 2000*, http://statistics.gov.uk/methods_quality/ns_sec/soc2000.asp (accessed 15/03/2006).

2 Kirsty McNeill, 'Interview with James Kelman', *Chapman*, 57 (Summer 1989), 1.

3 McNeill, 'Interview', 1.

4 James Mitchell, 'Politics in Scotland', in Patrick Dunleavy, Andrew Gamble, Richard Heffernan and Gillian Peele (eds), *Developments in British Politics 7* (Basingstoke: Palgrave Macmillan, 2003), 170.

5 Neil McMillan, 'Wilting, or the "Poor Wee Boy Syndrome": Kelman and Masculinity', *Edinburgh Review*, 108 (2001), 53.

6 Patricia Horton, '*Trainspotting*: A Topography of the Masculine Abject', *English*, 50 (2001), 227.

7 Douglas Gifford, 'Scottish Fiction Since 1945 I', in Douglas Gifford, Sarah Dunnigan and Alan MacGillivray (eds), *Scottish Literature: In English and Scots* (Edinburgh: Edinburgh University Press, 2002), 881.

8 Scottish novels set partly in the schoolroom include: J. F. Hendry, *Fernie Brae: A Scottish Childhood* [1947], in Liam McIlvanney (ed.), *Growing Up in the West* (Edinburgh: Canongate, 2003); Robin Jenkins, *The Changeling* [1958], (Edinburgh: Canongate, 1989); Muriel Spark, *The Prime of Miss Jean Brodie* (London: Macmillan, 1961); George Friel, *Mr Alfred M.A.* [1972], (Edinburgh: Canongate, 1987).

9 Alasdair Gray, *Lanark* [1981] (Edinburgh: Canongate, 2002), 149.

10 William McIlvanney, *Docherty* [1975] (London: Sceptre, 1996), 114–19. The most significant discussion of the tussle between Scots and English in literature, including coverage of *Docherty* and Kelman, is by Cairns Craig, *The Modern Scottish Novel: Narrative and the National Imagination* (Edinburgh University Press, 1999), 75–116.

11 McIllvanney, *Docherty*, 177.

12 James Joyce, *A Portrait of the Artist as a Young Man* [1916] (New York: Viking Press, 1969), 189.

13 Female prostitutes are encountered all over Kelman's fiction. The most startling representation is in the shape and content of the short story 'dear o dear', which is a prose pattern poem typeset to trace the outline of a woman. The speaker, startled by a 'certain pair of legs', while 'going through a bad patch with the wife' manages to 'go on past' nevertheless (*GFB* 186). The woman's shape is a typeset enactment of objectification.

14 Argyle, *The Psychology of Social Class*, 124.

15 Ben Knights, *Writing Masculinities: Male Narratives in Twentieth-Century Fiction* (Basingstoke: Macmillan, 1999), 181.

16 Knights, *Writing Masculinities*, 182.

17 Kelman has had stints as writer-in-residence for Renfrew District Libraries, the University of Texas, Austin, Goldsmith's College, London,

and latterly at the University of Glasgow as part of a Professorial
triumvirate with Alasdair Gray and Tom Leonard. Agnes Owens discusses
the impact of Kelman's tutelage in her autobiographical account in 'A
Hopeless Case', in Paul Henderson Scott (ed.), *Spirits of the Age: Scottish
Self Portraits* (Edinburgh: The Saltire Society, 2005), 75–80. Alasdair
Gray provides an account of the same scenario: see the 'Postscript' to
Lean Tales, James Kelman, Agnes Owens, Alasdair Gray [1985] (London:
Vintage, 1995), 283–7.
18 H. Gustav Klaus, *James Kelman* (Tavistock: Northcote House and British
Council, 2004), 78–83.
19 Jürgen Neubauer, *Literature as Intervention: Struggles Over Cultural
Identity in Contemporary Scottish Fiction* (Marburg: Tectum Verlag,
1999), 189.
20 Neubauer, *Literature as Invention*, 190.
21 For a discussion of Gray's publicly-accessible art, and some illustrations,
see Elspeth King, 'Art for the Early Days of a Better Nation', in Phil
Moores (ed.), *Alasdair Gray: Critical Appreciations and a Bibliography*
(Boston Spa and London: British Library, 2002), 93–121.
22 For a reproduction and brief description, see Juan José Junquera, *The
Black Paintings of Goya* (London: Scala, 2003), 80–1.
23 Robert Hughes, *Goya* (London: Vintage, 2004), 376. See also Nigel
Glendinning, *The Interpretation of Goya's Black Paintings* (London:
Queen Mary College, 1977).
24 McNeill, 'Interview', 2.
25 An overview of the influence of Russian writers on Kelman is offered
by Laurence Nicoll, 'Gogol's Overcoat: Kelman *Resartus*', *Edinburgh
Review*, 108 (2001), 116–22.
26 Cairns Craig, 'Resisting Arrest: James Kelman', in Gavin Wallace and
Randall Stevenson (eds), *The Scottish Novel Since the Seventies*
(Edinburgh: Edinburgh University Press, 1993), 111.
27 Duncan McLean, 'James Kelman interviewed', *Edinburgh Review*, 71
(1985), 80.
28 McNeill, 'Interview', 1–2.
29 'In the subsequent 13 Rebus novels, Rankin has continued to provide an
oblique guide to Scottish literature – "there's a rough housing estate
called the Kelman and Muriel Spark gets a few nods here and there"',
Nicholas Wroe, 'Bobby Dazzler', *Guardian*, 'Review', 28 May 2005, 22.
30 Roland Barthes, 'The Death of the Author' [1968], in Raman Selden
(ed.), *The Theory of Criticism* (London and New York: Longman, 1988),
319.
31 Dorothy McMillan, 'Constructed out of Bewilderment: Stories of
Scotland', in Ian A. Bell (ed.), *Peripheral Visions: Images of Nationhood
in Contemporary British Fiction* (Cardiff: University of Wales Press,
1995), 80–99.

32 Karl Miller, *Authors* (Oxford: Clarendon Press, 1989), 156–62.
33 Miller, *Authors*, 157.
34 Miller, *Authors*, 158.
35 Miller, *Authors*, 159.
36 Miller, *Authors*, 157.
37 Miller, *Authors*, 156.
38 Judy Goldhill, 'And the nominees are . . .', *The Times*, 'Weekend', 10 September 1994, 17.
39 Maya Jaggi, 'Speaking in tongues', *Guardian*, 'Weekend', 18 July 1998, 26.
40 In a revealing moment, Doyle avoids going into a café because someone he calls a 'dosser' is hanging about (*D* 134).
41 Kirsty Gunn, 'King of style', *Sunday Herald*, 2 May 2004, 12.
42 Russell Celyn Jones, 'Glasgow via California', *The Times*, 16 July 1998, 39.
43 Elizabeth Young's phrase is applied to Kelman, Tom Leonard and Alasdair Gray. 'Glasgow gothic', *Guardian*, 'Review', 3 September 1992, 23.
44 Gifford, 'Scottish Fiction Since 1945 I', 879.
45 Gifford, 'Scottish Fiction Since 1945 I', 879–82.

5

How late it was, how late (1994)

Contexts 1: Red Clydeside and the Year of Culture

In chronological terms, Kelman was a published short-story writer and a produced dramatist long before his first novel was in print. In 1978, for example, BBC Radio Scotland produced a play by Kelman called *Hardie and Baird: The Last Days*.[1] It concerns two leaders of a popular uprising of the radical reform movement in Glasgow in 1820. The uprising was put down brutally and quickly by British soldiers, having been manipulated and brought out into the open by government agents. Kelman's play is set in John Baird and Andrew Hardie's prison cells in Stirling and is largely based on surviving letters penned by the two men while in captivity that were brought to light by historical recovery work published in 1970.[2] It is unique in Kelman's work – across drama and prose – in being an historical subject from the long and distant past. Almost everything else he has written is explicitly set, or makes most sense as being set and expressed, in or near the contemporary moment, or in a near future (there are many short stories where time and place as context are not signalled and do not matter, where they do not have an active intrinsic function, but where the language appears to be contemporary and produced from a loosely definable place, so the text can therefore be extrinsically located).

There are obvious aspects to the 1820 uprising which made it attractive to Kelman as fit subject for his work: it suffered some historical neglect (and arguably continues to do so); it signals the dawn of the rich tradition of Glaswegian working-class radicalism; it confirms that British rule and English hegemony was (possibly is) based on the threat of force; it is plainly heroic; and it was a democratic and proto-socialistic uprising, and one not organised by the landed or the aristocracy, but by working men, by brave 'ordinary' people who were part of widespread social discontent and clamour for reform in the midst of the depression following the Napoleonic wars. The weavers Hardie and Baird were not on their own: the call for a strike on April 5th 1820 was responded to by as many as 60,000 workers, and lasted a week.[3]

Interestingly, Hardie and Baird's story was revisited in 1908 by the Independent Labour Party to stimulate the working man 'to play a man's part in the present-day struggle for Liberty, which can only be realised in Socialism'.[4] Subsequent to this publication, between 1915 and 1919 especially, the greater Glasgow area became known as 'Red Clydeside': widespread unrest over poor housing and poor pay flared into rent strikes and labour strikes, and most contentiously strikes during the war at munitions factories, which panicked Lloyd George's government. The unrest – not all of it socialist but most of it working-class – reached crisis point on 'Bloody Friday', January 31st 1919, when, as Iain Mclean puts it, a 'vast demonstration of unofficial strikers [was] roughly broken up by the police, and the next day six tanks lay in the Saltmarket with their guns pointing at the citizens of Glasgow'.[5] Small wonder that Lenin thought a British revolution would start in the city.[6] Stewart's historical pamphlet on Hardie and Baird was republished in 1920 by the Reformers' Bookstall of Glasgow.[7] In 1922 ten of the fifteen MPs representing Glasgow were Labour. The city remains a solid centre of power for the Labour party, and a fertile seedbed for more radical and left-wing activism.

By 1978, Hardie and Baird's martyrdom might well have been popularly and educationally neglected, as Kelman claims, but they were certainly held aloft as 'symbols for the future'[8] of socialist activism at the dawn of the twentieth century. Perhaps Kelman intended to revive their symbolic role in the struggle. A thoroughly researched knowledge of radical history is central to Kelman's own political activism, to his understanding of Glasgow, and to his purposeful rejection of authorised versions of history:

> Radical history is more complex than others. Not only is the history itself repressed, so too is the radical movement. Repression is exercised by any ruling authority, left or right. Individuals are marginalised when it appears in the interests of a party hierarchy. Names are marginalised, glossed over, forgotten. So too are the issues, the disagreements, the arguments.[9]

Like the 1920s, the late 1970s and early 1980s saw huge ideological battles between left and right – some of them violent – across the United Kingdom. While it is ostensibly historical, *Hardie and Baird* is as much about a period which signalled the decline of the power of unionised labour, as it is about the events of 1820 which foreshadow the Chartist, Trades Union and Labour movements of the nineteenth century. This is a play about working-class martyrs responding to a call for liberty, emancipation and social justice, though these putative leaders have already failed at the start of the play. It might be a play which therefore confirms the inevitable failure of revolutionary activity in the face of a violently oppressive and ruthless state machine. With Kelman's additional re-write for the stage, it becomes a play whose dates bookend the rise and fall of radical British socialism: 1820–1990. 1990 was the year Glasgow became Cultural Capital of Europe, something which Kelman, Tom Leonard and many other Glaswegians railed and rallied against. In 1989 Tom Leonard wrote 'A Handy Form for Artists for use in connection with the City of Culture' which lists optional reasons for declining participation in the 'City of Culture', among which are:

> a) places and people are worth something as to whether or not they can be described as "of Culture" b) that desirable thing-to-be-owned, Culture, is now owned by Glasgow.[10]

As we shall see below, the legitimate constitution of 'culture', its ownership and its governance, were to be debated furiously in responses to Kelman's work in 1994; the debate in 1990 was equally heated. For Leonard and Kelman, and many other artists and commentators in Glasgow,[11] the very name of the 1990 event meant it would omit, even suppress, working-class culture and left-wing artistic endeavour, covering the rough-hewn past of labour and unemployment with a pedestrianised, sanitised commodification for a city of consumers, merchants and tourists, not for its workers or dole queues. For People's Palace curator Elspeth King, the Year of Culture was 'not by, for or of the people of Glasgow. It is a classic example of cultural imperialism, done in the cause of economics.'[12] Most controversially of all the wrangles that characterised Glasgow in 1990, King herself was ousted from her job. The People's Palace she curated, on Glasgow Green, is a museum of the city's social history in which, significantly, a portrait of Kelman by Alasdair Gray now hangs. Glasgow Green continues to be the city's rallying point for demonstrations and protests and Kelman himself has spoken himself at mass meetings there.[13] That Glasgow council was determined to sell off a part of this historic Green in 1990, to a leisure company, added fire to growing resentment at the council's work towards the Year of Culture.[14]

If Glasgow Green signified the council's ignorance of social history for some, a parallel symbol of the Year of Culture's organisers' attitude to Glasgow art was located in their intention to hide Ian McCulloch's 'Strathclyde' mural – the 'Glasgow Guernica' – in the new Royal Concert Hall behind a curtain. This formed concrete evidence for many that art which did not fit the organisers' version of Glasgow was to be hidden from the purview of tourists, separated from officially-sanctioned work;[15] the Labour party leader of Glasgow council, Pat Lally, thought it 'looked bloody awful' and 'extremely garish'.[16] So, more broadly, to spend between £40 million[17] and £50 million[18] of public money on a cultural project which quite literally attempted to 'curtain off' art which did not fit the feel-good future the organisers wanted to promote, and to do so at a time when Glasgow was suffering acute social deprivation and mass unemployment, was unavoidably going to be controversial. It is important to remember that '22.6 per cent of Strathclyde Region's labour force were looking for work in April 1989'.[19] This painful context was the root of Kelman and Leonard's concerns; many other commentators felt the same way.[20]

The collusion between the right-wing national Thatcher government and the local Labour party led by Pat Lally seemed to be confirmed by the latter's hiring of the services of PR firm Saatchi and Saatchi to promote the Year of Culture, at a cost of £2 million. Saatchi and Saatchi had successfully worked for the electoral campaigns of the Conservative party. For Lally this was a 'commercial commission' not a political one;[21] for Kelman the involvement of Charles Saatchi, a very rich businessman, art collector and Conservative party donor, was confirmation that the Year of Culture was primarily in cahoots with 'big business'. Its aim was to put culture into the service of a Thatcherite post-industrial capitalist expansion of commerce and the widening corporate interests of mercantile Glasgow (*SRA* 3; 11–12). For Kelman, any art which, by accident or design, is complicit with the value system of its financial sponsors has lost the ability to call itself art, because it, and the artist, are no longer fully free of inherently coercive and exploitative market forces (*SRA* 27–36). Art has to be a guarantor of all manner of freedoms, which must include autonomy from any investment of institutions whose driving principal is the accumulation of capital.

For official organisers of the Year of Culture such as Neil Wallace (deputy director of festivals), Kelman, Leonard and King were part of a bitter group, promoting 'pathetic, factless, plank-walking anti-1990-ism' which was an 'embarrassment to this city and all of its cultural workforce.'[22] For Pat Lally, opposition to the events was led by 'a motley group of whingers', 'the little group of Scotia Bar Trotskyites and anarchists who paraded under the banner "Workers City"'.[23] The organisers eventually arrogated the rancour their events caused. Their official history of the year concludes:

> Glasgow's tradition of open political dissent was also serviced by the Year of Culture celebrations: if constructive debate and criticism was welcomed and engaged, unfounded diatribe was not, especially by the members of the city's cultural organisations who were striving to make 1990 a success. No one ever pretended that a year as Cultural Capital of Europe would solve deprivation in Glasgow, nor was that a direct objective.[24]

Kelman's responses to the 'Year of Culture' organisation were by no means entirely negative. Lally is quite right that the novelist was an active part of a collective called 'Workers City', based around the poetically and politically vibrant Scotia Bar (and subsequently the Transmission Gallery[25]) and established to counteract the mainstream event. The possessive plurality of the name 'Workers City' was designed to counter the rising profile of the 'Merchant City', a business district of central Glasgow which the council had redeveloped and rebranded. Both City labels were written and defined by class politics and competing versions of the city's history, as Kelman himself puts it:

> The name 'Workers' City' carries obvious connotations but it was chosen to directly challenge 'Merchant City', highlighting the grossness of the fallacy that Glasgow somehow exists because of the tireless efforts of a tiny patriotic coalition of fearless 18th century entrepreneurs and far-sighted politicians. These same merchants and politicians made the bulk of their personal fortunes by the simple expediency of not paying the price of labour. (*SRA* 1–2)[26]

Kelman was also active in an alternative intellectual organisation 'The Free University of Glasgow', and helped set up an international conference in Govan in January 1990. Two keynote speeches at 'The Self-Determination and Power Event' were made by Noam Chomsky, attending on Kelman's invitation (*AJS* 14–16). Chomsky discussed 'nationalism, the exercise of political power by leaders who do not answer to citizens, instruments of social control and isolationism'.[27] Kelman has written an extended essay on Chomsky and philosophy (*AJS* 140–86), and there are clear radical, anti-establishment, left-wing points of affiliation and allegiance between the two, illustrated in detail through Kelman's activities in 1990. When he feels it is necessary, Kelman surfaces as a vocal public figure of radical resistance to state-authorised activity, be it over the neglect of sufferers of asbestosis, the criminal justice bill, the closure of steelyards, the institutionalised racism of the police or the management of culture and history. To have a radical figure of international stature such as Chomsky attend a highly successful and innovative conference in Govan with over 300 delegates from all walks of life, at the very beginning of 1990, outside any institutional framework and without any establishment authorisation, was little short of a political and cultural coup for Kelman and his various event collaborators. So impressively high-profile was it, in fact, that the press assumed it was a part of the official Year of Culture.[28]

For both those in favour of the Year of Culture, and those against, 1990 marked a style-shift in Glasgow's public, authorised self-conception. This is not to say that there is any available evidence that Glasgow's citizenry noticed any substantial or material change in their city or in their actual lives, but rather that the *style* of understanding and representing Glasgow, for some, altered. Willy Maley shows how significant 1990 was to comprehending the major changes in twentieth-century Glasgow:

> In the last century Glasgow has passed through three stages, from being Second City of the Empire, after London, to being a centre of socialist agitation as the hub of Red Clydeside, to its promotion as European City of Culture in 1990. The transition from imperialist complicity, through masculinist workerism, to post-industrial heritage museum has been far from smooth.[29]

With this context in mind, the revival of *Hardie and Baird* in 1990 should be regarded as part of a communal project to develop and maintain awareness of rich working-class and socialist histories of Glasgow – what Maley calls 'masculinist workerism' – in a time of change, and from which the civic authorities seemed desperate to escape in the pursuit of an economic and mercantile valhalla. *Hardie and Baird* is overshadowed by the impending execution which was the lot of these two local heroes. Alongside fellow radical weaver James Wilson, Hardie and Baird are now fully memorialised by civic authorities in Glasgow, Strathaven and Paisley. Because the play starts after the heroes have been captured, the predominant direction is towards their inescapable doom.

Avoiding the 'I' through Sammy's eyes

In Kelman's 1994 novel, *How late it was, how late*, Hardie Street police station is the fictitious place where protagonist Sammy Samuels loses his sight, having been beaten senseless by 'sodjers' (*HL* 19). There is in reality a police station on Glasgow's Baird Street, but no Hardie Street in the city. Kelman puts that wrong to rights in his novel. His fictitious street might also be named in honour of the Lanarkshire-born working-class Keir Hardie (1856–1915), first leader of the Parliamentary Labour Party (1906), though given Kelman's critical take on party-sanctioned political activities, this is unlikely. Either way, Hardie is an evocative name in Glasgow. Like both historical Hardies from Red Clydeside's rich history though, Sammy is a working-class hero, albeit of a very different sort. The political dimension of the allusion to Hardie is significant: Sammy militarises his war with the authorities. He calls policemen 'sodjers' – which is both a phoneticisation of soldier, and a compact way of getting Sammy's relationship with the police into a playful name for them: 'sod you' sums up their response to Sammy, and his attitude to them too. Sammy marks a change from any previous novel's protagonist, as Kelman expresses it:

> *How Late* is different in a sense, because the central character I think is more positive, a character who's used to action, and is used to having to fend for himself and fight his way out of difficulties. In the other three novels I think characters are in a situation where, it's a kind of anti-existential thing in a way, it's almost like, when will action be pre-determined – and it's not going to happen.[30]

The whole novel is voiced from Sammy's perspective, if complicatedly so. The first word of the novel stands as an assertion of a fresh concentration of Kelman's developing stylistic confidence: 'Ye' (*HL* 1).

The second-person pronoun is phonetically rendered, is immediate and intimate, actually refers to Sammy himself, and is in Sammy's voice. This narrative is by no means exclusively in the second person, but in favouring 'ye' and 'he', it studiously avoids the 'I' form, unless in direct speech when Sammy is in conversation with someone else.

A Disaffection's Doyle suggests the ubiquitous nature of the first person is a key reason for dropping it:

> Naw but the I's were the worst. Everywhere you looked always this fucking I. I I I. I got really fucking sick of it I mean it was depressing, horrible. I mean that's exactly what you're trying to get rid of in the first damn bloody fucking place I mean christ sake, you know what I'm talking about. (*D* 145)

Typically, Doyle does not fully explain what he is in fact 'talking about', but we can imagine that he wants to resist the decadent and bourgeois fetishisation of the individual in writing; for Doyle, as for Kelman, the 'I' might not be inclusive, cannot be immediately and stylistically social, nor indeed socialist. But as Willy Maley notes, the problem is that 'to tackle the issue of class from the perspective of individual human beings, [is] a strategy that could be said to entail an adoption of a bourgeois standpoint, the individual itself being a construct of middle-class culture'. This version of the Marxist delineation of the conflict between bourgeois individualism and working-class collectivism, enables Maley to locate a problematic tension in Kelman's work:

> As a writer, Kelman wants to maintain close links with his roots, his origins, his culture, his working-class background, yet the characters he creates in his fiction find themselves out on a limb, isolated from the communities from which they arise.[31]

This argument could lead us to regard the novel as a form which is always already middle class, because it rose with and out of the rising middle classes and the concomitant expansion of capitalism in the late eighteenth and early nineteenth centuries. Nancy Armstrong confirms that the novel's 'original mission' was 'to open a space within the field of social positions for previously unacknowledged forms of individualism'.[32] Kelman could of course agree with this mapping of the development of the novel; indeed it could be a primary reason for his intention to break with inherited formal and national traditions. But Raymond Williams complicates matters. The application to fiction of a distinction between the individual and society is, he claims, a reductive bourgeois construct itself:

> The range of actual writing similarly surpasses any reduction of 'creative imagination' to the 'subjective', with its dependent propositions: 'literature' as 'internal' or 'inner' truth; other forms of writing as 'external' truth. These depend, ultimately, on the characteristic bourgeois separation of 'individual' and 'society' and on the older idealist separation of 'mind' and 'world'. The range of writing, in most forms, crosses these artificial categories again and again, and the extremes can even be stated in an opposite way: autobiography ('what I experienced', 'what happened to me') is 'subjective' but (ideally) 'factual' writing; realist fiction or naturalist drama ('people as they are', 'the world as it is') is 'objective' (the narrator or even the fact of narrative occluded in the form) but (ideally) 'creative' writing.[33]

Without wishing to dismiss Maley's anxieties entirely, I would like to focus a response to the problem he raises through Kelman's complex of resistances to the first person, and interpret his decisions across all of his work as the realisation of a criss-crossing of 'artificial categories again and again' that is offered as a possibility by Williams. When Maley elsewhere concludes that Sammy illustrates 'possessive individualism, bourgeois individualism, taken to its extreme',[34] he is reading Sammy as if he were inherently and ineluctably without society, social relation, social responsibility. But the narrative voice itself militates against that reading.

That the first word of How late. . . is 'ye', suggests that Kelman, through Sammy, is stylistically including 'you': the collective possibility of any reader. 'Ye' opens this particular, singular presentation of a human's experience through the possible plurality of the deictic second-person pronoun: 'Ye' could be plural or singular – and in fact is both at the same time. This in turn suggests that the sort of alienation the characters variously experience, while being specifically rooted to a locale, to a certain context of life and language, is also generally, socially applicable and in evidence in many – possibly any – other experiences. The 'ye' enacts a complicating resistance to the decadent, potentially anti-social(ist) focus of liberal humanism upon the individualised self. Complicating because not total, and complicating too in its overlapping and shifting use of the third person, but rarely the first person. If omniscience reconstitutes and enables authority, and if the 'I' atomises the social into individualised, bourgeois, anti-social units in capitalist competition with one another, then the narratological and grammatically non-standard combination of 'ye' and 'he' enacts a levelling set of communal artistic relations and effects even while constructing empathy for the suffering, alienated anguish of the existential male individual. Put more directly, the deictic possibilities of Sammy's 'ye' grants access to his 'I', an everyman's 'he' and by force of pluralising direction, both my singular reader's 'I' and our collective readers' 'we'. 'Ye' opens the novel into a non-standard voice of sociable inclusivity. Though Kelman has written numerous short stories in the first person (e.g. 'Old Francis', 'A History', 'The one with the dog', 'of the spirit', 'Renee', 'Manchester in July', all *GFB*), and his last two novels are also in the first person as we shall see, the formal avoidance of it for the first four novels up to and including *How late. . .*, can only be explained if he is concerned that the use of the 'I' voice might be reproductive of individualistic, bourgeois self-fashioning, rejection of which is foundational to his artistic project. At the same time, the first four of his novels are committed to the evocation of an individual, and that individual is not given an omnisciently-rendered community or social context in which that same individual is to be understood. The social emerges instead through the interaction of individuals, but always through the position and/or perspective of just one of those individuals, a focalised male lead. No matter how alienated the lead male might be, no matter how separated he is from friends or family in body or mind, he is always a social being, if problematically so. The individual is therefore always 'a manifestation of social life', to quote Williams, quoting Marx,[35] even if his thoughts are predominantly private. Maley's problem might therefore be solved by relaxing distinctions between subject and object, internal and external, individual and social. Kelman seems to be worrying at exactly those distinctions in his use of 'ye' and 'he' to problematise and reconstitute the 'I'.

Kelman will not replace the 'I' with omniscience, because like Alain Robbe-Grillet, he regards the author-god as being impossibly corrupted, and redolent of false consciousness:

> Who is this omniscient, omnipresent narrator, who is everywhere at the same time, who sees both sides of everything at the same time, who follows at the same time the movements of the face and those of a conscience, who is simultaneously aware of the present, the past, and the future of every adventure? He can only be a God.[36]

The existentialist dismissal of omniscience and the first person, is based upon an understanding of both as fictional mythological structures which deceive: they inhere a set of values which are secured by the comfort of the possibility of both complete knowledge, and the right of authority to judge and dispense a legitimised version of truth. Albert Camus suggests that use of the 'I' can likewise be a deceptive tool of appropriation by discourses of power, which point is both formally and thematically relevant to *How late. . . .* The distance between the language of authority and the language of the individual being spoken for, stylistically bridged by the use of 'I', actually serves to alienate the subject being referred to, according to Meursault's account in a key moment in his trial in *The Outsider*:

> I thought my lawyer's speech was never going to end. At one point though I listened because he said, 'It's true I killed a man.' Then he went on like that, saying 'I' every time he meant me. I was very surprised. I leant over to one of the policemen and asked him why this was. He told me to be quiet and a moment later added, 'Lawyers always do that.' It seemed to me that it was just another way of excluding me from proceedings, reducing me to insignificance and, in a sense, substituting himself for me.[37]

The subject is transformed into an object for the jury to conceive of; the appropriation of his identity is of course just an act, and is generated by Meursault's unwillingness to compromise his expressed reasons for the murder to help his defence counsel. The defence counsel's strategy is to negate Meursault completely in his choice of discourse, while grammatically becoming him. As I hope to show below, Sammy's real subject position is equally 'reduced to insignificance' by the linguistic strategies of his 'representatives', and employees of the state who use their linguistic codes to substitute Sammy's own. And like Meursault's, Sammy's situation is undermined by his refusal to compromise his own presentation of himself in the face of the welfare, police and legal systems and their demands for 'consistency' from the subject. On Sammy's departure at the end of the novel, he is aware that legal proceedings will continue without him (*HL* 362), as he has signed over certain representational rights to his 'rep' Ally: Sammy and Meursault are both deemed a hindrance to their representatives' work. Their function in the legal process is much less than secondary: it is nought. They are utterly negated by the legal process surrounding them. They no longer have a subject position of their own. Indeed, Ally ensures he can carry on with the case even if Sammy dies (*HL* 298–9).

Kelman, like Patrick Doyle, wishes to avoid the 'I'. In Sammy, he creates someone who loses his 'eye', his sight. This is not a simple pun: Sammy does not see, therefore he is. 'He', and 'ye', not 'eye', so not 'I'. The novel wakes him into blindness, into a transformation. He becomes the prophet of Glasgow, the blind seer, who has vision without sight, who feels every nook and cranny of his territory with his fingers, becoming the idealised model of the purist realist subject. He is a sensitised individual, expressing experience not through the individualising 'I' but through the still singular, yet always possibly plural, 'ye'. As he faces institutionalised language systems, like Meursault he is excluded from controlling how his language is represented by amanuenses – copying down statements, filtering his language, transforming evanescent, momentary, extempore fluidity of speech into the evidence, authority and history of permanent, stolid, typed transcription. The state in Sammy's world is that invasive, possessive lawyer in *The Outsider*, always pushing the individual in directions he does not wish to go, always demanding conformity to a set of assumptions and preconceptions by which the individual would be punished if unable to compromise his version of events. And compromise is what Sammy's legal 'rep' Ally both exemplifies and demands.

Sound and site

Sammy is Kelman's first fully formed celebrant of the musicality of Glasgow voice. The novel also shows an enriching development of Kelman's exploration of the relationship between site and sound, locality and accent, identity and speech. Because of Sammy's blindness, the sight of the eye is replaced by a raised awareness of sited voice, the voice of locality, of situation. Like most of Kelman's protagonists, Sammy is not wedded to the sounds of Glasgow alone. Sammy has a fully musical ear, always with a song in his head, always gathering remembered lyrics to console and empower; he is a budding songwriter too (*HL* 261). His musical passion is aroused most predominantly by American 'outlaw' country music (*HL* 60, 155), blues and folk singer-songwriters like Willie Nelson, Waylon Jennings, Kris Kristofferson, Bob Dylan and Patsy Cline; notably he rejects soul as propaganda (*HL* 155–6). Here it seems necessary to refute in part

Uwe Zagratzki's[38] reading of the novel as showing the structural influence of only African-American blues. Of necessity this interpretation has to ignore Sammy's *actual* musical tastes. Sammy 'needs' music (*HL* 60), and it is a music which is in fact predominantly 'white', not that the colour of the artist makes any difference at all to Sammy, as he certainly never mentions it. Like Patrick Doyle in *A Disaffection*, Sammy is very critical of racist language (e.g. *HL* 345); as Sue Vice points out Sammy 'is politically correct in his internal and external utterances on the subjects of women, gay men, and racial difference'.[39] But his musical taste has very little to do with African-American blues directly.

In fact Sammy's 'lone-star belt buckle' was to be his passport to the centre of his musical universe: Texas (*HL* 8). The 'lone-star state' is home to southern country, and 'western swing', the latter the subject of an extended account of a musical pilgrimage by fellow contemporary Scottish novelist Duncan McLean.[40] Sammy fantasises about a pilgrimage to Luckenbach, Texas, the place Jerry Jeff Walker recorded his groundbreaking 'outlaw country' *Viva Terlingua* live album of 1973. Luckenbach was memorialised further in Waylon Jennings' and Willie Nelson's 1970s hit single, 'Luckenbach, Texas (Back to the Basics of Love)'. Sammy responds to the romance of male community evoked by this song, wanting 'to team up with Willie and Waylon and the boys' (*HL* 250), quoting this impulse directly from the song itself; typically Sammy elsewhere censors this sentimental, romantic fantasy of international travel and musical pilgrimage (*HL* 255), though it comes up again at length (*HL* 285–6). Interestingly, 'Luckenbach' sounds exactly like 'looking back' when sung by Waylon Jennings; as I hope to show, Sammy's mind has to trawl through memories, simultaneously with reconfiguring itself in the present through its enhanced reliance on sound and remembered space. He has to 'look back' in memory because he cannot 'look around' visually. For all his retrieval of memories, like so many of Kelman's characters, the direction of Sammy's travelling mind is into the future and away from Glasgow. To mis-apply Wordsworth, Glasgow is too much with him, late and soon, and it is almost 'too late' to make a change. But change he feels he must.

While Sammy is blind to issues of a singer's colour, country and blues are clearly important as working-class forms for him, as song lyrics and half-remembered sounds are interwoven into his thoughts throughout the novel, especially when he is alone. In the absence of

trustworthy peers ('there was nay cunt ye could trust', *HL* 251), and
the continuing estrangement of his girlfriend Helen, music provides
Sammy with his most reliable social network, and it helps him voice
various experiences. In his study of country music and Texan working-
class culture Aaron A. Fox finds that 'voice' is everything:

> [F]or working-class Texans, the voice is a privileged medium for the
> construction of meaning and identity, and thus for production of a
> distinctive 'class culture.' Song and singing comprise the expressive
> apotheosis of this valued vocality, and song, in turn, is locally understood
> as a consciously elaborated discourse *about* (the) voice. Through song
> and its attendant forms of expressive, technical, critical, and playful talk
> (especially narrative and humor), working-class Texans construct and
> preserve a self-consciously rustic, 'redneck,' 'ordinary,' and 'country'
> ethos in their everyday life.[41]

So while the romance of travelling to Texas might well be beyond
Sammy, the working-class sociability of its sound, the articulacy of
its musical language, colours the tapestry of his newly aural world,
while also celebrating the 'ordinary' – a key facet of Kelman's project
form the start – providing a form of comradeship for Sammy which
encourages a playful, discursive coping with difficult circumstances.
In other words, even though it emanates from a world apart, the
music reaffirms Sammy's class identity. Following Fox's lead, we can
safely say that this particular style of music values the authenticity
of voice, all voices, and by implication Sammy's voice, while nearly
all other reported voices in the novel condemn his voice and his
language. The country music which is at the centre of his musical
passion is also subversive, and is therefore deliberately ignored by
the mainstream media because it might threaten the security of the
state if listened to widely: whatever the actual truth about 'outlaw
country' as a form of political subversion, Sammy's interpretation is
hugely significant. For Sammy, music is not an aesthetic experience
without political dimensions; his music of choice substantiates and
legitimises his antithetical positions and silently subversive intentions.
If more people were allowed to listen to 'adult' music of this kind
'there would be a fucking revolution' (*HL* 156).

At times voiceless music surfaces into the text as Sammy details
the sounds he hears in a pure musical notation, textualised in the
novel as concrete poems,[42] of his own creative making:

> He got down on his knees to feel the floor, cold but firm, cold but firm.
> The palms of his hands flat on it; he had this sensation of being

somewhere else in the world and a music started in his head, a real
real music, it was hypnotic, these instruments beating out the
tumatumatumti tumatumatumti tum, tum; tum, ti tum; tum, tum;
tum, ti tum, tumatumatumti tumatumatumti byong; byong byong byong
byong byong; byong, byong byong, byong, byong byong. (*HL* 11; cf 31)

Here Sammy is on the floor of his cell, having just realised he is
blind. Fleetingly he transcends his concrete situation through the
abstraction of imagined music. This silent music, fully conceptualised,
is quickly muffled by floods of pain and 'a whole crash of thoughts'
(*HL* 11), but it at least effects a temporary respite from awareness of
his imprisoned circumstances. The concrete musicality of the song-
poem lifts him momentarily out of his concrete cell. Sammy loses
his sight, loses perception of colour, dark and light, depth and
perspective, but regains his ear, elevates his sense of touch, and
reconfigures the importance of memory, of unseen rhythm, and of
unwritten story. Removed from access to written textuality, Sammy
inhabits a purified and intellectualised aurality and orality. In this
sense, Sammy is Kelman's ideal subject: articulacy and sound are
more important than writing for Sammy while blind, even if
paradoxically in the form and forum of this printed novel.

'he was reading all kinds of things'

It would be a mistake to conclude, as many critics have, that Sammy
is always illiterate, alien to the world of literature, blind or not: to do
so is to follow the underlying assumption Doctor Logan reveals when
he asks Sammy if he is 'a reader' (*HL* 218). Adam Mars-Jones for
example reads Sammy's world as a 'piling up of inarticulations', while
Kelman's control of punctuation 'belongs to a different world from
Sammy's'.[43] Likewise David Punter suggests Sammy's poor literacy
is graphically displayed by 'the perfect spelling of terms like
"dysfunctional" [in the speech of a council worker which] can have
a relation to Sammy's literacy that is only ironic'.[44] Punter assumes
that because Sammy does not often use words with Hellenic and
Latinate roots like 'dysfunctional' himself, he cannot therefore know
how to spell such words; he is, in effect, literarily and linguistically
dysfunctional. A parallel moment in Alex La Guma's *Time of the
Butcherbird*, set in South Africa, reveals how violent such a question
can be: a white Bantu Commissioner asks an 'old black man' the
question 'Can you read?'.[45] Both La Guma's commissioner and

Kelman's doctor Logan imply that reading is – perhaps should remain – the privilege of the powerful. It is not too crude to suggest that such divisions, policed as they are in both novels by the educated, empowered official of the state, form microcosmic instances of apartheid: in La Guma's world in terms of race, class and culture, in Kelman's in terms of class and culture. While the contexts differ hugely, the manner by which the two novelists reveal the prejudices of officialdom over the education and literacy of the people it officiates, is exactly the same, proffered in an unapologetically interrogative invasiveness.

The doctor's question of Sammy has to be addressed in detail, not only because it is illustrative of the social gulf between the two, which the doctor is positioned to police (for another relationship tense with class politics between a patient and a doctor, see the short story 'In with the doctor', *GFB* 118–132), but also because it opens up the question of Sammy's literacy. Sammy has frequent recollections of fiction, which range from explicit references such as *John Barleycorn* by Jack London (*HL* 29), to the more frequent unnamed references, such as:

> He once read a story about a Jewish guy and a black guy and they met in this New York cafe and drank coffee, they were both skint, and the way they knew one another was skint and used to being skint was because they both took triple helpings of cream and sugar. Fucking bullshit. (*HL* 198)

> He read a story once about a guy that vanished. But it was unbelievable. So fuck it. (*HL* 255)

> This story he had read once, about a German guy, maybe it was Scandinavia (*HL* 286)

'He once read. . .' and derivations of the same phrase almost acquire the status of a musical refrain. Each of these references is broken off by Sammy's blunt rejection of their relevance and value, or, in the latter's case, by his own hunger which elides the full-stop (a reference to Norwegian Knut Hamson's novel *Hunger* of 1890 perhaps). Nevertheless it is clear that literature is unproblematically a part of *his* culture, something which reactions to the novel almost always ignore, whether positive or negative. To ignore such references is necessary in the critical construction of Sammy as illiterate, but it also does damage to his frame of reference, and narrows the interpretative avenues for the novel as a whole. For example, Sammy, desperate for some blind role models, tries to remember a blind 'officer in some army' in a 'French novel maybe. Or Russian' (*HL* 127). This could be the partially sighted General Kutuzov in Leo Tolstoy's *War and Peace*. In the war with Napoleon, Kutuzov is Tolstoy's heroic spirit of Russia: a commonsensical general who is cautious with the lives of his troops and never tempted by the glorification of war, in contrast to the tyrannical vanity of Tolstoy's Napoleon. It is no stretch to read Sammy in his militarised fashion, continually 'battling on', as a Glaswegian Kutuzov: hard-nosed yet pragmatic; intellectual and combative; isolated and criticised on all fronts; weather-beaten and macho; disparaged but enduring.[46] There is another possible Russian reference which is also worth pursuing:

> He once read a story about that, some poor cunt that worked as a minor official for some government department and he beavered away all hours but everybody thought he was a dumpling, everybody he knew, they all thought he was a dumpling, poor bastard, that was what he was, a fucking dumpling. (*HL* 40)

The affectionate recollection is possibly of Akaky Akakievich from Nikolai Gogol's *The Overcoat*.[47] Akaky's surname is 'Baskmackin, which all too plainly was at some time derived from bashmak'.[48] 'Bashmak' is Russian for 'shoe'. Through Sammy's opening and subsequent references to the loss of his own stolen shoes (e.g. *HL* 1, 127, 247 and 325), and repeated considerations of the state of his feet, it might be that Kelman is trying to evoke both Akaky Akakievich, Gogol's bureaucratic functionary who is fatally robbed of his prized overcoat, and Estragon in Samuel Beckett's *Waiting for Godot* who, somewhat like Sammy, has slept in a ditch after having been beaten. The play opens with Estragon frantically trying to air his painful feet. His companion Vladimir philosophises: 'There's man all over for you, blaming on his boots the faults of his feet.'[49] Back in *How late . . .*, the police go on to abuse and humiliate Sammy physically by characterising his exposed toes as 'angry-looking', 'red and purplish', 'like a penis' (*HL* 180). The shoes, as Sammy confirms, are 'crucial, crucial' (*HL* 325). Sammy's ill-fitting, uncomfortable, borrowed or stolen footwear shows the delicacy of his survival, while the novel at the same time tries to put us 'in his shoes'. Kelman's wider point might be that our lives are as fragile and as absurd as Sammy's, and in wearing his shoes for the duration of the novel we are supposed to feel uncomfortable too.

How late. . . embeds allusions into the narrative of which Sammy does not ostensibly seem aware, while also confidently allowing Sammy to recall a wide range of world literature – an explicit surfacing of knowledge denied to Rab Hines and Tammas in previous novels, even though both are readers. To suggest Sammy is illiterate, un-literary or otherwise remote from writing and reading, is to carry the novel in that direction too. Very often, as we shall see, critics regarded both Sammy and the novel as sub-literary and beneath the concerns of culture. They are evidently mistaken. Ian Bell rightly proposes that Sammy's name might allude both to Kafka's Gregor Samsa and John Milton's *Samson Agonistes.*[50] Sammy and his novel are fully, and confidently, literate and literary. To suggest that Sammy would not know, *could* not know, how to punctuate or spell the way Kelman or council workers do, is an assumption verging on prejudice which Kelman is always fighting. To assume, as Mary McGlynn does, that Kelman deliberately draws characters who 'can access language likely to be beyond their purview' is to miss his fundamental point: broad and deep reading, complex metaphor and imagery, sophisticated and hybrid languages, *are* all within the possible range of any speaker, of any tongue, of any class, no matter what their 'limited education and background' as McGlynn says of Sammy.[51]

Apart from a note left to Helen – in which Sammy, like Kelman's narrator, inconsistently deploys contraction apostrophes but not all those that standard usage would (*HL* 360) – we do not have access to Sammy's writing. But this whole novel is, in a structural sense, *his* narrative, including the presentation of semi-colons and standard spelling of polysyllabic terms. A logical imperative of the conjoined voices of character and narrator, and the resulting singular subject position of Sammy with his neutralised narrator, is that we have to believe that he could write the novel too. If the novel does not explicitly construct Sammy as the novelist, as the writer of his own tale, we do know at least that he is a reader, and an avid one too. He is sorry that his blindness means he will not be able to read anymore. It is, he says, a 'pity about the reading. From now on it would have to be these talking books' (*HL* 66). In effect, Sammy enables Kelman to play with this novel as if it were a 'talking book', a book of voice, of sound, above and away from, blind to, print. Impossible of course: our access to this supposed oral world is always through print, and it 'talks' only through the activation of the reader – but it is still an artful illusion with which Kelman intricately plays.

The manner in which Sammy understands his blindness, from the start, is articulated through his reading, through remembered textual experience. In the passage that follows, Kelman manages to provide the materialisation of Sammy's blindness as a bleeding, and expanding, of the text itself, which any reader of *How late. . .* cannot help but 'see':

> Next time he woke it was black night again, and sore christ he was really really sore; aches all ower. The whole of the body. And then his fucking eyes as well, there was something wrong with them, like if it had still been daylight and he was reading a book he would have had double-vision or something, his mind going back to a time he was reading all kinds of things, weird things, black magic stuff and crazy religious experiences and the writing started to get thick, each letter just filled out till there was nay space between it and the next yin: no doubt just coincidental but at the time man he was fucking strung out with other sort of stuff so he took it extremely personal, extremely personal man ye know what I'm talking about. (*HL* 9–10)

This passage typifies the manner in which Sammy responds to and manages problems. He assesses his physical situation: his pains, his damage; then through simile, and then memory, he tries to express, ostensibly to himself, a conception of what he is experiencing. Here he has recourse to a black-out of the pages of texts which themselves are about 'crazy religious experiences': the print expands to cover the page. Kelman provides his readership with a materially imaginable process for Sammy's blindness, which is most readily imagined by making the print of *How late. . .* itself bleed across the page. At the moment Sammy realises his vision is transformed, Kelman's audience has to process an image which it will most easily imagine through the immediate physical presence of the page it is reading. Kelman makes the text become physically dynamic, spreading across, moving beyond its usual boundaries. I have pointed out how bookish Kelman's characters are: Hines, Tammas, Doyle – all are readers. But Sammy marks a development in the complexity of both literary and textual device, and in the way in which Kelman chooses to manage the text's own literariness, and Sammy's own textual life. His blindness here is conveyed by the text as both semiotic, lexical units, but also through text as icon, as image of black ink. And this is a secular spiritual experience, if only crazily so: it is a transformation, a darkening, an inverted road-to-Damascus moment remembered through the 'extremely personal' sensitised reading Sammy has enjoyed in the past.

To further enhance the spiritual and psychological effects of Sammy's transformation, Kelman offers other religious echoes. The waking into blindness is the third time that Sammy has awoken so far in the novel, indeed the novel starts with 'Ye wake' (see *HL* 1 and 7); just ten pages into the novel and we have had three mentions of Sammy waking, a trinity of risings, and on the third, a transformation. Because Sammy's body has been battered and beaten by state-legitimised, and militarised, authorities, a biblical echo is clearly made to the resurrected Christ who rises on the third day (Luke, 24.7). Christ's mocking, scourging soldiers become Sammy's kicking sodjers. A lower-case, talismanic 'christ' is summoned here by Sammy as he awakes into his transformed state, but idiomatically and secularly so. Sammy was brought up in 'an atheist house, a godless house' (*HL* 63). But in his gathering of embedded references to Christ together with other forms of allusions to other doomed heroes early on in the novel – such as Andrew Hardie, Estragon, Akaky Akakievich – it is unmistakable that Kelman is marking Sammy out as a martyr, a hero, doomed to suffer at the hands of the state. But like Christ's, Sammy's is a suffering that, to a degree, he brings on himself. He knows that 'it's the system' and that 'they're sodjers, trained to kill' (*HL* 63 and 64). Against such forces he can only finally admit that they will determine that he 'was the cause of the sight loss; him himself' (*HL* 248). He knows full-well when he makes his decision to punch and run (*HL* 3), that he might have a brief moment of all-important control in resisting the sodjers, but that they will punish him for it. He knows that his charge away from them, while joyful in its anapaestic imperatives – 'get to fuck get to fuck' (*HL* 5) – can only be a brief burst of laughter before the inexorable beating.

The beating the police administer is not detailed very much. The first two boots go into Sammy's stomach. The police then drag Sammy into a close and, as narrator, and in a delicate withdrawal typical of Kelman when dealing with violence or sexual activity, Sammy decides on 'drawing a curtain here' (*HL* 6). What is elided is the type of physical violence which Irvine Welsh, for example, revels in; this elision marks out how different Kelman's intentions are. He does not wish to exploit the potential of the horror scene, or stimulate the cheap thrills of watching torture: this is the generative moment of drama, the event which, with a little delay, causes Sammy's blindness. It is the springboard of the novel, no less so than Patrick Doyle's finding of the pipes. And yet we are not permitted to see it. Kelman

avoids prurience at all costs – avoiding sexual as well as violent detail
– perhaps to avoid the sentimentalism of a Zola-like naturalism[52] –
but also because the act which causes blindness is itself made blind
to us. Avoiding the gore enhances the subtle effect of mystery which
pervades this novel: it does not undermine Sammy's reliability, but
it does show him to be in control of his own story, even while this
is not a self-aware narrative (it does not explicitly know itself as a
book or as a story). It also shows that there will be some things to
which we will always be blind, no matter how seemingly 'honest' the
guiding narrative. Sammy does not wish to revisit this scene in the
retelling, does not see a need for a detailed scourging scene: as he
says 'nay point prolonging the agony' (*HL* 6). We are to know that
Sammy is a victim of disproportionate police violence, of a fight
where he is outnumbered and predetermined to lose, and these points
are enough for Kelman, and more than sufficient for Sammy. If
Kelman legitimised the use of vernacular for the narratives of
significant contemporary novelists like Niall Griffiths, Alan Warner
and Irvine Welsh, he was never a model for their various sub-
Clockwork Orange 'horror show' excesses.

Sammy's soft-palmed sensitivity

If Sammy's musical ear becomes more significant on the loss of
sight, equally an enhanced discovery of touch and sound is provoked,
of tactility and material renegotiation of private and public spaces.
The dynamics of the narrative are dominated by an active interpretation of space and sound; the loss of visual sight literally and
necessarily elevates Sammy's critical insight into matters material,
matters local, matters micro, matters of site and situation; but the
sight loss also abstracts his mental processing into recoveries of
memories and associations, which are both organisationally pragmatic
and aspirationally hopeful. Sammy becomes the sightless prophet
not of a possible or ideal future, but of a material, at times oppressively
close, concrete present: he has to concentrate on 'the day-to-day stuff,
the minute-to-minute points of order. The actual living' (*HL* 248):
in other words, the everydayness, the facticity of being. Sammy has
to touch his world more intimately, has to heighten his materialist
understanding of his local world, and the city starts to live through
this defamiliarising process, even through the agency of something
as day-to-day as Glasgow rain: 'These wee murmurs and groans and

fucking sighing noises; and these drips, like a burst pipe.' (*HL* 286)
In Sammy's ears, the city comes alive.

Sammy's new-found and vulnerable loneliness means he must
coax and motivate himself through a complex renegotiation of recollections of actions and space, while always reminding himself that
his defining characteristic is that he is 'a battler' (*HL* 47). Sue Vice
reads these two different modes as a Bakhtinian mixing of discourses:

> Sammy's inner discourse alternates between a material and precise
> realism (details of his struggles to walk home and use the lift when he
> is newly blind, the encounters with officialdom, such as DSS employees
> and the doctor) and a Beckettian existentialism (he ponders on the
> hardships of life, the reasons for carrying on, lessons to be learned
> from prison, and so on).[53]

The two modes of discourse intertwine: Sammy often starts a journey
with detailed considerations of precisely where he is in space, which
fraught situation he then copes with by existential pondering and
recollection as the journey gets underway. Immediately he is outside
and blind, he develops a technique for feeling out his world made
new to him. This 'patacaking' (*HL* 38) is a tool for the novelist's
defamiliarising of the familiar urban landscape – the laying of hands
onto walls, streets, the junctions of buildings, the shapes of closes,
kerbs, alleyways, doors, stairs: all become sites of comforting
reassurance when recognised, when felt out, when patted and petted,
but also they always threaten to dissociate, disorient, discompose and
destabilise. Fingers enquire and confirm the texture of his experience,
at the same time as Sammy is no longer able to access written text.
The recognition of places and noises is always possibly wrong, as
his usual cognitive processes are thrown into disarray by the lack of
definite visual information. In a sense, Sammy does become an
unreliable narrator and courier of his own story, as he is newly unsure
of his location. The children's game and nursery rhyme of the same
name soften Sammy's 'pat-a-cake' interpretation of his new environs
into a delicate infantilisation: 'How do ye walk' he asks himself,
as he 'patacakes' (*HL* 38). Patacaking opens his fighter's fists into
soft-palm sensitivity. Hands are unsure of themselves, leading an
unsteady, fragile and tentative body in its new explorations, reorien-
tations and relocations. When he is first turned out onto the street
outside the police station, it is the memory of the children's game
which nurses him, which constructs his technique for coping, for

moving, for enduring, for waiting. As Beckett puts it, he is to 'keep
going, going on':[54]

> The door shut behind him. There was the steps. He poked his foot
> forwards to the right and to the left jesus christ man that's fine, to the
> right and to the left, okay, fucking doing it ye're doing it; okay; down
> the steps sideways and turning right, his hands along the wall, step by
> step, reminding ye of that patacake game ye play when ye're a wean,
> slapping yer hands on top of each other then speeding it up. (*HL* 33)

This is the birth of a differently-sentient being: the police violence
has parented a newly vulnerable individual, thrust out into a busy
urban environment of modernist concrete and hard edges which is,
and is not, his own. This is a transforming inverted birth within a
realist frame, parallel to the surrealist swallowing, digesting and
ejecting of Lanark in Alasdair Gray's novel, by which process Lanark
ends up in an inverted hospital where the patients are food for the
sustenation of 'The Institute'.[55] The Institute's sole purpose is to
sustain itself by feeding on its patients. Gray's surreal parody is
developed by Kelman though in a more realist mode. Like Lanark,
Sammy is infantilised by the state, in the sense that his independent
and assertive strength to survive has been kicked out of him, leaving
him vulnerable, ironically enough, to further abuse by other wings
of the state through a dependency which the state itself created.
Subsequent boots of oppression will come from failing bureaucracy
rather than flailing policemen, though it is vital to remember that
Sammy has been witness to 'cunts fucking dying, getting fucking
kicked to death' (*HL* 57), and has had a cell-mate die at the hands of
prison officers (*HL* 189 and 202). It is not metaphorical *at all* for
Sammy to think of the state as violent, nor can it be deemed paranoid
or exaggerated if he considers the police to be always a threat to his
life. In summary, the state's blinding of Sammy is part of a continuum
of abuses he has suffered and witnessed since falling foul of it as a
teenager. The state does not work for this individual, but against
him; it does not trust him, it inspects and suspects him, and expects
him to conform.

   To return to the passage above, Sammy's version of the 'patacake'
game is solo rather than social as it would be for a child. The absence
of playing partners renders his isolation all the more threatening,
makes him a child in a world of danger. But the recollection of the
childhood game more directly reassures, makes the laborious task

of feeling out a way through adversity into dynamic, receptive play. Sammy finds comfort in the sure, repetitive, rhythmic sounds of his hands on hard surfaces. The mixture of second person and third person subjects in this passage, of past and present tenses and the repeated idioms of encouragement ('doing it ye're doing it; okay'), form a rapidly switching, multi-modal, potentially discombobulating, but ultimately confirmatory narrative style which typifies the novel when Sammy is alone. Sammy has to comfort himself, in the complete and continuing absence of anyone else to do it for him.

Sammy's blindness necessitates a heightened and newly unfamiliar, envisioned version of the city space, negotiation through which requires the continuous activation of memories at every tentative step: the articulation of reference points, the forging of multiple links to build scaffolding and ladders between what was seen with eyes before, and what is touched and heard now. The hero interprets through newly refreshed senses channelled to him by fingertips and feet, ears and nose, but the cautious reliance on these newly significant senses is bolstered and enriched by fragments of memories and remembered maps: the essential process by which Sammy is to gain safe passage, to ensure his own physical and mental security. Sammy's ventures into the outside world form psychological memorialisations of his recent and distant past, and often become relieved and happy celebrations, of his local sphere, his locality, the self-reflecting sounds of familiarity, of a language which comforts. Voice is orientation, location, and confirmation of identity. As part of his deposition to the police, Sammy admits how important accent is to him:

> He wasnay a homebird. He wasnay used to it. So he liked going out, he liked the pub, no just for the bevy, he liked the crack as well, hearing the patter. Even considering ye were home three years, ye still enjoyed it.
>
> I'm no kidding ye, he said, even just out walking first thing in the morning, ye forget where ye are, then that first Glasgow voice hits ye; it makes ye smile, know what I'm saying, cause it's a real surprise. (*HL* 160)

Here Sammy's deposition is conveyed as reported speech in the third person, then moves to direct speech with a mixture of the generalised second person and first person: it adopts and enacts many perspectives, forms an inclusive, collective, confident portrayal of his vibrant social context. Sammy might be using his happy recollection of

Glasgow voice and the confidence of his delivery to present himself as a relaxed, therefore innocent, man. Though the Glasgow voice seems properly significant to Sammy, the context of his describing its repeatedly happy 'surprise' as a part of his deposition to the police whose own 'voices came from different places' (*HL* 160), might mean that he is using the celebration of Glasgow partly to critique the non-Glasgow voices among the team of police interrogators, specifically a police officer whose 'accent sounded a bit English' (*HL* 162). The English accent might also be significant in that it suggests that police who are not local are investigating Sammy: Sammy has national detectives on his trail, which further suggests he is involved in something much more serious than just hitting a policeman (but we will never know for sure).

As his is a large and fully dynamic city, Sammy's encounters with other sighted inhabitants cannot be predicted. People he bumps into are mostly people he cannot blindly trust, because he simply does not know them, and cannot 'read' them. Throughout the novel there is an evident hunger for talking with 'somebody he could trust' (*HL* 150), not just because he is blind, but because he wants to recover his lost memory of the weekend which immediately precedes the start of the novel: it is a blindspot, a blank in his memory, and the journey of the novel is in part an exploration and a partial filling in of that blind spot (*HL* 26). This novel is a mystery, a socially-upended detective novel:[56] the victim-criminal tries to fill in that blank space of a lost Saturday, while studiously avoiding details of what exactly his criminal activities have been, leaving us to speculate, to do the detective work, if indeed we have a policeman's impulse to get to 'the truth'. If we do act on that impulse, we must also question its validity as the basis for a critical and interpretative tool, especially as Sammy himself is so determined to put his imprisoned past behind him. The sympathy of the novel is so fully with thirty-eight-year-old Sammy, perennially in and out of prison since the age of nineteen, that we can only define him as a 'criminal' if we reject him completely, and take the censorious position of the police. And the police are clearly not the arbiters of 'truth' in this novel. This was a frequent critical failing particularly among reactions to the novel on its winning the Booker prize in 1994, indeed not just from those critics who rejected the book outright. To ignore the huge questions the novel worries at – questions about the fairness and validity of the legal system, the state prison system, the police, the health and social security systems – is to ignore the novel's overall agenda, and to ignore Sammy's politics, to render him blind 'to history and politics and philosophy' as Willy Maley would have it.[57] This is a novel which asks questions about human rights from a local, practical, actualisable platform: what rights is Sammy actually, pragmatically allowed? Over what rights does he have sole control? How does the state help him? Is the state for or against the rights of the individual? Why does the state not function as a supportive prop for the vulnerable?

The blind populous anonymity of sighted city life, becomes in Sammy's newly individuated vision, a traumatic and fraught experience of fleeting moments of half-trusted or accidental intimacy: the touching on the arm as people help him cross the road (*HL* 53); the brushing against someone's clothes (*HL* 247); the fall into the street and the call for help (*HL* 41); sounds of passing laughter (*HL* 127); the feeling of someone walking beside him (*HL* 256); the offer from a prostitute (*HL* 287). Sammy's awkwardness with his new situation lies in his desire not to be helped, to blunder on, to follow his own path: as with Hines and Doyle, Sammy understands his transformation as one of a loss of control, of his own volition, his own independence. This confident independence – undermined and rendered at times impossible through his blindness – shows Sammy to be a very different personality from Doyle and Hines. Sammy is self-assured and self-contained in a manner to which Hines and Doyle can only aspire. For all his evident sensitivities, Sammy is more bluntly anarchic, more directly rebellious in the face of institutions, than either Hines or Doyle manage. Doyle and Hines are malcontent self-agitators for personal rebellion and reform. Their heated considerations of kicking against employers, state and institutions remain detached: extensively and potently articulated but nevertheless mostly unactivated. Sammy, by contrast, is a decider, a maverick soldier for his own cause, having associations with real – rather than Doyle's imagined – political radicals and, in the police's definition people who carry out 'acts of terrorism' (*HL* 178) (though we should be chary of trusting such blank definitions coming from the state authority. Any maintenance of 'truth' in this novel is located with Sammy). But all three leading men do have the same critical and politicised position in relation to the state; all three are suspicious of police, but only Sammy can be fully justified in thinking he is being watched. Evidence presented to him when he is arrested and interrogated for the second time, for example, is a photograph taken

of him eleven years ago, in London (*HL* 199–201), a photograph
which he cannot see (so like Sammy we cannot be sure it exists).
Even the dating of the photograph is unstable: the police say it was
ten years ago; Sammy asserts it was eleven (*HL* 201). Hines is
monitored by his employers' clocks, while Doyle imagines being
tracked by government spies, but only Sammy actually has been
under state-sponsored surveillance. The eyes of government are
everywhere, looking through his cell door (*HL* 8–9), possibly looking
at him in lifts (*HL* 91). The pressure of the police looking at Sammy
is immense, and increases (or threatens to increase) throughout the
novel: 'the more we look at you the more there is to see' they say
(*HL* 200) – and it is an indeterminate 'they' because Sammy has no
concrete idea who is actually interrogating him. He knows he would
have more power in the interrogation if he could look back at each
interlocutor (*HL* 204). The eyes of the oppressed individual are
blinded: he is no longer able to see himself, and his disability makes
him monstrous to others: as David Punter puts it 'Sammy becomes
"that which nobody wants to see"'.[58] Sammy, if representative of the
colonised masses as Punter reads him, is blinded and herded by
the all-pervasive control through observation and inspection of the
anonymous state machine. In this novel, looking is power, and Sammy
has none, because a boot of the state has stamped out his sight.

The blind gap between orality and textuality

This novel was published ten years after the setting of George Orwell's
Nineteen Eighty-Four. The state indoctrinator O'Brien provides his
charge, Winston Smith, with an image: '"If you want a picture of
the future, imagine a boot stamping on a human face – for ever."'[59]
Sammy is the product of that stamping: blinded by the oppression
of the state, imprisoned, provoked, questioned, bullied, threatened,
beaten and bribed. Sammy does not wilt like Smith, and the novel
projects no exaggerated distopia. Yet the focalisation of this individual who is perenially in conflict with authority is certainly meant
to provoke considerations of state authority and autocracy, particularly
in relation to the ways in which language is used to manage Sammy,
and to alienate him, and his own language, from the machina-
tions of standard English state processes and procedures. There is
not always a direct or simple conflict between Sammy's working-

class vernacular and state-authorised standard English, indeed such categories don't fully represent the far more nuanced and complicated linguistic world Sammy hears. At the DSS, the young man who takes his initial statement slips from official, formal language into talk of football – he talks to Sammy in two registers: the language of his own culture and the language of his job. In engaging in this exchange of mutual masculinity – shared memories of football in this case – Sammy also relaxes into trust. It is at this point that he slips further and admits that the police 'gave me a doing' (*HL* 96–8). His sight loss has disadvantaged him here – his memories of football perhaps dominating because he cannot 'see' where he is or to whom he is talking. Realising his mistake, remembering the function of the interview, Sammy swiftly requests that the involvement of the police – the causal relationship he had alluded to – be deleted from his deposition, but the keyboardist refuses, claiming he does not 'have the authority' (*HL* 98). Neither does Sammy, evidently. Sammy's life is out of control because it has fallen into a blind gap between orality and textuality. Because he has become fully oral, text is beginning to dictate his life, and he cannot control that text with any security. When his oral version of his life is written, it is nothing to do with him at all.

Perhaps following *Nineteen Eighty-Four*, Kelman also suggests that the state does not permit Sammy to construct his own version of history, the story that would most suit his cause. Because the register of this 'Preliminary Officer' is mixed, Sammy forgets that he is being 'assessed'. With the subsequent more senior Officer the same is true: she is given the markers of a Glasgow accent, but has recourse to an explicatory, legalistic discourse which is designed to control Sammy's account into due process. Sammy gets caught in a multiply-binding labyrinth: in order to pursue his claim of disability benefit, he has to say how he became blind. If he tells the truth, he then has to take legal action against the police, something he is determined not to do, because he wants the least trouble possible. Police mean trouble, and nothing but: 'There's nay such thing as a good fucking uniform' (*HL* 195). If he cannot secure the financial support of the state, what avenue, other than crime and the black market, is left open to him to ensure his survival? His criminality and now his blindness have made a monster of him, as David Punter points out, so nobody wants him. The Officer advises him:

I would point out the inconsistency however Mister Samuels: on the one hand you say that is the case; on the other hand I can imagine some saying, well if it's true why is he not taking any action? (*HL* 105)

Inconsistency will be Sammy's downfall: the standard process, the procedure, of the state demands consistency of its subjects' behaviour. Persistently the novel sets up a conflict between procedure and behaviour. The state is standardising, homogenising, essentialising; the individual is inconsistent, variegated, distinctive, but is repeatedly told not to be, or that he cannot be. 'No one is unique' says the Doctor (*HL* 222).

As Sammy navigates the corridors and officials of state bureaucracy, he encounters Ally. Ally wants to represent Sammy in the latter's claim against the police, a procedure in which Sammy is only involved because he could never be in full control of the way in which his oral account was written down by the Preliminary Officer. It is at a key conjunction of three agents involved in Sammy's 'case' that Sammy is most under pressure and stress: the police, having interrogated him at length, drop him off at the Doctor's with their by-now customary orders and threats – 'ye're going in alone' and 'we'll be waiting' (*HL* 211). Sammy is dealt with abruptly by the female receptionist he mentally names 'Missis La di da' (*HL* 212), his tension and stress elevated by his class reading of the power politics of her imperatives, her accent and her masterful management of silences (*HL* 216. She is therefore reminiscent of *A Disaffection*'s Old Milne, who Doyle characterises as being a master of conversational silence, which always gives the Headmaster the upper hand, *D* 151).

Here, inhabiting and exploiting Sammy's police-driven, medical, bureaucratic blind nadir, Ally awaits, a sighted predator of unknowable provenance. Practically, if Sammy can convince the Doctor of his blindness, if the interview goes well, he might eventually have some degree of financial security. As Sammy goes deeper into the labyrinth he gets increasingly disempowered and increasingly stressed, and at this low point, Ally appears: guardian angel or exploitative pariah? The provenance of Ally is kept from Sammy, and so from us: that Ally will not confess to his origins other than saying a 'wee bird' told him about Sammy (*HL* 214) renders Sammy's resistance to his intervention fully logical. The mainstay of Ally's advice is that because Sammy's case is not at all 'straightforward' (*HL* 215) whatever Sammy does, or whatever stories he tells about what he or the police did, he must at all costs be 'consistent' (e.g. *HL* 234–5, 294, 300 and 309).

Inconsistency will result in Sammy being engulfed yet further by the state machine. While it is impossible to be certain of Ally's specific origins, he says enough to suggest that he is probably of a working-class background. But he is some sort of legal representative, a functionary of the court system, perhaps an autodidact, and shows all the pragmatism of someone who wants to succeed materially. He is, at heart, a compromiser. Because of that, and because of Kelman's forthright condemnation of cultural compromise, Ally is not fully to be trusted. In a convincing reading of Ally, Matt McGuire adroitly suggests that, as Sammy's agent, he brings into question 'the role of the author as potential agent of subjugation within the act of literary creation'.[60] But the detailed construction of Ally's duplicity suggests that Kelman cannot logically have himself in mind, as McGuire suggests. McGuire might have a logical case if Ally can be read allegorically as representative of writers who do not write in 'their own language', and so who have, in Kelman's terms 'lost their culture'.[61]

Ally tries to talk Sammy's language, to close in on Sammy's position. He says to Sammy that he has been imprisoned, but he might be using this as a hook to get Sammy to trust him: it does not work as Sammy replies 'Dont con me' (*HL* 236). Ally clearly does know the processes and systems of the state machine as if he were an initiate, party to the inner workings of the enforcement of legislation. He provides both access to, and a slippery avoidance of, the material truths which are compressing and limiting Sammy's scope for manoeuvre. Aware of the legal process through bitter experience, Sammy still has no clear sense of his circumstances before Ally appears, magically, outside Doctor Logan's office to represent Sammy's case for him. Sammy bluntly, repeatedly rejects Ally's offer: Ally nevertheless manages to seize access to assist Sammy when he is most vulnerable, during an outburst of rage at the Doctor's intransigence. Ally is both insidious, and someone who claims Sammy's trust. He both speaks Sammy's language, and attempts to restrict and police it, telling Sammy to 'watch yer language; sorry, but every second word's fuck. If ye listen to me ye'll see I try to keep an eye on the auld words' (*HL* 238). Ally gives Sammy a rolling lesson in how and when to compromise, gives him advice on 'when ye bow and when ye scrape; when ye talk and when ye hold yer wheesht – ye follow me, when to shut the auld gub: all-important' (*HL* 239). Ally is ruthless in the pursuit of 'compen' for his clients, ruthless in the pursuit of his one-third share of all eventual payments. He is ruthless too in the sheer volume of his language: Sammy is more dominated, word-for-word, in conversations with Ally than he is even with the police or the doctor.

Ally also defines 'them' (state functionaries) against 'us' (working classes? the accused? victims of the state?), but quickly slips into an admittance that his position is actually in between the two parties: 'The closer I get to courts and tribunals the more like them I get. Ask the wife and she'll tell ye. If ye listen ye wouldnay know the difference.' (HL 240). George Orwell's 1945 satire of political revolution *Animal Farm,* throws stark light on Ally's position: the pigs, leaders of the animals' revolution against the humans, eventually become indistinguishable from those against whom they rebelled.[62] Ally is corrupted in his compromise, by his adoption of the language of state procedure, by his proximity to the state machine, by his collusion with it and by his occasional subservience to it. For Sammy, Ally's submission to the state is a sort of death; what Ally describes with pride – his negotiation of the language and culture of institutional power structures – is for Sammy exactly 'how they suffocate ye; all their fucking protocols and procedures, all designed to stop ye breathing' (HL 321). Language compromise is at the heart, it embodies, signifies everything in Ally's version of how to survive. This is clearly signalled in his story of a letter he wrote while in prison which, when published in a newspaper had 'SIC' beside his 'victomising' (HL 300). For Ally, this was his fault, and he should have known better, should have controlled his language more; for Kelman, the SIC is the tool of oppression, the tool of judgement, the place where violence happens, where authority stamps its boot on the language of the powerless. As Primo Levi says, the SIC asks how can we trust the author? It puts a sterilising distance of condemnation between us (writer and reader) and the fool quoted.[63] Ally spells his own 'victomhood' 'wrong': Kelman's point is that he is a victom of his own language use, because the power of standard language polices and denigrates and effectively criminalises non-standard use, just as the legal system defines and punishes 'non-standard' behaviour.

The critical question here is whether Sammy is right to eventually resolve himself to trust Ally albeit in a limited fashion, 'as far as it went' (HL 362). To begin an answer, we should turn to a linguistic feature of Kelman's work which I identified in the introduction to this book. Kelman, along with Tom Leonard, is committed to the value of inconsistency as a linguistic policy in the rendition of authenticity in their textual practices. As I outlined in the introduction, some critics have identified this as a strength (e.g. Edwin Morgan) and some as a weakness (e.g. Mac Daly). But Kelman defends his right to orthographic and punctuational inconsistency in the face of publishers' homogenising standards just as he defends his right to the utilisation of oral Glaswegian working-class language practices in literature in the face of the primacy and normalisation in literary practice of the linguistic variety usually called Standard English. Relevant to this battleground is the rationale through which Ally begins to coerce Sammy into types of behaviour which the legal system will recognise as 'consistent'. Ally wants Sammy's behaviour to be consistent, because he wants it to be recognised as logical and coherent by the judging state machinery. Inconsistency is therefore rendered into a weakness, into unacceptability always with the inbuilt threat of being converted into guilt.

Tangential to Sammy's perceived inconsistency is Ally's assessment of the legal efficacy of the 'language' Sammy uses. Of course, Ally is not the only person to warn Sammy that his language is not appropriate: his word 'cunt' is not accepted for input into the police computer (*HL* 160); the Doctor finds Sammy's language 'offensive' (*HL* 225). But Ally is the most persistent and materially self-interested agent of all in the governing of Sammy's manner of communication. Ally speaks in an accent like Sammy's, but he also deploys at much greater length the language of 'the system'. But he is able, and willing, to see, assess and judge Sammy through the eyes of the state: he is, therefore, ultimately a compromiser, and someone who seeks behavioural, linguistic and cultural compromise from his client, so that the 'best' outcome can be achieved from any litigation. Ally asks that Sammy 'look at it from the big picture' (*HL* 239). In other words, and reading this suggestion through Kelman's understanding of traditional realist narrative forms, Sammy should take the omniscient perspective of the courts on his own situation, and so adopt the value system inherent in the makeup of that perspective.

If the client, Sammy, is obdurate in his initial assertion of independence from any need for representation at first, Ally is equally stubborn and relentless in pursuing this possible client. Ally's name as he gives it to Sammy (just 'Ally', with no surname) puns on a number of possible aspects to his multifaceted positions: he presents himself as an *allied* force in the service of Sammy, as someone with whom Sammy ought really to have natural *allegiance*; Ally occupies the *alleys* of the legal labyrinth, knows passages through the backways and narrow thoroughfares of the legal system; he is a tough, embattled *alley* cat; and finally he presents himself as being in the business of *allaying* his clients' fears. These multiple meanings emerge slipperily from his name, and model the mode of loquacious effluence Ally adopts to drown out the doubts and fears of his clients. In Ally's floods of legalese, Sammy does indeed seem limited of awareness, narrow of experience and blunt of intent. By sheer volume of speech alone, Ally bullies Sammy's own very limited spoken responses into submission. Ally eloquently sets out how vulnerable Sammy is, thereby attempting to increase Sammy's dependence on Ally himself. And he occasionally adopts an understanding of the situation which seems diametrically opposed to Sammy's arch enemy, the Doctor. For example, Ally makes Sammy smile when he asserts that 'every case is unique in its own way' (*HL* 310), which is clearly opposite to the Doctor's own assertion (*HL* 222). Yet Ally still maintains an objectifying presentation of Sammy's position, and in fact is suggesting that although all cases are in fact unique, in court the safest presentation of a case is to make it seem 'unexceptional' and 'consistent'.

Ally's unwanted intrusion into Sammy's life means that he is a potent threat to the latter's dominant intention to be independent. The ease with which Ally inveigles his way into Sammy's world is further evidence of just how vulnerable the latter is. The prime example of Ally's ability to permeate Sammy's life is his utilisation of Sammy's fifteen-year-old son to take photos of his father's bruises: Sammy did not give Ally permission to contact Peter, nor did Ally even forewarn Sammy that this might be a possibility. Peter's visit to Sammy, and his help in his father's departure from Glasgow, close the novel. Inadvertently, Ally has ensured that Sammy has finally encountered someone he can fully trust, resolving one aspect of the novel's quest at least. In reply to Peter's questions, Sammy feels compelled to lie three times (*HL* 343, 353 and 354). This triple repetition is surely designed to echo and invert the Biblical Peter's triple betrayal of Christ (John, 13.38–18.27), and it balances perfectly with Sammy's trinity of wakings which precedes his blindness. In contrast with the Biblical Peter's lying for self-preservation, Sammy's lying twice about the cause of his blindness, and once about his relationship with Helen, seems to be designed to ensure Peter does

not worry excessively. The otherwise open conversation enabled by
the mutual trust includes Sammy's account of the effects of prison
on his youthful relationship with Peter's mother. Although Peter's
friend Keith is also present, this is the first fully intimate conversation
Sammy has had in the novel. Because of the book-length absence of
any mutual trust and intimacy until the arrival of Peter, when it
finally does arrive, it has a powerful emotional effect (*HL* 336). Peter
asks to go with his father on his bus journey south; rebuffed, he
helps his father prepare for and fund the journey, secretly giving
Sammy all of his savings (*HL* 373). The final three words of the novel
are 'out of sight': we leave the novel as Sammy leaves Glasgow and
his son. Like so many of Kelman's protagonists, Sammy joins the
Scottish diaspora, helped along by an intensely moving inversion
of the usual provision of economic security from father to son. The
final scenes with Peter prove the strength of Sammy's core code
of honourable and loving trust, a paternal warmth mostly hidden
until now.

Contexts 2: *The Glasgow Gospel* and the Booker

As discussed above, Sammy repeatedly refers to the police as 'sodjers'.
Notably one English reviewer of *How late. . .* thought they were literal,
military soldiers, in so doing denying Sammy the power of
metaphor.[64] Kelman's phonetic spelling of 'sodjers' is consistent in
the novel. This particular word can offer a micro-case-study for the
status of the Glasgow accent. The word forges a bridge to another
text, published in 1992, which is written in 'Glasgow's distinctive
vernacular', or so its back-cover blurb claims. Scots dictionaries
confirm that 'Sodger' is the legitimised standard spelling. In his
Glaswegian-dialect translation of parts of the *New Testament*, Jamie
Stuart uses this standard Scots spelling:

> The sodgers forced Jesus tae cairry his ain cross tae the place o execution,
> Golgotha, oan the ootskirts o the city. But oan the wey, Jesus wis
> staggerin under the great weight o it an a man in the crowd, Simon
> fae Cyrene, wis made tae cairry the cross instead.
>   At Golgotha the sodgers nailed Jesus tae the cross, hoistin him up
> alang wi two robbers, wan oan either side.[65]

Stuart's book is one of the most bizarre products in the resurgence
of publishing confidence in the Glasgow dialect. If Kelman and

Leonard are partly responsible for that renewed confidence, then the behemoth of the Year of Culture also has a PR claim, convincing publishers as it did that Glasgow was a marketable commodity after 1990. *The Glasgow Gospel* is relevant otherwise for three reasons. Firstly, it shows how varied the politics of purpose for dialect writing can be across the Scottish publishing scene. Secondly, it shows how much Kelman's own dialect forms actually lack the phonetic or Scots density about which reviewers often complain. And thirdly, its prefatory pieces, all written in standard English, incredibly re-inscribe prejudices about the Glasgow tongue while supposedly celebrating its value: Hugh R. Wyllie's foreword calls Glasgow's language 'pithy and pungent patter'; in the introduction John Campbell says 'the Glaswegian can't be anonymous. His brashness makes that impossible.'[66] Jamie Stuart and his two supporters are self-avowedly Glaswegian, and foreground the 'pungent' 'brashness' – among whose pejorative synonyms we could choose 'overpowering aggression' – of the language their city speaks. Their characterisation indicates a pride in a minoritarian language which is insecure of its boasts in the face of the dominance of the major textual tongue, standard English. That the prefatory pieces have to be written in standard English in order to guarantee legitimacy for the project adds to the blighted self-positioning of Glaswegian dialect.

What defence can remain then, when that same 'overpowering aggression' is perceived by critics and reviewers of *How late. . .?* If Glaswegians themselves characterise and anthropomorphise their own language this way, even as they purport to defend it, it is small wonder that when Kelman's novel generated widespread international attention through winning the 1994 Booker prize, it was roundly attacked for its language on many different fronts. But Kelman was long used to this. *The Busconductor Hines* was rejected by Richard Cobb, chairman of the Booker panel in 1984, because it was ' "written entirely in Glaswegian". "I found him very heavy-going and only read two chapters," confessed Cobb. "It was in dialect, like Burns's poems." '[67] Ten years later, Simon Jenkins of *The Times* thought that *How late. . .* had a language neither 'Older Scottish, or Scots English, or Lallas, or any dialect of Burns's "Guid Scots Tongue" ' but instead, was 'merely Glaswegian Alcoholic With Remarkably Few Borrowings'.[68] For many English reviewers – especially those whose interest in Kelman was generated by the glitzy cultural gossiping of the Booker prize rather than by intrinsic literary pursuits – the language of Kelman is brutalising, amoral, desensitised, difficult and unsophisticated: Jenkins compared reading his work with being accosted by a Glaswegian drunk on a train. Eric Jacobs concurred: the novel was 'like an encounter in a Glasgow pub when you are sober and the man who buttonholes you is seriously drunk. He jabs you in the chest, blows smoke in your face, dribbles his drink all over and rambles incoherently on.'[69] Another critic said the book should have been rejected by the Booker panel because his wife pointed out that it was not written in English.[70] The Leader in the *Daily Telegraph* claimed that, together with Conservative Cabinet Minister Michael Heseltine punning on the word 'balls', the novel's success indicated a worrying 'pollution of the language which forms an essential part of our culture.'[71] The Leader in *The Times* was happier that the novel had won because of the 'factitious row' that ensued, but summarised it as a 'rambling monologue of Glaswegian low life, narrated by the sort of lumpenproletarian Scottish drunk one might cross Sauchiehall Street to avoid'.[72] Max Davidson dismissed the novel as 'the ravings of a Glaswegian drunk' and declared that its prize-winning was not the product of 'literary preference, but guilt.'[73] Of course, among the furore over the novel, Kelman had many defenders. Robert Crawford predicted that negative critical response would be produced by a 'reductive stereotype of the Scottish writer as working-class bruiser',[74] and he was right. Ian Bell thought the 'blindness of so many commentators to the book's deep humanity is a terrible indictment of their limitations in sympathy and understanding'.[75] But even positive reviewers like David Buckley heard 'the fierce rhythms of Glasgow vernacular',[76] a characterisation not far removed from the 'overpowering aggression' to which the prefatory comments to *The Glasgow Gospel* concede. Years later, the legacy of the initial uproar over the language of the novel continues to distort understanding of Kelman's work: writing in 2000, Susan Taylor Chehak contends that the novel 'employs the "ordinary" language of modern Scottish thugs, complete with just about every slang word that you've ever heard, and then some.'[77]

Many issues clashed when Kelman won the Booker, and because the prize has such cultural cachet, the novel has been the focus of a lot of serious and extended criticism too. Anxieties over literariness, national language and nationality (both Englishness and Scottishness), morality and class were to the fore. Even if two of the judges, Alastair Niven and Alan Taylor, were Scottish, the elevation of Kelman's novel to a pedestal of London-based establishment esteem exposed deep-seated concerns not just about the novel as a piece of fiction, but also about the historical realities of its supposed origins. To give any status to these origins would be to damage the nature, value and purpose of 'culture'. By far the most extreme version of this perception was offered by Gerald Warner:

> That the novels which are the main contenders for the prize should be characterised respectively by expletives and anal sex speaks volumes about the values of 'serious' literature today. Kelman has defended the monotonously foul-mouthed vocabulary of his books: 'If the language is taboo, the people are taboo. A culture can't exist without the language of the culture.'
>
> He fails to recognise that, in reality, what he is describing is not properly a 'culture', but the primeval vortex of undevelopment that precedes culture. If the literary gurus who consider his work 'daring' had any real instinct for adventure, they would unfashionably proclaim that there is a good cultural case to be made for Kelman's people remaining taboo.[78]

Warner's article emerged at the time of the announcement of the shortlist of finalists for the prize. Warner's moral fibre was also rubbed up the wrong way by the shortlisting of Alan Hollinghurst's *The Folding Star*, which contained offensive 'limp-wristed attractions' and which, if it won the prize, would become 'endorsement of sodomy as an eligible "lifestyle"'. Warner makes explicit here that he wishes not only such literature to remain beneath the interest of culture as he defines it, but the *real* people, milieu and moralities Kelman and Hollinghurst are variously concerned with too. They are to be deliberately ignored because they are beneath the processes and interests of societal valuation and cultural acknowledgement. Warner's understanding of the management of culture is bleakly hierarchical and blankly élitist (to use a word to which Kelman often has recourse): it determines that some better people own, maintain and deserve the benefits of culture, and that some worse people do not, should not and cannot. Certain literatures and certain peoples are not as 'cultured' as Warner and his world, indeed they are not 'cultured' at all. Kelman predicted it all, in 1988:

> Writers have to develop the habit of relying on themselves. It's as if there's a massive KEEP OUT sign hoisted above every area of literature. This is an obvious effect of the hopeless elitism referred to earlier. But there are other reasons. The very idea of literary art as something alive

and lurking within reach of ordinary women and men is not necessarily the sort of idea those who control the power in society will welcome with open arms. It is naive to expect otherwise. Literature is nothing when it isn't being dangerous in some way or another and those in positions of power will always be suspicious of anything that could conceivably affect their security.[79]

Warner's article and the many others which came close to it in intention, raised that 'KEEP OUT' sign high, daubed in brash Tory blue English letters, against which Kelman was compelled to kick. Kelman gave varying reports as to why he did not attend the Booker award ceremony in 1989 when *A Disaffection* was shortlisted: either he 'had a previous engagement, teaching an evening class',[80] or he could not afford the price of travel to London, nor the required formal dinner jacket, a material reality the organizers could not comprehend, according to Kelman.[81] In 1994, however, he did attend, attempted to deliver his winner's speech, and was cut off after thirty seconds. His speech was published in various newspapers the same week of the ceremony. Kelman was as forthright as Warner:

> A couple of weeks ago a feature writer for a quality newspaper suggested that the use of the term 'culture' was inappropriate in relation to my work, that the characters peopling my pages were 'preculture' or was it 'primeval'? This was explicit, generally it isn't. But, as Tom Leonard pointed out more than 20 years ago, the gist of the argument amounts to the following, that vernaculars, patois, slangs, dialects, gutter-languages might well have a place in the realms of comedy (and the frequent references to Billy Connolly or Rab C Nesbitt substantiate this) but they are inferior linguistic forms and have no place in literature. And a priori any writer who engages in literature of such so-called language is not really engaged in literature at all. It's common to find well meaning critics suffering the same burden, while they strive to be kind they still cannot bring themselves to operate within a literary perspective; not only do they approach the work as though it were an oral text, they somehow assume it to be a literal transcription of recorded speech.
>
> This sort of prejudice, in one guise or another, has been around for a very long time and for the sake of clarity we are better employing the contemporary label, which is racism. A fine line can exist between elitism and racism and on matters concerning language and culture the distinction can sometimes cease to exist altogether.[82]

Further on Kelman announces his allegiance to a 'movement, towards decolonisation and self determination'. This self determination is postcolonial and one that sees the literary establishment, including the Booker prize process itself, as one which inherently tries to appropriate and so negate the effect of anything that is dissident, or outwith its remit. So, logically, at the supreme moment of public inclusion of Kelman within the contemporary British canon – at the moment of his sanctification as an author by an establishment which deems his work worthy of interest – he rejects the foundation and hierarchies of capitalising prize culture itself; he takes the money, but attacks the commodifying and judging process which grants it. Logically perhaps, one of the judges, Julia Neuberger, rejected Kelman, saying that his winning of the prize was a 'disgrace'.[83] The book likewise revealed itself to be resistant to absorption into the capitalist current: the usually highly fertile boost to sales generated by winning the prize was widely perceived not to have happened in the case of *How late. . .*,[84] though the actual success was evident in terms of sales at least according to Kelman's publisher, who, in February 1995, claimed that the novel 'sold 30,809 copies since winning the Booker prize on October 11, 1994, bringing total sales to 41,165. It entered the *Sunday Times* bestseller list in May, and went to number 2 on October 23'.[85] The perception of its poor marketability was generated by a widespread sense of the novel's lack of literary worth (led in kind by the Director of Dillons who did not want his stores to stock it[86]); this moralising conjecture, combined with the impatience of business, seems to have blinded some to its real success in terms of actual sales.

There is a wider critical problem here, which has dogged the writing of this book, which arguably dogs all criticism of Kelman. Kelman's version of criticism is that it always seeks to appropriate that which it wants to control and manage. Criticism therefore has a colonising structure of relation to the texts or subjects it discusses: it is territorially aggressive, asserting its language and value systems as ways of understanding the other; and it is linguistically discriminatory, because it maintains itself in a language which keeps that same other out. If the relationship between a standard-speaking omniscient narrator and regionally or class-accented character is inherently reproductive of a social hierarchy of power which disenfranchises those who do not speak the standard and empowers those who do, then what of the relationship between critical language and Kelman's texts? At times I have raised the issue of the appropriateness of terms critics use to discuss both Kelman's world and working-class life and

culture in general, especially where the vocabulary seems to be un-
necessarily remote from the language of the culture being described,
explained and/or accounted for, and especially where the critical
language seems implicitly to effect a judgement or condemnation of
characters, contexts, actions and words. But my own critical language,
the language you are reading, is standard English, with the occasional
lapse into the abstruse and academic lexis of someone desperate both
to impress, and to be as accurate as possible. I have tried to inflect
my critical methodology self-reflexively at times (as I am doing now),
as a direct response to the way in which Kelman constructs the
relationship between his own work, and critical work, as he describes
it, reported in interview as follows:

> 'A lot of the ritualistic behaviour that goes on in the literary establish-
> ment, it's charades, really. It's a form of colonization, or a form of
> imperialism, and one of the effects of that is colonization.'

> Write a book, he says, on whatever subject you choose – South Africa,
> Aids, drugs, someone dying of asbestos disease – and you will be
> regarded as part of the establishment, as one of the perpetrators of
> the crimes. 'Their act of fellowship with the writer is a kind of appro-
> priation, a method of extending domination over the subject, as if they
> also owned the experience of the novel. It's a kind of continuing
> disenfranchisement.'[87]

If Kelman is right, the critic is caught in a double bind: a monograph
like the one you are reading is a product of a system of professionalised
academic life in cahoots with an academic press, produced through
research leave partly funded by a government body. In that, its
publication could be read as a 'ritualistic' material product of a culture
industry and educational establishment, even if its commitment to
the subject of study is indeed a sort of 'fellowship', even if it respects
and considers the politics and processes of its own relationship
to its subject. With this model to hand, all criticism is an act of
'appropriation' and 'domination': there is simply, and sadly, no way
out. This very sentence disenfranchises Kelman's subject matter,
because it attempts to explain and so control his ideas; his position
would be that the standard language of this book is commonly
regarded as edifying, whereas the discourse of working-class culture
is relegated by the very act of critical interpretation, explanation and
accounting. Elsewhere Kelman has defined the creative against the
critical – as if the two were mutually and morally exclusive absolutes.[88]

The model suggests that creativity should always be genuine and sincere, honest and pure of intention; criticism on the other hand is nefarious and double-dealing, corrupting and territorial. The 'wider process, or movement, towards decolonisation and self determination' which Kelman reads his work into, through his understanding of criticism, is denied that same self-determination through an encroaching colonisation by criticism. The only way out of this relationship is critical silence.

Notes

1 The play was re-written for a stage production at the Traverse Theatre in Edinburgh in 1990 (*HB* 102–80).
2 The most detailed investigation, and a source of the letters Kelman uses for his play is *The Scottish Insurrection of 1820*, Peter Berresford Ellis and Seumas Mac A'Ghobhainn, 3rd edn (Edinburgh: John Donald, 2001). Their claim that the uprising was driven by a nationalist imperative does not convince other historians, for example, W. Hamish Fraser, *Conflict and Class: Scottish Workers, 1700 –1838* (Edinburgh: John Donald, 1988), 109–13.
3 T. C. Smout, *A History of the Scottish People, 1560–1830* (London: Fontana Press, 1969), 419. Although Hardie and Baird are not mentioned by name, Smout does offer an extended account of the 'Radical War' of 1820 and credits it as the start of 'proletarian'-led workers' reform movements.
4 William Stewart, *Fighters for Freedom in Scotland: The Days of Baird and Hardie* (London: Independent Labour Party, 1908), 6.
5 Iain Mclean, *The Legend of Red Clydeside* (Edinburgh: John Donald, 1983), 1.
6 Alasdair Gray, *Lanark* [1981] (Edinburgh: Canongate, 2002), 244.
7 William Stewart, *Fighters for Freedom in Scotland*, 2nd edn (Glasgow: Reformers' Bookstall, 1920).
8 Fraser, *Conflict and Class*, 169.
9 From Kelman's introduction to Hugh Savage, *Born up a Close: Memoirs of a Brigton Boy* (Glendareul: Argyll Publishing, 2006), 19. This introduction is Kelman's most substantial historical account of socialist activism in twentieth-century Glasgow.
10 Tom Leonard, *Reports from the Present. Selected Work: 1982–94* (London: Jonathan Cape, 1995), 212–13, Leonard's italics.
11 See Kelman, 'Art and Subsidy, and the Continuing Politics of Culture City', *SRA*, 27–36. See also Kelman's introduction to Savage, *Born up a Close*, 9–16. For succinct accounts of the controversies of 1990 and 1994, see Moira Burgess, *Imagine a City: Glasgow in Fiction* (Glendaruel:

Argyll Publishing, 1998), 297–311 and Don Mitchell, *Cultural Geography: A Critical Introduction* (Oxford: Blackwell, 2000), 7–11.

12 Quoted in David Kemp, *Glasgow 1990: The True Story Behind the Hype* (Gartocharn: Famedram, 1990), 31.

13 For example, in June 2002 Kelman spoke at a rally on Glasgow Green, organised by the Scottish Socialist Party, designed to offer an alternative republican critique of official celebrations of the Queen's jubilee. See Kay Jardine, 'Sheridan and his citizens hold an alternative party', *Herald*, 4 June 2002, 2. According to Graeme Esson, 'as Kelman reminded the crowd, [Glasgow Green] has a rich history of left-wing gatherings down the decades', 'A city divided over the Jubilee', *BBC Scotland News Online*, 3 June 2002, http://news.bbc.co.uk/1/hi/scotland/2023059.stm (accessed 8/08/2006).

14 For council leader Pat Lally's defence of both the 'Elspeth King Affair' and the selling of Glasgow Green, see Pat Lally, with Neil Baxter, *Lazarus Only Done it Once: The Story of My Lives* (London: Harper Collins, 2000), 83–9.

15 Kemp, *Glasgow 1990*, 32.

16 Lally, *Lazarus Only Done it Once*, 93–5.

17 Lally, *Lazurus Only Done it Once*, 67.

18 Savage, *Born Up a Close*, 9.

19 Carl MacDougall (ed.), *Glasgow's Glasgow: The Words and the Stones* (Glasgow: The Words and the Stones, 1990), 14. Ironically enough, this book was funded by Glasgow District Council as part of 'Glasgow 1990: Cultural Capital of Europe'. For a withering critique of the £3.5 million publicly funded exhibition of which this publication was a part, see Kemp, *Glasgow 1990*.

20 See Seán Damer, *Glasgow: Going for a Song* (London: Lawrence & Wishart, 1990) and Mark Boyle and George Hughes, 'The Politics of the Representation of "The Real": Discourses from the Left on Glasgow's Role as European City of Culture, 1990,' *Area*, 23 (1991), 217–28.

21 Lally, *Lazurus Only Done it Once*, 67.

22 Quoted in Kemp, *Glasgow 1990*, 19.

23 Lally, *Lazarus Only Done it Once*, 87 and 91.

24 Dominic D'Angelo, Joseph Farrell *et al*, *The 1990 Story: Glasgow Cultural Capital of Europe* (Glasgow: Glasgow City Council, 1992), 34.

25 William Clark, 'Remembering Hugh Savage and Workers City', in Savage, *Born up a Close*, 251.

26 See also Farquhar McLay (ed.), *Workers City: The Real Glasgow Stands Up* (Glasgow: Clydeside Press, 1988), 1–4.

27 Robert F. Barsky, *Noam Chomsky: A Life of Dissent* (Cambridge, Mass.: MIT Press, 1997), 217.

28 See Olga Wojtas, 'Shrugging off the guru's mantle', *Times Higher Education Supplement*, 26 January 1990, 15.

29 Willy Maley, 'Denizens, Citizens, Tourists, and Others: Marginality and Mobility in the Writings of James Kelman and Irvine Welsh', in David Bell and Azzedine Haddour (eds), *City Visions* (Harlow: Pearson, 2000), 60.

30 Michael Gardiner, 'James Kelman interviewed', *Scottish Studies Review*, 5:1 (2004), 106.

31 Maley, 'Denizens, Citizens, Tourists', 66.

32 Nancy Armstrong, 'The Fiction of Bourgeois Morality and the Paradox of Individualism', in Franco Moretti (ed.), *The Novel. Vol. 2: Forms and Themes* (Princeton and Oxford: Princeton University Press, 2006), 387.

33 Raymond Williams, *Marxism and Literature* (Oxford: Oxford University Press, 1977), 148.

34 Willy Maley, 'Swearing Blind: Kelman and the Curse of the Working Classes', *Edinburgh Review*, 95 (1996), 107.

35 Karl Marx, *Economic and Philosophical Manuscripts* (Moscow, 1961), 105, quoted in Williams, *Marxism and Literature*, 194.

36 Alain Robbe-Grillet, 'New Novel, New Man' [1961] in '*Snapshots*' and '*Towards a New Novel*', trans. Barbara Wright (London: Calder and Boyars, 1965), 139.

37 Albert Camus, *The Outsider* [1942], trans. Joseph Laredo (London: Penguin, 1983), 100.

38 Uwe Zagratzki, '"Blues Fell This Morning" – James Kelman's Scottish Literature and Afro-American Music', *Scottish Literary Journal*, 27:1 (2000), 105–17.

39 Sue Vice, *Introducing Bakhtin* (Manchester: Manchester University Press, 1997), 102. For another Bakhtinian analysis, see J. C. Bittenbender, 'Silence, Censorship, and the Voices of Skaz in the Fiction of James Kelman', *Bucknell Review*, 43:2 (2000), 150–65.

40 Duncan McLean, *Lone Star Swing: On the Trail of Bob Wills and his Texas Playboys* (London: Jonathan Cape, 1997).

41 Aaron A. Fox, *Real Country: Music and Language in Working-Class Culture* (Durham and London: Duke University Press, 2004), 20.

42 See Ken Cockburn and Alec Finlay (eds), *The Order of Things: An Anthology of Scottish Sound, Pattern and Concrete Poems* (Edinburgh: Pocketbooks, 2001).

43 Adam Mars-Jones, Review of *HL*, *Times Literary Supplement*, 1 April 1994, 20.

44 David Punter, *Postcolonial Imaginings: Fictions of a New World Order* (Edinburgh: Edinburgh University Press, 2000), 116.

45 Alex La Guma, *Time of the Butcherbird* (Oxford: Heinemann, 1979), 11. See Kelman's essay on La Guma (*AJS* 95–102).

46 Prince Vasili characterises Kutuzov as follows: 'He can't ride a horse, he falls asleep at meetings, and he's completely immoral! He earned a marvellous reputation in Bucharest! Never mind his qualities as a general, at a time like this how can we appoint a man who's on his last legs and

blind? Yes, blind! What a splendid idea – a blind general! He can't see a thing. All right for a spot of blind-man's bluff! . . .', Leo Tolstoy, *War and Peace* [1863–69], trans. Anthony Briggs (London: Penguin, 2005), 785.

47 Akaky Akakievich leaves the living world with the following summary: 'So vanished and disappeared for ever a human being whom no one ever thought of protecting, who was dear to no one, in whom no one was in the least interested . . .', Nikolai Gogol, *The Overcoat* [1842], trans. Ronald Wilks (London: Penguin, 1972), 102.

48 Gogol, *Overcoat*, 72.

49 Samuel Beckett, *Waiting for Godot* [1955], in *The Complete Dramatic Works* (London: Faber and Faber, 1986), 13.

50 Ian A. Bell, 'Empty Intensifiers: Kelman Wins "The Booker" (At Last)', *New Welsh Review*, 27 (Winter 1994–95), 14.

51 Mary McGlynn, '"Middle-Class Wankers" and Working-Class Texts: The Critics and James Kelman', *Contemporary Literature*, 43:1 (Spring 2002), 61.

52 For a comparative analysis of Zola and Kelman, see Graeme MacDonald, 'Writing Claustrophobia: Zola and Kelman', *Bulletin of the Émile Zola Society*, 13 (1996), 9–20.

53 Vice, *Introducing Bakhtin*, 102.

54 Samuel Beckett, *The Unnamable* [1959] in *The Beckett Trilogy* (London: Calder, 1994), 293.

55 Gray, *Lanark*, 48–9.

56 Thanks to Graeme MacDonald for making this point to me in 1995.

57 Maley, 'Swearing Blind', 107.

58 David Punter, *Postcolonial Imaginings: Fictions of a New World Order* (Edinburgh: Edinburgh University Press, 2000), 118.

59 George Orwell, *Nineteen Eighty-Four* [1949] (London: Penguin, 1989), 280.

60 Matt McGuire, 'Dialect(ic) Nationalism? The Fiction of James Kelman and Roddy Doyle', *Scottish Studies Review*, 7:1 (Spring 2006), 91.

61 Duncan McLean, 'James Kelman interviewed', *Edinburgh Review*, 71 (1985), 72.

62 George Orwell, *Animal Farm* [1945], (London: Penguin, 1989), 95.

63 Primo Levi, '*Sic!*', in *The Mirror Maker: Stories and Essays,* trans. Raymond Rosenthal (New York: Schocken Books, 1989), 93–4.

64 Eric Jacobs, 'Eyeless and legless in Glasgow', *Spectator*, 2 April 1994, 33–4.

65 Jamie Stuart, *The Glasgow Gospel* (Edinburgh: Saint Andrew Press, 1992), 49.

66 Stuart, *The Glasgow Gospel*, vii and ix.

67 P.H.S., 'Diary: Closed book', *The Times*, 13 October 1994, 18.

68 Simon Jenkins, 'An expletive of a winner', *The Times*, 15 October 1994, 20.

69 Jacobs, 'Eyeless and legless', 33–4.
70 Miles Kington, 'Revealed: how the Booker changed Cheltenham', *Independent*, 17 October 1994, 15.
71 [Hastings, Max?], [Leader:] 'Polluting the language', *Daily Telegraph*, 14 October 1994, 26.
72 [Stothard, Peter?], [Leader:] 'Traditional bookmanism', *The Times*, 12 October 1994, 19.
73 Max Davidson, 'Critic's view', *Daily Telegraph*, 13 October 1994, 9.
74 Robert Crawford, 'Northern exposure', *Sunday Times*, 17 April 1994, 8.
75 Bell, 'Empty Intensifiers', 14.
76 David Buckley, Review of *HL*, *Observer*, 'Review', 3 April 1994, 19.
77 Susan Taylor Chehak, *Don Quixote Meets the Mob: The Craft of Fiction and the Art of Life* (Philadelphia: Xlibris, 2000), 234.
78 Gerald Warner, 'Time for a disaffection from literary slumming', *Sunday Times*, 25 September 1994, 8.
79 James Kelman (ed.), *An East End Anthology* (Glasgow: Clydeside Press, 1988), 2.
80 Julia Llewellyn Smith, 'The prize will be useful. I'm skint', *The Times*, 13 October 1994, 17.
81 Sue Wilson, 'Battling on', *The List*, 25 March–7 April, 1994, 9.
82 See for example: 'Elitist slurs are racism by another name', *Scotland On Sunday* 'Supplement', 16 October 1994, 2; 'The speech he had no time to make at the Booker ceremony', *Sunday Times*, 16 October 1994, 21; 'Vernacular', *Brick: A Literary Journal*, 51 (Winter 1995), 68–9.
83 Dalya Alberge, 'Booker judge says winner is disgrace', *The Times*, 12 October 1994, 1.
84 See for example: Gillian Bowditch, 'Glasgow disowns prize novel', *The Times*, 13 October 1994, 2; Marianne Macdonald, 'Bookshops bemoan "Mogadon" Booker', *Independent*, 2 October, 1994, 1.
85 John Potter (Managing Director, Secker & Warburg), Letter, *Sunday Times*, 19 February 1995, 2. A week later, bookshop manager Cynthia Reavell asked 'whether the 30,000 copies sold are actually copies bought by individuals from the bookshops; or does this impressive figure represent copies subscribed in most cases on a sale-or-return basis by the book trade?' Her question went unanswered. *Sunday Times*, 26 February 1995, 2.
86 Gardiner, 'James Kelman interviewed', *Scottish Studies Review*, 5:1 (Spring 2004), 109.
87 Ian Bell, 'Four letter truths', *Observer*, 'Review', 27 March 1994, 16.
88 *An East End Anthology*, ed. Kelman, 1–2. Rob Pope suggests otherwise: 'the relation between "criticism" and "creativity" . . . is better conceived as a *connection* rather than a *distinction*, reciprocally defining rather than mutually exclusive', in *Creativity: Theory, History, Practice* (London and New York: Routledge, 2005), xviii (Pope's italics).

6

Translated Accounts (2001) and You Have to be Careful in the Land of the Free (2004)

Language in exile: abrogation and supranationality

Throughout this study, I have used standard interchangeable terms to describe generally the type of language Kelman uses in his fiction: 'vernacular' or 'dialect'. The problem with such terms is that they signify both a degree of subordination to a standard form of language and, perhaps as a consequence, a quality of pejorative provincialism in contradistinction to the metropolitan assumptions of universalism which the standard is granted, in the very act of defining one against the other. While there may be many dialects, a dialect in isolation is always the binary though unequal opposite of the standard form. In application to Kelman, neither term is fully appropriate because his language use – and the politics of discourse which are expressed through it – question the viability of any hierarchies implicated between language types. Indeed the fluid, heteroglossic hybridity of language in his novels brings into question the comfortable definition even of language typologies. For example, he persistently denies the definition of certain words he uses as 'swearing' or 'profanity', asserting that to censor such terms is to censor the culture in which they are used. Such words are only defined as 'swearing' by a culture which should not assume the power to define – often to castigate – their usage.[1]

This area of Kelman's work has been hotly, brashly, contested more than any other, predictably by cultural commentators, but most bizarrely by academics. An upsurge of 'prolier-than-thou' Glaswegian critical machismo raged briefly between Willy Maley and Macdonald Daly. The tussle masqueraded as a fight over Kelman, but was also brazenly about their competing claims for the territory of authentic

Glasgow working-class masculinity. Most curiously, Daly and Maley
adopt Kelman's style in their respective attack upon and defence of
the novelist – which decision affects simultaneous homage and parody
in both. Both of these male Glaswegian academics expose contesting
anxieties about their own class and masculine authenticities, piqued
by Kelman's language use. Kelman's Patrick Doyle offends Daly's
social roots: 'This is straight bourgeois intellectual wank. How dae
ah know? Cause ah fuckin lived in the Red Road fucking flats masel.'[2]
He makes a similar point, this time in standard English, five years
later:

> a reader of Kelman's work who is intimately familiar with the *patois*
> of the Glaswegian working class – and the present writer can claim the
> distinction of having thrived from the ages of three to fifteen in a public
> housing district which a character in one Kelman novel knowledgeably
> calls 'an awful place to live' – is highly unlikely to find his rendering
> of it 'uncompromising'.[3]

This version of authoritative legitimacy is countered by Willy Maley,
who likewise foregrounds his own claims to authenticity:

> Kelfuckingman, know what I'm talking about? JamesbastardingKelman.
> . . . Sworn enemies of Kelman think that by out-swearing him they have
> answered his call, his challenge, as though it all came down to a swearing
> contest. This is the kind of macho posturing, the intellectual equivalent
> of armwrestling, that we get from Macdonald Daly. The more working-
> class-than-thou attitude. You can get a good price on the open market
> for working-class credibility these days. I've floated my own company
> there at times, and never been bought out yet.[4]

Daly subsequently withdrew from the fray, diffidently claiming that
he 'cannot be bothered reading anything else about Kelman'.[5] Maley
however, continues to promote Kelman,[6] and to worry at his own
Glaswegian working-class validity in print:

> You wouldn't know it now from my title or my professorial demeanour,
> but listen carefully and beneath this quiet air of majesty you'll hear the
> rapid heartbeat of a "Ghetto Child" . . . . The seventh of nine children,
> I had parents who weren't box-makers, picture-framers or candlestick
> makers. They were manual workers at the bottom end of the scale.[7]

Kelman's father was a 'picture-framer and restorer'.[8] In claiming
more authentic working-class roots than the novelist, the professor
scores a hollow point. Another Glaswegian writer, Johnny Rodger,

astutely observes: 'it seems impossible, in Glasgow at least, to go beyond this sort of laying one's class cards on the table'.[9]

Whatever the rights and wrongs of it, Kelman's position is consistently clear: he denies the validity of anyone's definition of 'correct' language use, and denies the categorisation of some language varieties as subordinate to a standard, while at the same time he works with and adapts from within a version of the hegemonic major tongue that is English. Therefore, Kelman is involved in what post-colonial theorists call 'abrogation':

> Abrogation refers to the rejection by post-colonial writers of a normative concept of 'correct' or 'standard' English used by certain classes or groups, and of the corresponding concepts of inferior 'dialects' or 'marginal variants'. The concept is usually employed in conjunction with the term appropriation, which describes the processes of English adaptation itself, and is an important component of the post-colonial assumption that all language use is a 'variant' of one kind or another (and is in that sense 'marginal' to some illusory standard). Thus abrogation is an important political stance, whether articulated or not, and even whether conscious or not, from which the actual appropriation of language can take place.[10]

While Kelman attempts to resist the reductive marginalisation and othering of a language and a culture, he also abrogates standard bearers on another front: nationality. In his last two novels, he questions the validity of national definition, and looks at the violence and oppressions carried out through establishment state politics in the name of national 'integrity' and cultural tribalism. Kelman worries at nationality because, as a libertarian anarchist in the tradition of Pierre-Joseph Proudhon and Rudolf Rocker,[11] but also as someone deeply versed in post-colonial theories of nationality and culture,[12] he questions the value of essentialising, universalising ideas about national character and its potential to enervate, or even obliterate, the independent sovereignty of the individual. Kelman would concur with Rocker that language is 'no characteristic of a nation; it is even not always decisive of membership in a particular nation'[13]. Kelman sees no problem in regarding Scotland through a post-colonial prism, and critics have fruitfully mined this aspect of his work.[14] In the name and service of the state, nationalities can militate against individual rights to think and act freely, and can deny the right to difference, equality and expression. Similarly, 'dialect' or 'vernacular' are vehicles by which a language variety can be managed into a pigeon-holed hideaway of cosy kailyard subordination. The labels admit a language's difference from and deference to the linguistic norm while at the same time devaluing it, castigating it, forcing it into a circumscribed regionalism of limited relevance, where it no longer has consequence in establishment literary power. This is certainly descriptive of the cultural powerhouse called 'The Booker' which chewed Kelman's work up, baulked at a taste which did not suit its palate, and spat it out nervously. A dialect so treated, becomes a foreign language within a major tongue: the language variety if distinguished as a dialect, becomes an internal exile, diminished of status, patronised into parochialism, treated as an alien citizen, but also fixed and ordered into constants, which for Deleuze and Guattari, language use never offers. Inferiorisation of the non-standard is achieved, unless the categorisation process itself is invalidated. Kelman abrogates the categorisation process of language and of nationality to the point of becoming a hybridising supranationalist.

Any lingering critical tussles over the authenticity of Kelman's masculine Glaswegianess are made utterly irrelevant by the last two novels' supranationality. In these last two novels, *Translated Accounts* (2001) and *You Have to be Careful in the Land of the Free* (2004), Kelman approaches the violence of nationality through two very different frames, but in both language varieties are in confrontation. Continuing thematically in areas exposed in previous work, the most recent two novels explore tensions in relations between individual and society, between subject and subjection, between story and history, between male and female, between language and nation. But an abrupt break contextually and narratologically with the preceding novels is stark. Kelman takes both novels out of Glasgow. In *Translated Accounts*, his most experimental novel to date, the removal includes the total erasure of identifiable context and locatable accent in the language. In *You Have to be Careful in the Land of the Free*, the building up of desire to move away which runs through all four of the previous male protagonists, has given birth, finally, to a member of the Glaswegian diaspora, living in the United States.

Both novels also give more lucid reign to implicit analyses of global and state politics which – albeit problematically – show tangible traces of Kelman's continuing experiences as a political activist. Indeed, if we can continue to take the liberty of ignoring Kelman's own declaration that his politics are consistently separate from his art, these two novels might well be seen as part and parcel of his political activism. *Translated Accounts* is set in a militarised, probably occupied, state, which is either going through, or has recently gone through, a terrible violent war. It details the fragmented, constantly battered and buffeted lives of thoroughly anonymised individuals, reported in a no-man's land of a language which, by the stage it reaches us, has been reproduced by poor machinic translation, and so becomes neither theirs, nor ours. It is a nowhere language for a nowhere place. The homeless world it represents is in internal exile:

> And for how many languages? One may know all languages thus inferior to all peoples. I know all languages, I am inferior to all peoples. It is not sarcasm. I am capable of sarcasm, this is not it. They spoke a dialect that rendered them inferior but they were not inferior, they did not allow of it. But myself, yes. If it mattered, it did not. (*TA* 317)

This passage starts an account entitled 'who asks the question': who indeed (all the titles of the accounts carry double quotation marks, marking out the distance doubly, as it were, between reader and each original narrator). The removal of identifiable subjects, the absence of any of the pronouns' referents, the resort to generalised terms, the conditionals which are opened and half answered, statement followed by counter-statement, together effect a language which is English, yet in an alienated form of distancing and perplexing abstraction.

The full title is *Translated Accounts: A Novel,* and the force of determining the genre at the outset is required because actually this work functions more like a collection of short stories which only loosely interrelate. As a novel, it breaks with all of the preceding four in terms of narrative, and shows more allegiances to Kelman's numerous short story collections. It is shattered into fifty-four narratives: two are dramatic dialogues (*TA*, 125–31); the rest are voiced by first-person narrators. These fragmentary accounts – fragmented from each other, but also fragmented in rendition, in style, in syntax – are deliberately formulated so as to be difficult to re-build into a collected whole, while having stylistic and thematic consistencies. Some of the stories might be told by the same individuals, but that is almost impossible to be sure about. Society is dismembered, torn limb from limb, rendered just an ideal, a dream-story, rather than a narratological possibility. There are moments of union, of love and lust amidst the rubble, but they are transitory, founded in grief, in permanent absence. The language of the accounts is the fractured

terrain of splintered peoples who are almost completely lost to war,
to oppression, to foreign invasion, to the humiliation and degrada-
tion of a violent abuse fired repeatedly by a destructive masculine
sexual urge to annihilate. All the speakers are vulnerable in their
own isolated first-person individualisms, even as they desperately
cling to collective, yet factional, 'campaigning formations'. Ideals are
espoused as pithy aphorisms, which sometimes seem to proffer a
way of understanding not only the narrative structure, but the political
principles underlying it:

> It is with difficulty we refer to 'all individuals' as humanity, leading as
> it must to misunderstandings and confusions. Regard humanity as one
> wide-ranging community of individuals where difference begins from
> that one fact, community, where one law may be applied. Economic
> and social difference are individual qualities, sometime properties, and
> will enter the process of individual cases. (*TA* 87)

Here the speaker, who appears to be giving a lecture to an audience
of 'colleagues' bonded edgily around an anonymised 'campaigning
formation' (*TA* 87) whose purpose is to 'confront authorities' (*TA*
78), pithily summarises the importance of resisting universal categori-
sations to manage diverse human lives, while at the same time urging
commitment from his audience to the 'fact' of community. By no
means all the speakers show the hallmark of Kelman's politics as
clearly as this lecturer but there are many similar mentions of
'campaigning formations', and accounts of how they function and
disable themselves through factional discord (e.g. 97, 169, 200). This
passage appears in an account entitled 'lecture, re sensitive periods'.
The next account, 'old examples', is voiced from the position of
someone in the audience of a lecture. But it is not the same lecture
which precedes it, because the lecturer in 'old examples' grabs the
narrator by the throat, choking him and forcing him onto his back,
in a physical demonstration of the techniques of disembowelling with
a knife (though the narrator is not sure of this, *TA* 89–96). This is
typical of the manner in which the novel works as a whole: each story
might have some link to the preceding one, but will voice a differing
perspective, or a different abuse of a similar-seeming situation. The
perspectives are multiplying, refracting and dizzying. As Drew Milne
puts it, the novel 'lacks the sense of location [of earlier work] and
forces the reader into imagining more paranoid perspectives.'[15] The
loosening from a locatable context and the erasure of regional voices

means this novel, stylistically speaking, is more of a dystopic political allegory than an exercise in mimetic realism, and so immediately it becomes more widely applicable and more plurally referential in terms of history and context, than any of the preceding novels. For Robert Maslen, the accounts are 'common property, freed from the encumbrances of ownership'.[16] This is a novel of dispersal, of people frenetically on the move: 'Anywhere, it was just to anywhere, needing that I had, yes escape from this territory' (*TA* 306).

The quotation marks the faceless team of compositors, translators and editors places around each chapter heading are as alien to Kelman's stylistic universe in 2001 as their absence might be to someone reading his first novel in 1984. Between the translated texts and the anonymous author of the 'Preface', and the team of modifiers and translators, the quotation marks function like *sic*, maintaining a safe distance. The editor explains in a brief 'Preface' that some of the accounts 'arrived with titles already in place; others had none and were so assigned' (*TA* ix). To get round the logical problem of first-person accounts, Kelman borrows the tool of the extradiegetic editor's collecting hand from James Hogg's *The Private Memoirs and Confessions of a Justified Sinner* (1824), as he explains in 1985:

> So you have someone saying 'He walked across the hill and BUMP Jill stuck the axe in the head, you know.' And you start to say 'Well how did you write it down, if there's an axe in your head? Was that your dying breath?' That type of problem, for instance, is a genuine problem in the sense that people have to tackle it – James Hogg has to tackle it. Wringhim – I mean what happens there? because that is the I-voice, right, and you find out the guy has written it all down and buried it at the cross roads, or whatever, and somebody discovers it.[17]

In a similar way to Margaret Attwood who places 'Historical Notes' at the end of *The Handmaid's Tale* (1985) to offer some degree of complicating structural viability to the whole novel, Kelman is concerned to make the structure of *Translated Accounts* as credible as possible. Instead of concluding his novel with a voice of editorial authority, as Hogg and Atwood do, he opens with a brief passage on the provenance of the accounts to mount a defence against predictable quiddities raised by the language of the succeeding narratives.

The quotations from the novel above supply evidence of how standard and English the orthography and vocabulary is (certainly in comparison with *You Have to Be Careful. . .*) and this might be a part of Kelman's larger point. Standard language is always alienating, and is the product not of identity or locale, but of collusion with a mythical centre, that same mythical centre of authority which has reproduced, collected, collated and deracinated these accounts. Critic Susanne Hagemann clarifies the position of the editorial 'Preface':

> As the preface makes clear, narrative authority in *Translated Accounts* is characterised by anonymity and dispersal. Power is exercised over the text, but it remains unclear who exercises it and at what concrete point and why. The only exception is the preface. The preface's standard-English bureaucratic voice denies all responsibility for the shape of the main text, but by reporting on the genesis of the text it does constitute itself as the last and highest authority in this genesis; and in addition it creates a certain degree of coherence and meaning.[18]

Hagemann points us to an important question: who is the intended audience? The accounts once translated are foreign to audience, to editor and would be to the original authors too: so what and who do they represent? The speaker of the 'Preface' does not know and is not him/herself, the editor. Foreignness is as key to this novel as it is to *You Have to be Careful*. . . . The speakers are foreign to one another: the 'martial law' in this 'occupied territory' has estranged everybody into atomised voices in pain, all of them speaking from 'awkward situations, situations of adversity' (*TA* 91). All find it difficult, stressful, fraught, dangerous, even life-threatening, to communicate. Even so, the sheer necessity of story-telling, of remembering and recording, is drummed home repeatedly (e.g. *TA* 61, 167, 257), as are the dangers of being misunderstood, appropriated by foreign agents, journalists, observers and 'authoritys' (e.g. *TA* 147, 208, 229, 268).

Many of the accounts must have been posthumously retrieved, as the speakers are repeatedly concerned with mortality and evidently under very serious threat of murder, execution or disappearance: everyone, every bond, every surety, lives under constant threat. The ghostly nature of the language with its repetitions, jarring collocations, frequent fragmentary conditional clauses, destabilising interrogatives with no question marks, and lack of any tangible context-specific detail, mean the accounts as a whole become an assemblage of stuttered syntax brought together for some form of abstracted documentation. While there are moments of levity and hope, as a whole the accounts document human suffering in many different, individualised, forms. If the documentation and translation procedures can be understood as an attempt at a sympathetic historical recovery of lost lives, then perhaps Hagemann's reading polarises the hierarchy between the editor-translator and the edited accounts too much. Still the historical recovery is fractured and dissembled by mutual foreignness, if not intentionally so.

On occasion the text seems to descend into computer gobbledegook, especially in account 5 '¿FODocument' which the 'Preface' singles out as being 'in the form it emerged from computative mediation' (*TA* ix). But D. J. Taylor is not entirely right in thinking that such 'typewriter explosions' are 'just mucking about'.[19] Though the resultant text can seem to be overwhelmed by messy meaninglessness, actually, if the text is approached like a poetic jigsaw puzzle, as Robert Maslen recommends,[20] some meanings begin to coalesce. Often, what is struggling to be expressed, is too horrific for language to cope; if the text seems meaninglessness, it is because the event cannot be accounted for, cannot be fully accepted into language. Gang rapes of men and women, murders, intimidations and humiliations of all kinds rage around the speakers, always about to engulf the furtive narratives. I would like to focus now on one such instance in some depth. One line of account 5 reads, margin to justified margin:

whatlanguage pleas onbayntsbaybybaybyfatherisfather&a (*TA* 20)

This is striking because the damaged, compacted language contains identifiable items such as 'what', 'language', 'pleas', 'baby' and 'father' and, surfacing less distinctly, is the part-anagram of a weapon, which emerges sharply a few lines further along: 'bayonetsbabyof' (*TA* 20). The same pairing of 'bayonet' and 'baby' formed an important weapon of British propaganda for First World War recruitment, in the notorious Bryce report of 1915. Here is an excerpt which is supposedly an eye-witness account of the behaviour of German soldiers in Belgium. Its full impact necessitates a lengthy quotation:

> It is clearly shown that many offences were committed against infants and quite young children . . . A shocking case of the murder of a baby by a drunken soldier at Malines is thus recorded by one eye-witness and confirmed by another:
> 'I saw eight German soldiers, and they were drunk. They were singing and making a lot of noise and dancing about. As the German soldiers came along the street I saw a small child, whether boy or girl I could not see, come out of a house. The child was about two years of age.

The child came into the middle of the street so as to be in the way of the soldiers. The soldiers were walking in twos. The first line of two passed the child; one of the second line, the man on the left, stepped aside and drove his bayonet with both hands into the child's stomach lifting the child into the air on his bayonet and carrying it away on his bayonet, he and his comrades still singing. The child screamed when the soldier struck it with his bayonet, but not afterwards.'[21]

Whether it is a 'true' account or not, Bryce's report served as propaganda to recruit soldiers for the First World War, and to encourage American sympathy for Britain's military action. There are two areas of possible shame here: the murder of babies by soldiers (which may not have occurred) and the construction of stories of murdered children spun to whip up a frenzy of hoards of boy soldiers to feed the machinery of war. It is a most unforgettable scene, a nadir of war imagery which appears in altered states in every human conflict: the purely innocent victim of a dehumanisation which is absolute. The baby on the bayonet does not surface definitely in '¿FODocument', but it is a repeated collocation which threatens to take place in the narrative at every turn, once set up initially in the condensed alchemical formula that is 'onbayntsbaybybaybyfatherisfather&a'.

The speaker of '¿FODocument' is a young man who is about to be caught out by a curfew, in a town he is quite new to. The curfew is being enforced by 'securitys', this being perhaps the most repeated noun of import in this book: securitys are everywhere. The speaker recognises a 'foreign guest in our country, famous man, political man' (TA 22), who is chased past him by securitys, who then murder him. The speaker hears the securitys laugh off the murder as a suicide. He is a witness, and as such, is in grave danger. Two of the soldiers are 'young, 16, 17 years, 18 years' and they carry weapons 'having bayonets certainly' (TA 24). They interrogate the speaker about his proximity to the curfew deadline, but let him go to what he has pointed out is his 'home' (TA 25). He is begrudgingly let into the house (evidently not his actual home) and again recognises one of the occupants, this time a 'trade unionist, famous, framing the famous documents [which shame] the State Security Council' (TA 30). In other words, a person also in grave danger. Among the small domestic group, is a baby:

I saw the baby on the floor by the fireside, the other child was with it, the baby, now as in mid movement, its image forever there for me, laughing and on one hand, the other raised as balancing itself, on its knees looking up to the child, its sister, brother, I cannot remember, girl I think, but the baby, the interested look that a baby gives, I see my own daughter, and its laughingand andto the guest in our country . . . (TA 30)

Upon the consideration of the emotional significance of the baby, the 'computative mediation' fragments the account again. When textual clarity is regained, the speaker is recalling the comic scene of a friend learning to march in the military. And his recollection moves *Translated Accounts* temporarily to 1915:

Bayonets, I remember too, old fashioned, design from years back. They could fix their bayonets and throw sacks of grain one to another, they could catch the sack on the bayonet and throw to the next man, this was practice for them, if they might use babies, of course. (*TA* 31; repeated again as fragments, 36 and 39)

The securitys come to the door of the house. The baby is wide-eyed and curious. The speaker takes the baby from its mother, and holds it as the securitys ask 'where is your woman' (*TA* 34). The non-standard plural securitys are always male in this novel, and they invariably threaten sexual violation and torture. Rape of women, men and children lurks everywhere (e.g. *TA* 137, 222, 227 and 254). The violation implicated in this story is equally obscene. The speaker has the baby taken from him, and language and comprehension cannot cope with the impending horror, so it breaks into meaninglessness (*TA* 35). It returns again to a faltering coherence but to an earlier stage in the account, taking us back over the same story again, never quite going beyond the moment after the baby is taken by the securitys. A repetition of the compound appears amid computerised mess as the story dissolves: 'baybyonets' and 'baybybyebynets' (*TA* 40 and 44). We are never told clearly that the baby and bayonet meet, but the language brings the two together anyway, bidding a repressed bye bye to a murdered child.

The event resurfaces elsewhere. In 'a pumpkin story', a bookish speaker, in the midst of a Mark Anthony-inflected invective against '[h]onourable militarys, honourable securitys, all honourable operatives' (*TA* 123), watches as a boy throws a rotten pumpkin at a security, and is immediately shot for it. This speaker raises the bye bye bayonet baby for different purposes:

How not to use bayonets bay on-ets for goodbye babeee. Bay on-ets may be used on younger fellows as on babies, sacks of grain as it may be done for children when all are surrounded and by heavy numbers face bravely our infants, why not if these are the foreign fabulists who may write it, academic experts who are into our country as servants and clowns to our master authoritys, all monies and riches from our colleges to these foreign professors, specialty experts who may say we do exist, or not so, who is to buy my words, all newspaper media, other servants all servants, such politicians and other personnel, allied at foreign office. Why not use such. Sacks of grain also are human beings. Yes. Come to our country... (*TA* 121)

The questions a passage such as this raises are manifold. Outside 'academic experts' are clearly formulated both as leeches, and as 'fabulists', but what is their function in a land being ripped apart? How can we understand them allegorically? The speaker clearly suspects them of collusion with his own corrupted state, and of selling their wares to the highest bidders such as news media and diplomatic services. Perhaps he is pointing out the self-serving non-participation of international observers (UN officials? Reporters? Researchers?), watching the militarised mayhem, but never being involved, never taking a moral stance or an interventionist approach to ensure social justice. Whatever the reason, the novel despairs at the misunderstandings generated by poor communication across national divides, while it also problematises the nationalisms which serve to sever mutual trust. In some senses, to class this novel as allegorical is to deny the existence of war atrocities carried out in the name of the state. Writing about the history of the socialist movement in Scotland, and worldwide, Kelman writes:

> In an occupied country indigenous history can only be radical. It is a class issue. The intellectual life of working class people is 'occupied'. In a colonised country intellectual occupation takes place throughout society. The closer to the ruling class we get the less difference there exists in language and culture, until finally we find that questions fundamental to society at its widest level are settled by members of the same closely knit circle, occasionally even the same family or 'bloodline'. And the outcome of that can be war, the slaughter of working class people.[22]

'this furin stranger varmint'

Suspicions about foreigners in *Translated Accounts* are directed constantly at Jeremiah Brown, the lead male of *You Have to be Careful in the Land of the Free*. From the graphic horrors and multiple tragedies of *Translated Accounts*, Kelman turns his hand to create his most humorous male lead to date. As with *Translated Accounts*, a first-person narrative structure reflects the state of the exiled individual, and the state of the nation he is in. When the novel starts, Jeremiah has been in the United States for twelve years. Like so many of Kelman's characters, he is about to take a line of flight, only this time the hero is moving in the opposite direction: he is on his way back to Glasgow. Jeremiah's journey is to happen from the outset of the novel: the body of his narrative is analeptic, as he considers his life in America on the last night before his flight, tomorrow's flight providing a frame of reference, and tomorrow's flight never coming by the novel's close. Like Tammas, we never know whether Jeremiah makes it. What we do know is that the journey home will have 'nothing to do with homesickness or notions of a motherland. Fuck the motherland' (*YH* 25).

The novel amounts to one evening's act of recovery – 'memories to dump' (*YH* 261) – as Jeremiah sifts through his American experience, concerning at its heart his recently estranged partner Yasmin and their daughter, a nameless four-year-old 'wean'. It becomes clear that the 'mystery' of Yasmin (*YH* 403) will remain unresolved by the novel's closure. Comedic though this novel is, and light though Jeremiah's voice always is, the consciousness presented has a background of psychological pain.

Jeremiah is, by his own constant estimation, a 'unassimiliatit furnir'. Whenever he mentions nationality, he resorts to an idiosyncratic quasi-phonetic presentation of the proper nouns, playfully denigrating the sanctity of those same national categories as he does so. So, when he spells 'American' 'Uhmerkin' (e.g. *YH* 120), the visual rhyme with gherkin serves to tease, stretch and defamiliarise the idea of nation into a strange, comic shape. The sound of the word could represent an American pronunciation, or more likely, Jeremiah's exaggerated comic parody of an American accent. The alien quality of such presentation of nation, is designed to present Jeremiah's own alienation from nationality: he is, officially an alien, but in his own terms 'a member of the alienigenae' (*YH* 81). And it seems he is alienated from all forms of nationalism, including any sentimental attachment to himself as a 'Skatchman' (*YH* 6), the country of 'Skallin' (*YH* 15) or his 'Skarrisch' nationality (*YH* 12). In terms of nationality, Jeremiah is without 'hame' (*YH* 15).

Phoneticisation is used as much for play, as it is for politics. When Jeremiah phoneticises 'individyouells' for individuals, 'sakyr' for soccer, 'tayyingallon' for ten-gallon (*YH* 37, 94 and 97), he is doing so out of a playful joy in difference. Everybody he meets is a product of hybridity, of cultures meeting and mating. There is no such thing as a pure monologic national identity in the people Jeremiah has encountered in America. In fact the only body that seems to hold the idea of national purity in any esteem is the state machine. In order to manage its immigration problem, the America of this novel has formulated a system of colour ID cards which set down, in the most basic, primary terms, the aspects of an alien's identity which the state determines are most important to that individual's assimilation, or lack thereof. Jeremiah is constantly reminded of his status as an alien by the dystopic fact of his 'Red Card' (*YH* 11), which exposes him, to any 'true-born' American who wishes to ask to see documentation of his identity, as a socialist and an atheist (though he is, by his own estimation, 'mair an anarchist. . . opposed to authority on principle, *YH* 12). Jeremiah is repeatedly exposed and so abused by an alienating procedure that the State reinforces and polices. Kelman pushes the context of this novel a little into the future, and exaggerates American politics incrementally further to the right, satirising by implication political developments in the wake of terrorist attacks on the USA in September 2001, such as the US 'Patriot' Act of 2001, the ensuing 'War on Terror' in Iraq, Afghanistan and elsewhere. Following Noam Chomsky's lead, Kelman's America is divided between an imperial state policed by and in the interests of a militarised ruling élite, and a relatively liberal, if blinkered and paranoid, populace of ordinary citizens.[23]

For Jeremiah, alien by birth, by politics, by accent and by faith, the United States can only offer repeated reinforcement of that alienation, can only make him aware of the fragility of his existence, of his subjection to rules and stipulations of immigration management, unless of course he shifts his subject position to one which is acceptable to the state authority. Jeremiah's first-person narrative could signal Kelman's raising of the possibility that only 'I's can exist in the United States for those who are new to the country. Indeed Jeremiah's encounters with the state seem only to be about securing his identity, ensuring every natural-born American knows, and has a right to know, who he is and what he might threaten America with, all in the name of domestic national security. In true political satire mode, and with deliciously subversive irony, unassimilatable Jeremiah becomes a Security operative in an airport, that most testy and fluid of borderlands, the space of internal borders, of moving peoples, of nationalities in febrile, populous contact. Airports are always multi-linguistic, multinational, always transient, always homeless, are spaces offering the promise of freedom but marshalling individuals more rigorously than anywhere else. As David Pascoe points out, after terrorist atrocities of the 1970s 'airspace would officially become a police state whose electrified borders were crossed as one passed into the [. . .] airport.'²⁴ The 'security' that airports and flying attempt to embody, is undermined by a complex parodic interplay between gambling, flying and insurance. This is where Kelman implicitly reflects a widespread anxiety about flying in the wake of the September 2001 use of airplanes as vehicles of destruction. Taking a gamble himself, Kelman teases those anxieties into a comic shape. Jeremiah details at great length the history of 'persian bets' – persian being derivative of 'perishing'. Again, the pun could effect an implicitly topical critique of American intervention in Persia which could readily be described as perishing as a policy, and one which certainly has involved the perishing of many thousands of innocents. Back in the novel, persian bets see the American poor gamble on whether they will survive an internal, domestic flight or not. If they are injured or die, the 'insurance' – the gambling winnings – will be paid to their families. If they do not, they fly (*YH* 91–4 and 115–22). Kelman's complex parody here is aimed at the sanctity of flying, undercutting the modernist promise of supreme technological safety while also attacking the laughable but prevalent notion that America is a classless society. Airports become filled with gamblers waiting for a cheap flight on which they might make their fortune. There is therefore increased demand for airport security operatives (*YH* 128), and in the mad rush to secure airspace, even 'libertarian socialist atheist' Jeremiah is employed (*YH* 142). Through this conceit, Kelman also pokes his critical stick at the reliability of insurance companies, which fundamentally rely on odds and probabilities to survive in the capitalist market place. And he takes a satirical swipe at the airline industry, the health of which is always used as a yardstick to measure the wealth of capitalist economies, and the progress of society. One of the homeless poor comes to haunt the airport, pushing its shopping trolley and dissolving into thin air (no one is sure of 'its' gender). Jeremiah's fellow low-level security guards draw on their various superstitious inheritances from their wide variety of cultures and become certain 'it' is a ghost. The exception is the existential rationalist Jeremiah who empowers it with the name 'Being'. In a scene parodic of the widespread fear of terrorist plots at airports, the Being unaccountably explodes into a conflagration of used lottery tickets 'right inside the VIP suite' in the airport terminal (*YH* 232).

More insidiously, hidden from the sight of low-ranking alien security officials like Jeremiah, airports are the site of 'Patriot Holding Centres' (*YH* 157), in which fresh immigrants are vetted and processed, rubber stamped or returned to sender. The immigrant is squeezed in the coldpress of a state machine which cannot brook what the novel offers in bucketloads: the heat and mixtures of plural multiculturalism. Jeremiah revels in his own Glaswegian language variety – this novel is peppered with more Gaelic, Scots idiom and quasi-phonetic spelling than any before it – but at the same time, like all Kelman heroes, Jeremiah avoids sentimental nationalism at all costs, and constantly dances in other language types and cultural forms he encounters in the whirlpool that is immigrant America. He might well be alienated from the American state machine, but he revels in both his own difference from everyone he meets, and in the playful hybridity of American cultures, always in the plural, always meticulously shown to be different, in stark contrast to the deadening hand of the state machine. In revelling in that multiplicity, flawed as he is, Jeremiah is Kelman's most garrulous and comic vehicle yet for a bold politics of persistent and risk-taking subversions: Jeremiah subverts Scottishness and all national or state allegiances; like all Kelman heroes he embodies a reconsideration of Glaswegian masculine stereotypes; this in turn entails a liberation from any remaining traces of a working-class work ethic, the ideology which suggests that hard, boring work is an unquestioned good. A frustrated and unproductive writer in what little spare time he has, Jeremiah gnaws with fervid articulacy at his own isolation. But he is never a misanthrope, resolutely maintaining ideals of socialist and sociable freedoms in the face of stern state policing, and a relationship which recently fell apart. Talking about himself to an unwitting elderly couple in a bar, he sums up his position in Uhmerika:

> this young feller with the Red Card, this self-avowed anarchist, unassim-
> ilatit socialist and atheist with a hatred of ruling bodies everywhere;
> religious, monarquic, political, corporate or financial, who gies a fuck,
> pardon the language, sorry, yet here he is at this very moment in time

– sorry about that, I do apologize – why he is so close to ye, is sitting so close, so close ye could reach out yer hand and stroke his face, this seeker of sanctuary within, so close ye could close yer eyes and sense his breath on yer face this furin stranger varmint, congenital member of the evil undead. (*YH* 356–7)

Though, as I have said, the last two novels are a formal departure from the preceding four, the critique of nation and language they display is perfectly consistent with traits developing out of Kelman's evident sense of foreignness within English, perhaps out of an alienation from Scottishness, but certainly a disappointment with Scottish politics. He is markedly still a minoritarian writer of the masses who refuses to generalise about human experience. He is someone who maintains an integral sense of political purpose and artistic agency in styles which are maturing into cogent expressions of radical dissent, persistently in complex, fraught engagements with immoveable, absurd realities. His fictional sense of humour increases in relation to an increasing political urgency and horror at state interventions and travesties upon individual rights and freedoms. That there continues to be something alien and 'furin' about Kelman's writing – in style, substance and subject – is an effect carefully crafted by the author. He is a foreigner in his own tongue.[25] He pushes his polyvalent work away from any monologic literary grouping or tradition, to ensure the determined minoritarian supranational distinction of his work, so that it might continue to irritate those in search of comfortable reading or placating platitudes.

Notes

1 'I object to taking part, for instance, in a discussion that hinges on the use of swear words in literature, because right away you've begged the question of what those words are, you know, and you're involving me again in a value system that *isn't your own to deny.*' Duncan McLean, 'James Kelman interviewed', *Edinburgh Review*, 71 (1985) [McLean's or Kelman's emphases]. Geoff Gilbert provides the most useful critical analysis of this issue in 'Can Fiction Swear? James Kelman and the Booker Prize', in Rod Mengham (ed.), *An Introduction to Contemporary Fiction: International Writing in English since 1970* (Cambridge: Polity, 1999), 219–34.

2 MacDonald Daly, 'Your Average Working Kelman', *Cencrastus*, 46 (Autumn 1993), 16.

3   MacDonald Daly, 'Politics and the Scottish Language', *Hard Times*
    (Berlin), 64/65 (1998), 22. http://nottingham.ac.uk/critical-theory/
    papers/Daly.pdf (accessed 17/07/2006).

4   Willy Maley, 'Swearing Blind: Kelman and the Curse of the Working
    Classes', *Edinburgh Review*, 95 (1996), 106–8.

5   Mac Daly, *Crackpot Texts: Absurd Explorations in Modern and Post-
    modern Literature* (London: Zoilus Press, 1997), 202.

6   Willy Maley and Ellen-Raisa Jackson co-edited the only collection of
    critical essays on Kelman to date: 'Committing to Kelman: The Art of
    Integrity and the Politics of Dissent', *Edinburgh Review*, 108 (2001).

7   Willy Maley, 'Who Let the Underdogs Out?', *The Drouth*, 18 (Winter
    2005–06), 78–9.

8   Lesley McDowell, 'Look back in anger', *Independent*, 21 May 2004, 20–1.

9   J[ohnny] R[odger], 'Omniscience or Existence? That is the Question', *The
    Drouth*, 18 (Winter 2005–6), 5.

10 Bill Ashcroft, Gareth Griffiths and Helen Tiffin, *Post-Colonial Studies:
    The Key Concepts* (London and New York: Routledge, 2000), 5. See also:
    Bill Ashcroft, Gareth Griffiths and Helen Tiffin, *The Empire Writes
    Back: Theory and Practice in Post-Colonial Literatures* (London and New
    York: Routledge, 1989), 41–51; Gareth Griffiths, 'Imitation, Abrogation
    and Appropriation: The Production of the Post-Colonial Text', *Kunapipi*,
    IX: 1 (1987), 13–20.

11 See for example Pierre-Joseph Proudhon, *What is Property?* trans. Donald
    Kelley and Bonnie Smith (Cambridge: Cambridge University Press, 1994)
    and Rudolf Rocker, 'The Nation as Community of Language', in
    Nationalism and Culture [1933], trans. Ray E. Chase (Montreal, New York
    and London: Black Rose Books, 1998), 276–97. For accounts of both,
    see George Woodcock, *Anarchism: A History of Libertarian Ideas and
    Movements*, 2nd edn (Ontario: Broadview, 2004). For an analysis of
    Kelman's anarchism, see H. Gustav Klaus, 'Anti-authoritarianism in the
    Later Fiction of James Kelman', in H. Gustav Klaus and Stephen Knight
    (eds), *'To Hell with Culture': Anarchism and Twentieth-Century British
    Literature* (Cardiff: University of Wales Press, 2005), 162–77.

12 'I'm not involved with any parties, you know, the idea that this guy's an
    anarchist, is a bit of a laugh in some ways . . . The kind of non-debates
    we have now in Scotland are shocking. I think we need Frantz Fanon
    to talk about the kind of stuff we have here', Michael Gardiner, 'James
    Kelman interviewed', *Scottish Studies Review*, 5:1 (Spring 2004), 112.
    For relevant discussions of post-colonial nationality see Frantz Fanon,
    The Wretched of the Earth, trans. Constance Farrington (London:
    Penguin, 2001). For Kelman's engagement with post-colonial writers,
    see the discussion of Saadat Hasan Manto (*SRA* 23–6), and the essays
    'Alex La Guma (1925–1985)' (*AJS* 95–102), 'An Interview with John La
    Rose' (*AJS* 229–59) and 'The Caribbean Artists Movement, 1966–1972'
    (*AJS* 260–4).

13 Rocker, 'The Nation as Community of Language', 297.

14 For readings of Kelman in relation to post-colonial texts and theories, see: Roderick Watson, 'Postcolonial Subjects? Language, Narrative Authority and Class in Contemporary Scottish Culture', *Hungarian Journal of English and American Studies*, 4:1–2 (1998), 21–38; Ismail S. Talib, *The Language of Postcolonial Literatures: An Introduction* (London and New York: Routledge, 2002); David Punter, *Postcolonial Imaginings: Fictions of a New World Order* (Edinburgh: Edinburgh University Press, 2000); Stefanie Lehner, 'Towards a Subaltern Aesthetics: Reassessing Postcolonial Criticism for Contemporary Northern Irish and Scottish Literatures. James Kelman and Robert McLiam Wilson's Rewriting of National Paradigms', *eSharp: Electronic Social Sciences, Humanities, and Arts Review for Postgraduates*, 5 (Summer 2005), 1–14. www.sharp.arts.gla.ac.uk/issue5/lehner.pdf (accessed 3/05/2006).

15 Drew Milne, 'Broken English: James Kelman's *Translated Accounts*', *Edinburgh Review*, 108 (2001), 113.

16 R. W. Maslen, Review of *TA*, *Scottish Studies Review*, 3:2 (Autumn 2002), 86.

17 McLean, 'James Kelman interviewed', 80.

18 Susanne Hagemann, 'Postcolonial Translation Studies and James Kelman's *Translated Accounts*', *Scottish Studies Review*, 6:1 (Spring 2005), 77.

19 D. J. Taylor, 'Eh?', Review of *TA*, *Literary Review* (June 2001), 48. The general consensus among reviewers was, as Robert Hanks put it, *Translated Accounts* 'is too difficult'. Robert Hanks, ' "What I am to say"; This book is too difficult', *Daily Telegraph*, 9 June 2001, 5.

20 Maslen, Review of *TA*, 86.

21 [James Bryce], *Report of the Committee on Alleged German Outrages* (London: H.M. Stationery Office, 1915), 32.

22 From Kelman's introduction to Hugh Savage, *Born up a Close: Memoirs of a Brigton Boy*, ed. James Kelman (Glendareul: Argyll Publishing, 2006), 20.

23 Chomsky's latest in a long line of critiques of American international politics is *Hegemony or Survival: America's Quest for Global Dominance* (London: Penguin, 2004).

24 David Pascoe, *Airspaces* (London: Reaktion Books, 2001), 196.

25 'It is in one's own language that one is bilingual or multilingual. Conquer the major language in order to delineate in it as yet unknown minor languages. Use the minor language to *send the major language racing*. Minor authors are foreigners in their own tongues.' Gilles Deleuze and Felix Guattari, *A Thousand Plateaus: Capitalism and Schizophrenia*, trans. Brian Massumi (London and New York: Continuum, 2004), 116 (Deleuze and Guattari's emphasis).

Select bibliography

Major works

An Old Pub Near the Angel (Orono, Maine: Puckerbrush Press, 1992 [1973]).

Three Glasgow Writers: A collection of writing by Alex.Hamilton, James Kelman, Tom Leonard (Glasgow: Molendinar Press, 1976).

Short Tales from the Night Shift (Glasgow: Print Studio Press, 1978).

Jim Kelman. Writers in Brief 11 (Glasgow: National Book League, 1980).

Not not while the giro (London: Minerva, 1993 [1983]).

The Busconductor Hines (London: Phoenix, 1984).

A Chancer (London: Picador, 1985).

Lean Tales, with Alasdair Gray and Agnes Owens (London: Jonathan Cape, 1985).

Greyhound For Breakfast (London: Vintage, 1999 [1987]).

An East End Anthology, ed. Jim Kelman (Glasgow: Clydeside Press, 1988).

A Disaffection (London: Vintage, 1999 [1989]).

The Burn (London: Vintage, 1999 [1991]).

Hardie and Baird and Other Plays (London: Secker & Warburg, 1991).

Some Recent Attacks (Stirling: AK Press, 1992).

How late it was, how late (London: Minerva, 1995 [1994]).

Seven Stories, Audio CD (Edinburgh: AK Press Audio, 1997).

Tantalising Twinkles: some thoughts on a First Order Radical of European Standing (Breckan, Stenness, Orkney: Emergency Eyewash Press, 1997).

The Good Times (London: Vintage, 1999 [1998]).

Translated Accounts (London: Secker & Warburg, 2002).

"And the Judges Said. . .": Essays (London: Secker & Warburg, 2002).

You Have to be Careful in the Land of the Free (Orlando: Harcourt, 2004).

Born up a Close: Memoirs of a Brigton Boy, by Hugh Savage, ed. James Kelman (Glendareul: Argyll Publishing, 2006).

Major interviews

Clark, William, 'A conversation with James Kelman', *Variant*, 2:12 (Spring 2001), 3–7. http://variant.randomstate.org/pdfs/issue12/Kelman.pdf.

Gardiner, Michael, 'James Kelman interviewed', *Scottish Studies Review*, 5:1 (2004), 101–15.

Kane, Pat, 'Underclass, under-what? Fictions and realities from Glasgow to Prague: an interview with James Kelman', *Regenerating Cities*, 7 (1995), 18–20.

McLean, Duncan, 'James Kelman interviewed', *Edinburgh Review*, 71 (1985), 64–80.

McNeill, Kirsty, 'Interview with James Kelman', *Chapman*, 57 (Summer 1989), 1–9.

Toremans, Tom, 'An Interview with Alasdair Gray and James Kelman', *Contemporary Literature*, 44:4 (Winter 2003), 565–86.

Torrington, Jeff, 'In conversation with Jim Kelman', *West Coast Magazine*, 12 (1993), 18–21.

Newspaper coverage used in this book

Alberge, Dalya, 'Booker judge says winner is disgrace', *The Times*, 12 October 1994, 1.

[Anon.], 'The scribbler', *Sunday Business Post*, 18 January 2004, http://archives.tcm.ie/businesspost/2004/01/18/story460699552.asp.

[Anon.], 'Better Late than Never: Profile – James Kelman', *Scotland on Sunday*, 20 March 1994, 19.

Bell, Ian, 'Four letter truths', *Observer*, 'Review', 27 March 1994, 16.

Bowditch, Gillian, 'Glasgow disowns prize novel', *The Times*, 13 October 1994, 2.

Buckley, David, Review of *HL*, *Observer*, 'Review', 3 April 1994, 19.

Crawford, Robert, 'Northern exposure', *Sunday Times*, 17 April 1994, 8.

Davidson, Gina, 'De Bernières scorns "sordid" Scots writers', *Scotland on Sunday*, 26 August 2001, 3.

Davidson, Max, 'Critic's view', *Daily Telegraph*, 13 October 1994, 9.

Goldhill, Judy, 'And the nominees are. . .', *The Times*, 'Weekend', 10 September 1994, 17.

Gunn, Kirsty, 'King of Style', *Sunday Herald*, 2 May 2004, 12.

Hanks, Robert, '"What I am to say"; This book is too difficult', Review of *TA*, *Daily Telegraph*, 9 June 2001, 5.

[Hastings, Max?] [Leader:], 'Polluting the language', *Daily Telegraph*, 14 October 1994, 26.

Hunter, William, 'A voice of Glasgow with a withering effect on apostrophes', *Herald*, 12 February 1983, 8.

Jacobs, Eric, 'Eyeless and legless in Glasgow', *Spectator*, 2 April 1994, 33–4.

Jaggi, Maya, 'Speaking in tongues', *Guardian*, 'Weekend', 18 July 1998, 26.

Jardine, Kay, 'Sheridan and his citizens hold an alternative party', *Herald*, 4 June 2002, 2.

Jenkins, Simon, 'An expletive of a winner', *The Times*, 15 October 1994, 20.

Jones, Russell Celyn, 'Glasgow via California', *The Times*, 16 July 1998, 39.

Kington, Miles, 'Revealed: how the Booker changed Cheltenham', *Independent*, 17 October 1994, 15.

Lockerbie, Catherine, 'Lighting up Kelman', *Scotsman*, 'Weekend', 19 March 1994, 3.

MacDonald, Marianne, 'Bookshops bemoan "Mogadon" Booker', *Independent*, 2 October 1994, 1.

McDougall, Liam, 'Author and artist Alasdair Gray reveals double blow to health', *Sunday Herald*, 5 October 2003, 3.

McDowell, Lesley, 'Look back in anger', *Independent*, 21 May 2004, 20–1.

Marshall, Alasdair, 'Hot tip for the top', *Evening Times*, 27 September 1989, 10.

Mars-Jones, Adam, Review of *HL*, *Times Literary Supplement*, 1 April 1994, 20.

Martin, Lorna, 'Dreary, deprived, awful – a Scot on the Scots', *Observer*, 13 February 2005, 1.

Massie, Allan, 'Rude awakening for complacent Scots', *Sunday Times*, 23 November 1997, 19.

Massie, Allan, 'The way to literature's urban kailyard', *Scotsman*, 23 August 2001, 12.

Naysmith, Stephen, 'Author seeks arrest over torture claims', *The List*, 21 March–3 April 1997, 4.

P.H.S., 'Diary: closed book', *The Times*, 13 October 1994, 18.

Phipps, Sam, 'The age of the page', *Herald*, 11 March 2006, 4.

Smith, Julia Llewellyn, 'The prize will be useful. I'm skint', *The Times*, 13 October 1994, 17.

Smith, Ken, 'Kelman fans flames at demonstrations against Bill', *Herald*, 3 November 1994, 3.

[Stothard, Peter?] [Leader:], 'Traditional bookmanism', *The Times*, 12 October 1994, 19.

Sutherland, John, 'Janet Todd: a novel mission', *Guardian*, 'Education', 21 March 2006, 11.

Warner, Gerald, 'Time for a disaffection from literary slumming', *Sunday Times*, 25 September 1994, 8.

Wilson, Sue, 'Battling on', *The List*, 25 March–7 April 1994, 9.

Wojtas, Olga, 'Pubs, power and the Scottish psyche: Olga Wojtas reports from Govan on a conference on self-determination', *Times Higher Education Supplement*, 26 January 1990, 15.

Wroe, Nicholas, 'Bobby Dazzler', *Guardian*, 'Review', 28 May 2005, 22–3.
Young, Elizabeth, 'Glasgow gothic', *Guardian*, 'Review', 3 September 1992, 23.

Critical bibliography

Anon., 'Changing patterns in the consumption of foods at home, 1971–2000: Social Trends 32' (London: National Statistics, 2002), http://statistics.gov.uk/StatBase/ssdataset.asp?vlnk=5234&More=Y.

Argyle, Michael, *The Psychology of Social Class* (London and New York: Routledge, 1994).

Armstrong, Nancy, 'The Fiction of Bourgeois Morality and the Paradox of Individualism', in Franco Moretti (ed.), *The Novel. Vol. 2: Forms and Themes* (Princeton and Oxford: Princeton University Press, 2006), 349–88.

Ashcroft, Bill, Gareth Griffiths and Helen Tiffin, *Post-Colonial Studies: The Key Concepts* (London and New York: Routledge, 2000).

—— *The Empire Writes Back: Theory and Practice in Post-Colonial Literatures* (London and New York: Routledge, 1989).

Baker, Simon, '"Wee stories with a working-class theme": The Reimagining of Urban Realism in the Fiction of James Kelman', in Susanne Hagemann (ed.), *Studies in Scottish Fiction: 1945 to the Present* (Frankfurt: Peter Lang, 1996), 235–50.

Bakhtin, Mikhail Mikhailovich, *The Bakhtin Reader*, ed. Pam Morris (London: Edward Arnold, 1994).

Balfour, Campbell, *Unions and the Law* (Farnborough, Hants and Lexington, MA: Saxon House and Lexington Books, 1973).

Barsky, Robert F., *Noam Chomsky: A Life of Dissent* (Cambridge, Mass.: MIT Press, 1997).

Barthes, Roland, 'The Death of the Author', in Raman Selden (ed.), *The Theory of Criticism* (London and New York: Longman, 1988), 318–20.

Beckett, Samuel, *The Unnamable*, in *The Beckett Trilogy* (London: Calder, 1994).

—— *Waiting for Godot*, in *The Complete Dramatic Works* (London: Faber and Faber, 1986).

Bell, Ian A., 'Empty Intensifiers: Kelman Wins "The Booker" (At Last)', *New Welsh Review*, 27 (Winter 1994–5), 12–14.

Bergson, Henri, *Henri Bergson: Key Writings*, ed. Keith Ansell Pearson and John Mullarkey (New York and London: Continuum, 2002).

Berresford Ellis, Peter, and Seumas Mac A'Ghobhainn, *The Scottish Insurrection of 1820*, 3rd edn (Edinburgh: John Donald, 2001).

Bernstein, Stephen, 'James Kelman', *Review of Contemporary Fiction*, 20:3 (Fall 2000), 42–79.

Bex, Tony and Richard J. Watts (eds), *Standard English: The Widening Debate* (London and New York: Routledge, 1999).

Birrell, Ross and Alec Finlay (eds), *Justified Sinners: An Archaeology of Scottish Counter-Culture (1960–2000)* (Edinburgh: pocketbooks, 2002).

Bittenbender, J. C., 'Silence, Censorship, and the Voices of Skaz in the Fiction of James Kelman', *Bucknell Review*, 43:2 (2000), 150–65.

Bogue, Ronald, *Deleuze on Literature* (New York and London: Routledge, 2003).

Boyle, Mark and George Hughes, 'The Politics of the Representation of "The Real": Discourses from the Left on Glasgow's Role as European City of Culture, 1990', *Area*, 23 (1991), 217–28.

Brown, Gordon, and Robin Cook, *Scotland: The Real Divide: Poverty and Deprivation in Scotland* (Edinburgh: Mainstream, 1983).

[Bryce, James], *Report of the Committee on Alleged German Outrages* (London: H.M. Stationery Office, 1915).

Burgess, Moira, *Imagine a City: Glasgow in Fiction* (Glendaruel: Argyll Publishing, 1998).

Cannadine, David, *The Rise and Fall of Class in Britain* (New York: Columbia University Press, 1999).

Chehak, Susan Taylor, *Don Quixote Meets the Mob: The Craft of Fiction and the Art of Life* (Philadelphia: Xlibris, 2000).

Chomsky, Noam, *Hegemony or Survival: America's Quest for Global Dominance* (London: Penguin, 2004).

Clark, William, 'Remembering Hugh Savage and Workers City', in Hugh Savage, *Born up a Close: Memoirs of a Brigton Boy*, ed. James Kelman (Glendareul: Argyll Publishing, 2006), 251–61.

Cockburn, Ken and Alec Finlay (eds), *The Order of Things: an anthology of Scottish Sound, Pattern and Concrete Poems* (Edinburgh: pocketbooks, 2001).

Corbett, John, *Language and Scottish Literature; Scottish Language and Literature* (Edinburgh: Edinburgh University Press, 1997).

Cosgrove, Stuart, 'The Edinburgh Lecture: Innovation and Risk – How Scotland Survived the Tsunami', 16 February 2005, download.edinburgh.gov.uk/lectures/StuartCosgrove.pdf.

Craig, Cairns, *The Modern Scottish Novel: Narrative and the National Imagination* (Edinburgh: Edinburgh University Press, 1999).

—— 'Resisting Arrest: James Kelman', in Gavin Wallace and Randall Stevenson (eds), *The Scottish Novel Since the Seventies* (Edinburgh: Edinburgh University Press, 1993), 99–114.

Crowley, Tony, *The Politics of Discourse: The Standard Language Question in British Cultural Debates* (Basingstoke: Macmillan, 1989).

D'Angelo, Dominic, Joseph Farrell *et al* (eds), *The 1990 Story: Glasgow Cultural Capital of Europe* (Glasgow: Glasgow City Council, 1992).

Daly, Macdonald, 'Politics and the Scottish Language', *Hard Times* (Berlin), 64/65 (1998), 21–6. http://nottingham.ac.uk/critical-theory/papers/Daly.pdf.

—— *Crackpot Texts: Absurd Explorations in Modern and Postmodern Literature* (London: Zoilus Press, 1997).

—— 'Your Average Working Kelman', *Cencrastus*, 46 (Autumn 1993), 14–16.

Damer, Seán, *From Moorepark to 'Wine Alley': The Rise and Fall of a Glasgow Housing Scheme* (Edinburgh: Edinburgh University Press, 1989).

—— *Glasgow: Going for a Song* (London: Lawrence & Wishart, 1990).

Deleuze, Gilles and Felix Guattari, A *Thousand Plateaus: Capitalism and Schizophrenia*, trans. Brian Massumi (London and New York: Continuum, 2004).

—— *Anti-Oedipus: Capitalism and Schizophrenia*, trans. Robert Hurley, Mark Seem and Helen R. Lane (London and New York: Continuum, 2004).

—— *Kafka: Toward a Minor Literature*, trans. Dana Polan (Minneapolis: University of Minnesota Press, 1986).

Deleuze, Gilles and Claire Parnet, *Dialogues II*, trans. Hugh Tomlinson and Barbara Habberjam (London and New York: Continuum, 2002).

Duguid, Lindsay, 'Before it Becomes Literature: How Fiction Reviewers Have Dealt with the English Novel', in Zachary Leader (ed.), *On Modern British Fiction* (Oxford: Oxford University Press, 2002), 284–303.

Edgley, Alison, *The Social and Political Thought of Noam Chomsky* (London and New York: Routledge, 2000).

Engledow, Sarah, 'Studying Form: The Off-the-Page Politics of A Chancer', *Edinburgh Review*, 108 (2001), 69–84.

Fox, Aaron A., *Real Country: Music and Language in Working-Class Culture* (Durham and London: Duke University Press, 2004).

Fraser, W. Hamish, *Scottish Popular Politics: From Radicalism to Labour* (Edinburgh: Polygon, 2000).

—— *Conflict and Class: Scottish Workers, 1700–1838* (Edinburgh: John Donald, 1988).

Frede, Dorothea, 'The Question of Being: Heidegger's Project', in Charles Guignon (ed.), *The Cambridge Companion to Heidegger* (Cambridge: Cambridge University Press, 1993), 42–69.

Freeman, Alan, 'The Humanist's Dilemma: A Polemic Against Kelman's Polemics', *Edinburgh Review*, 108 (2001), 28–40.

Geertz, Clifford, 'Deep Play: Notes on the Balinese Cockfight', in Rachel Adams and David Savran (eds), *The Masculinity Studies Reader* (Oxford: Blackwell, 2002), 80–98.

Gifford, Douglas, 'The Authentic Glasgow Experience: James Kelman's A Chancer', *Books in Scotland*, 19 (Autumn 1985), 9–13.

—— *The Dear Green Place? The Novel in the West of Scotland* (Glasgow: Third Eye Centre, 1985).

Gifford, Douglas, Sarah Dunnigan and Alan MacGillivray (eds), *Scottish Literature: In English and Scots* [1981] (Edinburgh: Edinburgh University Press, 2002).

Gilbert, Geoff, 'Can Fiction Swear? James Kelman and the Booker Prize', in Rod Mengham (ed.), *An Introduction to Contemporary Fiction: International Writing in English since 1970* (Cambridge: Polity, 1999), 219–34.

Glendinning, Nigel, *The Interpretation of Goya's Black Paintings* (London: Queen Mary College, 1977).

Gogol, Nikolai, *The Overcoat*, trans. Ronald Wilks (London: Penguin, 1972).

Gray, Alasdair, *Lanark* (Edinburgh: Canongate, 2002).

—— *1982 Janine* (Harmondsworth: Penguin, 1985).

—— (ed.), *The Book of Prefaces* (London and New York: Bloomsbury, 2002).

Griffiths, Gareth, 'Imitation, Abrogation and Appropriation: The Production of the Post-Colonial Text', *Kunapipi*, IX:1 (1987), 13–20.

Hagan, Anette I., *Urban Scots Dialect Writing* (Frankfurt: Peter Lang, 2002).

Hagemann, Susanne, 'Postcolonial Translation Studies and James Kelman's Translated Accounts', *Scottish Studies Review*, 6:1 (Spring 2005), 74–83.

Harvie, Chistopher, *No Gods and Precious Few Heroes: Scotland 1914–1980* (London: Edward Arnold, 1981).

Haywood, Ian, *Working-Class Fiction: From Chartism to Trainspotting* (Plymouth: Northcote House and British Council, 1997).

Heidegger, Martin, *Ontology – The Hermeneutics of Facticity*, trans. John van Buren (Bloomington and Indianapolis: Indiana University Press, 1999).

Hobsbaum, Philip, 'The Glasgow Group: An Experience of Writing', *Edinburgh Review*, 80:1 (1988), 58–63.

Honey, John, *Language is Power: The Story of Standard English and its Enemies* (London: Faber and Faber, 1997).

—— 'The Language Trap: Race, Class and the 'Standard English' Issue in British Schools', *Kay-Shuttleworth Papers on Education*, No. 3. (Kenton: National Council for Educational Standards, 1983).

Horsey, Miles, *Tenements & Towers: Glasgow Working-Class Housing, 1890–1990* (Edinburgh: The Royal Commission on the Ancient and Historical Monuments of Scotland, 1990).

Horton, Patricia, 'Trainspotting: A Topography of the Masculine Abject', *English*, 50 (2001), 219–34.

Huggan, Graham, The *Postcolonial Exotic: Marketing the Margins* (London and New York: Routledge, 2001).

Hughes, Robert, *Goya* (London: Vintage, 2004).

Jackson, Ellen-Raïssa and Willy Maley, 'Committing to Kelman: the Art of Integrity and the Politics of Dissent', *Edinburgh Review*, 108 (2001), 22–7.

Jefferson, Ann, *The Nouveau Roman and the Poetics of Fiction* (Cambridge: Cambridge University Press, 1980).

Joyce, James, *A Portrait of the Artist as a Young Man* (New York: Viking Press, 1969).

Junquera, Juan José, *The Black Paintings of Goya* (London: Scala, 2003).

Kemp, David, *Glasgow 1990: The True Story Behind the Hype* (Gartocharn: Famedram, 1990).

King, Elspeth, 'Art for the Early Days of a Better Nation', in Phil Moores (ed.), *Alasdair Gray: Critical Appreciations and a Bibliography* (Boston Spa and London: British Library, 2002), 93–121.

Kirk, John, *Twentieth-century Writing and the British Working Class* (Cardiff: University of Wales Press, 2003).

Klaus, H. Gustav, 'Anti-authoritarianism in the Later Fiction of James Kelman', in H. Gustav Klaus and Stephen Knight (eds), *'To Hell with Culture': Anarchism and Twentieth-Century British Literature* (Cardiff: University of Wales Press, 2005), 162–77.

—— *James Kelman* (Tavistock: Northcote House and British Council, 2004).

Knights, Ben, *Writing Masculinities: Male Narratives in Twentieth-Century Fiction* (Basingstoke: Macmillan, 1999).

Kowalewski, Krzysztof, 'Exiles in Their Own Country: The Problem of Gender and Identity in the Work of James Kelman and Janice Galloway', in Wojciech Kalaga and Tadeusz Rachwal (eds), *The Writing of Exile* (Katowice: Slask, 2001), 105–16.

Laing, Stuart, *Representations of Working-Class Life, 1957–1964* (Basingstoke: Macmillan, 1986).

Lally, Pat, with Neil Baxter, *Lazarus Only Done it Once: The Story of My Lives* (London: Harper Collins, 2000).

Lehner, Stefanie, 'Towards a subaltern aesthetics: Reassessing Postcolonial Criticism for Contemporary Northern Irish and Scottish Literatures. James Kelman and Robert McLiam Wilson's Rewriting of National Paradigms', *eSharp: Electronic Social Sciences, Humanities, and Arts Review for Postgraduates*, 5 (Summer 2005), 1–14. htpp://sharp.arts.gla.ac.uk/issue5/lehner.pdf.

Leonard, Tom, *Intimate Voices* (Buckfastleigh: Etruscan Books, 2003).

—— *Nora's Place and Other Poems, 1965–1995*. Audio CD. (Edinburgh: AK Press Audio, 1997).

—— [untitled essay], in Bob Mullan (ed.), *R. D. Laing: Creative Destroyer* (London: Cassell, 1997), 89–91.

—— *Reports from the Present: Selected Work, 1982–94* (London: Jonathan Cape, 1995).

—— *Radical Renfrew: Poetry from the French Revolution to the First World War by Poets Born, or Sometime Resident in, the County of Renfrewshire* (Edinburgh: Polygon, 1990).

—— *Ghostie Men* (Newcastle: Galloping Dog Press, 1980).

—— *Three Glasgow Writers: A Collection of Writing by Alex.Hamilton, James Kelman, Tom Leonard* (Glasgow: Molendinar Press, 1976).

Levi, Primo, 'Sic!', in *The Mirror Maker: Stories and Essays*, trans. Raymond Rosenthal (New York: Schocken Books, 1989), 93–4.

Lindsay, Isobel, 'Migration and Motivation: A Twentieth-Century Perspective', in T. M. Devine (ed.), Scottish *Emigration and Scottish Society: Proceedings of the Scottish Historical Studies Seminar, University of Strathclyde, 1990–91* (Edinburgh: John Donald, 1992), 154–74.

Little, Stuart M., *A Handbook of Glasgow Corporation Motorbuses: 1924–1971* (Glasgow: Scottish Tramway Society, 1971).

—— *Glasgow Buses* (Glossop: Transport Publishing Co. Ltd. and Scottish Tramway and Transport Society, 1990).

Lowndes, Sarah, *Social Sculpture: Art, Performance and Music in Glasgow. A Social History of Independent Practice, Exhibitions and Events since 1971* (Glasgow: Stopstop, 2003).

Macarthur, J. D., 'The Narrative Voice in James Kelman's The Burn', *Studies in English Literature* [Tokyo], 71 (1995), 181–95.

Macaulay, R. K. S., *Language, Social Class, and Education: A Glasgow Study* (Edinburgh: Edinburgh University Press, 1977).

MacDonald, Graeme, 'A Scottish Subject? Kelman's Determination', *Études Écossaises*, 8 (2002), 89–111.

—— 'Writing Claustrophobia: Zola and Kelman', *Bulletin of the Émile Zola Society*, 13 (1996), 9–20.

MacDougall, Carl (ed.), *Glasgow's Glasgow: The Words and the Stones* (Glasgow: The Words and the Stones, 1990).

McGlynn, Mary, '"Middle-Class Wankers" and Working-Class Texts: The Critics and James Kelman', *Contemporary Literature*, 43:1 (Spring 2002), 50–84.

McGuire, Matt, 'Dialect(ic) Nationalism? The Fiction of James Kelman and Roddy Doyle', *Scottish Studies Review*, 7:1 (Spring 2006), 80–94.

McIlvanney, Liam, 'Give or take a dead Scotsman', Review of YH, *London Review of Books*, 26:14, 22 July 2004, 15–16.

—— 'The Politics of Narrative in the Post-war Scottish Novel', in Zachary Leader (ed.), *On Modern British Fiction* (Oxford: Oxford University Press, 2002), 181–208.

McIlvanney, William, *Docherty* (London: Hodder & Stoughton, 1985).

—— 'Plato in a Boiler Suit: William McIlvanney', in Isobel Murray (ed.), *Scottish Writers Talking* (East Linton: Tuckwell Press, 1996), 132–54.

Mcintyre, Sally, 'Socio-economic inequalities in health in Scotland', in *Social Justice Annual Report Scotland 2001* (Edinburgh: Scottish Executive Department of Health, 2001), http://scotland.gov.uk/library3/social/sjar-41.asp.

McLay, Farquhar (ed.), *Workers City: The Real Glasgow Stands Up* (Glasgow: Clydeside Press, 1988).

Mclean, Iain, *The Legend of Red Clydeside* (Edinburgh: John Donald, 1983).

McMillan Porter, Dorothy, 'Imagining a City', *Chapman*, 63 (1991), 42–50.

McMillan, Dorothy, 'Constructed Out of Bewilderment: Stories of Scotland', in Ian A. Bell (ed.), *Peripheral Visions: Images of Nationhood in Contemporary British Fiction* (Cardiff: University of Wales Press, 1995), 80–99.

McMillan, Neil, 'Wilting, or the "Poor Wee Boy Syndrome": Kelman and Masculinity', *Edinburgh Review*, 108 (2001), 41–55.

McMunnigall, Alan and Gerard Carruthers, 'Locating Kelman: Glasgow, Scotland and the Commitment to Place', *Edinburgh Review*, 108 (2001), 56–68.

Maley, Willy, 'Who Let the Underdogs Out?', *The Drouth*, 18 (Winter 2005–6), 78–9.

—— and Ellen-Raisa Jackson, 'Committing to Kelman: The Art of Integrity and the Politics of Dissent', *Edinburgh Review*, 108 (2001), 22–7.

—— 'Denizens, Citizens, Tourists, and Others: Marginality and Mobility in the Writings of James Kelman and Irvine Welsh', in David Bell and Azzedine Haddour (eds), *City Visions* (Harlow: Pearson, 2000), 60–72.

—— 'Swearing Blind: Kelman and the Curse of the Working Classes', Edinburgh Review, 95 (1996), 105–12.

—— 'History's Mandate: Alasdair Gray and the Art of Independence', *The Glasgow Review*, 3 (Summer 1995), htpp://arts.gla.ac.uk/sesll/STELLA/COMET/glasgrev/issue3/maley.htm.

Malthus, Thomas, *An Essay on the Principle of Population*, ed. Geoffrey Gilbert (Oxford: Oxford University Press, 1993).

Malzahn, Manfred, 'Aspects of Identity: The Contemporary Scottish Novel (1978–1981) as National Self-Expression', *Scottish Studies*, Vol. 2 (Frankfurt: Peter Lang, 1984).

Mapstone, Sally, 'Common Sense', Review of *TA*, *London Review of Books*, 23:22, 15 November 2002, 25–7.

March, C. L., *Rewriting Scotland* (Manchester: Manchester University Press, 2002).

Margery Palmer McCulloch, 'What Crisis in Scottish Fiction?: Creative Courage and Cultural Continuity in novels by Friel, Jenkins and Kelman', *Cencrastus*, 48 (Summer 1994), 15–18.

Maslen, R. W., Review of *TA*, *Scottish Studies Review*, 3:2 (Autumn 2002), 86–7.

Maver, Irene, *Glasgow* (Edinburgh: Edinburgh University Press, 2000).

Millar, A., *Strathclyde. British PTEs: 1* (London: Ian Allan, 1985).

Miller, Karl, *Authors* (Oxford: Clarendon Press, 1989).

Milne, Drew, 'The Fiction of James Kelman and Irvine Welsh: Accents, Speech and Writing', in Richard J. Lane, Rod Mengham and Philip Tew (eds), *Contemporary British Fiction* (Cambridge: Polity Press, 2003), 158–73.

—— 'Broken English: James Kelman's *Translated Accounts*', *Edinburgh Review*, 108 (2001), 106–15.

—— 'Dialectics of Urbanity', in James A. Davies and Glyn Pursglove with M. Wynn Thomas and Andrew Varney (eds), *Writing Region and Nation: A Special Number of the Swansea Review* (Swansea: Department of English, University of Wales, 1994), 393–407.

Mitchell, Don, *Cultural Geography: A Critical Introduction* (Oxford: Blackwell, 2000).

Mitchell, James, 'Politics in Scotland', in Patrick Dunleavy, Andrew Gamble, Richard Heffernan and Gillian Peele (eds), *Developments in British Politics 7* (Basingstoke: Palgrave MacMillan, 2003), 161–80.

Moran, Michael, *The Politics of Industrial Relations: The Origins, Life and Death of the 1971 Industrial Relations Act* (London and Basingstoke: Macmillan, 1977).

Morgan, Edwin, 'Glasgow Speech in Recent Scottish Literature', *Crossing the Border: Essays on Scottish Literature* (Manchester: Carcanet, 1990), 312–29.

Murphy, Terence Patrick, 'Durational Realism? Voice over Narrative in James Kelman's *An Old Pub near the Angel, and Other Stories*', *Journal of Narrative Theory*, 33:3 (Fall 2003), 335–56.

Neubauer, Jürgen, *Literature as Intervention: Struggles Over Cultural Identity in Contemporary Scottish Fiction* (Marburg: Tectum Verlag, 1999).

Nicoll, Laurence, 'Gogol's Overcoat: Kelman *Resartus*', *Edinburgh Review*, 108 (2001), 116–22.

—— ' "This is Not a Nationalist Position": James Kelman's Existential Voice', *Edinburgh Review*, 103 (2000), 79–84.

O'Hagan, Andrew, 'Beast of a Nation' [review of Neal Ascherson, *Stone Voices: The Search for Scotland* (London: Granta, 2002)], *London Review of Books*, 24:21, 31 October 2002, 11–12.

Orwell, George, *Nineteen Eighty-Four* (London: Penguin, 1989).

—— *Animal Farm* (London: Penguin, 1989).

Owens, Agnes, 'A Hopeless Case', in Paul Henderson Scott (ed.), *Spirits of the Age: Scottish Self Portraits* (Edinburgh: The Saltire Society, 2005), 75–80.

Parker, Peter (ed.), *The Reader's Companion to Twentieth-Century Writers* (London: Fourth Estate, 1995).

Parr, Adrian (ed.), *The Deleuze Dictionary* (Edinburgh: Edinburgh University Press, 2005).

Pascale, Casanova, *The World Republic of Letters*, trans. M. B. DeBevoise. (Cambridge, MA: Harvard University Press, 2004).

Pascoe, David, *Airspaces* (London: Reaktion, 2001).

Pitchford, Nicola, 'How Late It Was for England: James Kelman's Scottish Booker Prize', *Contemporary Literature*, 41:4 (Winter 2000), 693–725.

Pope, Rob, *Creativity: Theory, History, Practice* (London and New York: Routledge, 2005).

Punter, David, *Postcolonial Imaginings: Fictions of a New World Order* (Edinburgh: Edinburgh University Press, 2000).

Richards, Andrew J., *Miners on Strike: Class Solidarity and Division in Britain* (Oxford and New York: Berg, 1996).

Riddell, Peter, *The Thatcher Era And its Legacy* (Oxford: Blackwell, 1991).

Rocker, Rudolf, *Nationalism and Culture*, trans. Ray E. Chase (Montréal, New York and London: Black Rose Books, 1998).

Robbe-Grillet, Alain, *Snapshots and Towards a New Novel*, trans. Barbara Wright (London: Calder and Boyars, 1965).

Rodger, Liam, 'Tense, Aspect and *The Busconductor Hines* – the Literary Function of Non-Standard Language in the Fiction of James Kelman', *Edinburgh Working Papers in Applied Linguistics*, 3 (1992), 116–23.

Rodger, Johnny, 'Omniscience or Existence? That is the Question', *The Drouth*, 18 (Winter 2005–6), 5.

Rosie, Michael, *The Sectarian Myth in Scotland: Of Bitter Memory and Bigotry* (Basingstoke: Palgrave MacMillan, 2004).

Ryan, Ray, *Ireland and Scotland: Literature and Culture, State and Nation, 1966–2000* (Oxford: Oxford University Press, 2002).

Sarraute, Nathalie, *The Age of Suspicion*, in *Tropisms and The Age of Suspicion*, trans. Maria Jolas (London: John Calder, 1963).

Sartre, Jean-Paul, *Being and Nothingness: An Essay on Phenomenological Ontology*, trans. Hazel E. Barnes (London and New York: Routledge Classics, 2003).

—— *Existentialism and Humanism*, trans. Philip Mairet (London: Methuen, 1948).

Savage, Hugh, *Born up a Close: Memoirs of a Brigton Boy*, ed. James Kelman (Glendareul: Argyll Publishing, 2006).

Shaw, Andrew, Anne McMunn and Julia Field (eds), *The Scottish Health Survey 1998*, Vol. 1 (Edinburgh: Scottish Executive Department of Health, 2000), http://show.scot.nhs.uk/scottishhealthsurvey/.

Smout, T. C., *A History of the Scottish People, 1560–1830* (London: Fontana Press, 1969).

Spinks, Lee, 'In Juxtaposition to Which: Narrative, System and Subjectivity in the Fiction of James Kelman', *Edinburgh Review*, 108 (2001), 85–105.

Stewart, William, *Fighters for Freedom in Scotland: The Days of Baird and Hardie*, 2nd edn (Glasgow: Reformers' Bookstall, 1920).

—— *Fighters for Freedom in Scotland: The Days of Baird and Hardie* (London: Independent Labour Party, [1908]).

Stuart, Jamie, *The Glasgow Gospel* (Edinburgh: Saint Andrew Press, 1992).

Stuyvenberg, J. H. van (ed.), *Margarine: an Economic and Social History, 1869–1969* (Liverpool: Liverpool University Press, 1969).

Talib, Ismail S., *The Language of Postcolonial Literatures: an Introduction* (London and New York: Routledge, 2002).

Tandon, Bharat, 'The furnirs in the compound: James Kelman's portrayal of American disappointment', Review of YH, *Times Literary Supplement*, 21 May 2004, 19.

Taylor, D. J., *A Vain Conceit: British Fiction in the 1980s* (London: Bloomsbury, 1989).

—— 'Eh?' Review of *TA*, *Literary Review* (June 2001), 48.

Todd, Richard, *Consuming Fictions: The Booker Prize and Fiction Today* (London: Bloomsbury, 1996).

Tolstoy, Leo, *War and Peace*, trans. Anthony Briggs (London: Penguin, 2005).

Vice, Sue, *Introducing Bakhtin* (Manchester: Manchester University Press, 1997).

Watson, Roderick, 'Postcolonial Subjects? Language, Narrative Authority and Class in Contemporary Scottish Culture', *Hungarian Journal of English and American Studies*, 4:1–2 (1998), 21–38.

Williams, Raymond, 'Culture is Ordinary', in Ann Gray and Jim McGuigan (eds), *Studying Culture: An Introductory Reader* (London: Edward Arnold, 1993), 1–14.

—— *Marxism and Literature* (Oxford: Oxford University Press, 1977).

Woodcock, George, *Anarchism: A History of Libertarian Ideas and Movements*, 2nd edn (Ontario: Broadview, 2004).

Zagratzki, Uwe, '"Blues Fell This Morning" – James Kelman's Scottish Literature and Afro-American Music', *Scottish Literary Journal*, 27:1 (2000), 105–17.

Zamyatin, Yevgeny, *We*, trans. Mirra Ginsburg (New York: Avon, 1972).

Zola, Émile, *Germinal*, trans. Havelock Ellis (London: Dent, 1946).

After this book was finished, Michael Gardiner's *From* Trocchi *to* Trainspotting: *Scottish Critical Theory Since 1960* (Edinburgh: Edinburgh University Press, 2006) became known to me. Its chapter on Kelman is essential reading.

Index

n. after a page number indicates the number of a note on that page

Chomsky, Noam 5, 127, 180
Christ, Jesus 116, 141, 154
Cicero, Marcus Tullius 109
class
  America 181
  grammaticality and 27
  inarticulacy and 17
  narrative and 12–18, 128–33
    see also narrative
  the novel and 12–15
  occupation and 88–94, 98–9,
    103, 118n.1
    see work
  relationships 22
  stratification 13
  town planning and 57–8
  transport and 39–40
  war 4, 9, 11
  see also Glasgow; masculinity;
    middle class; poverty; reading;
    ruling class; unemployment;
    work; working class
Clockwork Orange, A 142
Cobb, Richard 156
Coleridge, Samuel Taylor 14
colonisation 95, 178
  criticism as 160–2
Conservative party 3, 80, 91, 125, 157
control 46, 50, 52–4, 72, 83–4, 97,
    99, 104–7, 142, 147, 148–50
Copernicus, Nicolaus 109
Corbett, John 20, 66
Cosgrove, Stuart 2–3
Craig, Cairns 13, 47, 73, 83–5, 110
Crawford, Robert 157
Criminal Justice Bill (1994) 6
criminality 146, 149
Crowley, Tony 13
culture 6, 8–11, 22, 26, 28, 42, 58,
    75, 89–90, 111–13, 124–6, 149,
    157–8, 167, 169, 180

Daly, Macdonald 35n.62, 153,
    167–8
Damer, Seán 50–1
Dante Alighieri 12

Davidson, Max 157
'dear o dear' 119n.13
deep-sea oil 78
Deleuze, Gilles 27–9, 43–4, 113,
    170, 185n.25
Dent 25
Descartes, René 106, 109–10
dialect 13, 27, 155–6, 167, 169–70
Dickens, Charles 15
Dillons 160
Disaffection, A 9, 21, 60, 77, 84,
    88–121, 129, 133–4, 141, 147,
    150, 159, 168
Dostoevsky, Fyodor 109, 112, 115
Dylan, Bob 133

education 31n.11, 45, 88–9, 94–9,
    111–14, 118n.1, 119n.17, 137,
    139
Empedocles 109
Engledow, Sarah 74, 84
English accent 146
English hegemony 6, 28, 91, 93–5,
    102, 122, 169
existentialism 5, 10, 19, 34n.54, 49,
    52, 73, 109, 128, 132, 143, 182

facticity 10, 60, 66, 73–7, 142
Fernando VII (King of Spain) 107
flying 181–2
folk voice 13
foreignness 30, 174, 178–9, 182–3
Fowles, John 11
Fox, Aaron A. 135
Frame, Ronald 2
free indirect style 18, 52, 69–70
'Free University, The' 5, 126–7
freedom 21, 53, 74, 76–7, 105,
    123, 169, 181
Freeman, Alan 75
Freud, Sigmund 116
Friel, George 119n.8

Gaelic 182
Gaitens, Edward 15
Galloway, Janice 1, 3